MISSION TRENDS NO. 4

Mission Trends No. 4

*Liberation Theologies
in North America and Europe*

Edited by
Gerald H. Anderson
and
Thomas F. Stransky, C.S.P.

PAULIST PRESS
New York/Ramsey/Toronto
and
WM. B. EERDMANS PUBLISHING CO.
Grand Rapids

Copyright © 1979 by
Paulist Fathers, Inc.
and Wm. B. Eerdmans Publishing Co.

Library of Congress
Catalog Card Number: 78-70827

Published by
Paulist Press
Editorial Office: 1865 Broadway, N.Y., N.Y. 10023
Business Office: 545 Island Road, Ramsey, N.J. 07446

ISBN: 0-8091-2185-9

and
Wm. B. Eerdmans Publishing Co.
255 Jefferson, S.E., Grand Rapids, Mich.

ISBN: 0-8028-1709-2

Reprinted, December 1982

Printed and bound in the
United States of America

The Editors

GERALD H. ANDERSON, director of the Overseas Ministries Study Center in Ventnor, New Jersey, is editor of the *Occasional Bulletin of Missionary Research,* and secretary-treasurer of the American Society of Missiology. He was formerly professor of church history and ecumenics, and academic dean of Union Theological Seminary, Manila, Philippines, and president of Scarritt College for Christian Workers, Nashville, Tennessee.

THOMAS F. STRANSKY from 1970–1978 was president of the Paulist Fathers, the first missionary society of priests founded in the United States (1858). He is a member of the Joint Working Group between the World Council of Churches and the Roman Catholic Church, an official consultant to the Vatican Secretariat for Promoting Christian Unity, and a participant in the Scholars' Group sponsored by the Southern Baptist Convention and the U.S. Catholic Bishops' Ecumenical Commission. Presently enjoying a one-year research fellowship from the Maryknoll Center for Mission Studies, he is concentrating on the variety of mission thinking and practices among evangelical Christians both in the United States and in Africa.

Contents

Foreword

Mission Trends No. 3 offered reflections on Christian mission from Asia, Africa and Latin America ("Third World Theologies"). We suggested that Europe and North America are no longer the centers of influence in theological construction, and that new centers are appearing elsewhere. But this radical realignment tries not to spawn new provincialisms. It is accepting critical partnership.

The present volume attempts to show the growing influence also in North America of a strong theological current first developed outside the North Atlantic community, primarily in Latin America.

"Liberation theology" falls easily into the double trap of faddism: a flash of enthusiasm that quickly is played out before it is understood, challenged and refined into varied but related theologies; or an in-label that considers any theology using "liberation" a liberation theology.

Only the naive would claim that in the discussions—*pro et contra*—there is rigor in methodology, clarity in all the terms, and accuracy in all the analyses of the predictable and unpredictable practice of Christians and their faith communities. Rather than confidence about one's own interpretations, the very insecurity of positions may have had much to do with the rhetoric of either/or's and the dismissal of differing viewpoints, with the judgments about the exact present plight of humankind, and with the predictions about its future.

But now there seems to be a sufficient body of writing and reflective experience to invite serious analyses and criticisms, and thus to avoid slogans and glib descriptions. These new insights arise from the shattering experiences of men and women who feel the burden especially of political, economic, racial and sexual dependence, even oppression, and who long for a liberation from whatever vitiates human projects, and aspire for total reconciliation in communion with God through the Saviour Jesus Christ. Integral salvation and full liberation.

Christian mission in and to North America thus does not ignore the liberation aspirations and reflections of the Black, Native, Asian American and Hispanic communities. Nor of the women in any community or in any church. Nor of any human being, race or society, anywhere.

The resulting critique of Christian individual and communal living, the re-examination of existing patterns of systematic theology, the confirmation by a transforming acceptance of the Word of God—together this more than hints at the implications of liberation theology on present and future Christian missionary understanding and practice.

With this fourth volume of *Mission Trends* we continue a modest means of sharing mission reflections and experiences. Although each volume has been self-contained, the delight of one, we hope, provokes the reading and re-reading of the others. We thank our consultants, the authors, editors and publishers of the journals in which the articles first appeared—and our own ecumenical- and mission-minded publishers. Explicit reactions to this venture will indeed be welcomed, as we now prepare *Mission Trends No. 5*, dealing with the encounter of Christians with people of other faiths.

Gerald H. Anderson
Thomas F. Stransky, C.S.P.

I: Mission and Liberation

Liberation Theology:
Paralyzing Threat
or Creative Challenge?

Robert McAfee Brown

A new way of "doing theology" has emerged from Latin America, called liberation theology, that radically challenges traditional concepts and practices of *who* does theology, of *how* and *where* it is done, and *what* the focus should be. Robert McAfee Brown describes it as an "attempt to look at the world in terms of involvement with the under-privileged and oppressed, and to find within the Christian gospel both the analytic tools and the energizing power to work for radical change in that world." Brown participated in a conference at Detroit in the summer of 1975 where Latin American liberation theologians met with representatives of various minority and marginal peoples in North America, along with some white male North Americans, for dialogue about common (and some uncommon) concerns they have for doing "theology in the Americas." Dr. Brown, who is Professor of Ecumenics and World Christianity at Union Theological Seminary in New York, describes here the major features of liberation theology and responds to the charges against it. He concludes with suggestions for those "who are not oppressed . . . who are relatively comfortable, whose daily existence is not seriously threatened," if they are to "play any role in developing a 'theology in the Americas.' " This chapter is reprinted with permission from the published proceedings of the Detroit conference, *Theology in the Americas,* edited by Sergio Torres and John Eagleson (Maryknoll, N.Y.: Orbis Books, 1976). Brown's most recent book, *Theology in a New Key: Responding to Liberation Themes* (Westminster Press, 1978), carries this discussion forward.

Over the past few years there has been growing up in the Third World, and particularly in Latin America, a movement called "liberation theology"—an attempt to look at the world in terms of involvement with the underprivileged and oppressed, and to find within the Christian gospel both the analytic tools and the energizing power to work for radical change in that world. The "analytic tools" have also, and often initially, involved sociological and economic analysis, frequently along Marxist lines, and the biblical and ecclesiastical resources have involved a critical stance toward institutional religion's long alliance with the status quo. Thanks to theologians of liberation, a rereading of Christian history and Christian documents has become possible, in terms of what they contribute to a new understanding of God as one who sides with the oppressed and works with them for their own liberation.[1]

A New Way of "Doing Theology"

In the past, theology has usually been done by the "experts," who, although they sometimes worked in the heat of the battle, more often worked in the relative calm and detachment of the seminary or university or monastery, using texts of·the past as their basic resources, producing large and scholarly tomes of "systematic theology," replete with footnotes, foreign phrases, and intricate arguments that could conserve and interpret the past for the sake of the present. The orientation was in large measure to books, ideas, concepts, and modes of argument, rather than to human struggle, anguish, pain, and exploitation. A finished position was being sought, a restatement of "the faith once delivered to the saints," that, if not destined to be definitive forever, might at least be normative for a long time to come.

There is no point in trying to demean or put down the need for such discursive, rational, and somewhat abstract endeavor. There is, however, a point in suggesting that no matter how valuable such activity has been in the past, and might once again be in the future, it is not the crying need of the present.

The crying need of the present is for further experimentation with the sort of theologizing that the present volume represents. In it we see the "doing" of theology as a *process*—a word introduced with some hesitation, for fear it would be confused with the process-philosophy of Alfred North Whitehead. Prefacing the word with a few adjectives may help to clarify what it means in the present context.

1. The process is *an open-ended process*. It is not assumed that theology will come to fixed positions that will be securely defined and nailed down for generations of inspection. Instead, theology will involve ongoing reflection, alternating between looking at its past conclusions and reviewing them in the light of the present world seen from the standpoint of the oppressed. This will mean rethinking past conclusions, which in turn will be tested in the light of present conditions, which themselves will be subject to re-evaluation as new data come to light and as the conditions themselves change. For awhile at least, the writing of theology needs to be done in loose-leaf notebooks. New pages will continue to be needed, and some older pages will need to be replaced.

2. The process is *a corporate process*. Input will come from many sources and many disciplines. The reflection will be done by many people, and the results will be disseminated in many ways. It is crucial to the meaning of the present book that it is *not* a new theology by an individual, but the expression of a theological process engaged in by a large number of individuals, who have worked together and struggled together, and who only by going through that corporate struggle have gained some fresh insights for the next round.

3. Therefore, the process is also a *a self-correcting process*. ("Conflictive process" was a tempting term, save that it does not contain any inherent hope; conflicts do not always have creative outcomes, whereas acts of self-correction almost always can.) In such a process, the end result may be very different from the initial conception. The 1975 Detroit conference of Latin American and North American theologians and practitioners is a case in point. Early in the planning for this conference it was seen that the original design was "elitist," in that it did not involve a sufficiently widespread representation of different classes, points of view, backgrounds, sexes, and so forth. The complaints arose out of those involved in the process

itself; they were heeded, and corrections were made. Further corrections continued to be needed all along the way, many of them within the dynamics of the week at Detroit itself. More corrections will be needed as the process continues, particularly as the net is widened yet further to include new voices and perspectives. But the process itself makes possible such self-correction.

There is another way in which the self-correcting aspects of the process are important. Each special interest group at Detroit needed the help of other groups to get beyond some of its own biases. The Latin Americans, it turned out, had barely awakened to the fact that they had ignored the oppression of women in their own cultures. North American women took great pains to point out that deficiency. North American black theologians have given little attention to economic sources of their own oppression: Latin Americans insisted on a new degree of economic analysis. Middle class white women were told that they may have overlooked the class dimension of their own internal struggle for womens' liberation; a black woman Marxist gave help at this point. And so on. Each group could point more skillfully to the mote in someone else's theological eye than to the beam in its own, and the corporate self-correction in these matters was immensely fruitful.[2]

4. The process is finally an *engaged process*. From start to finish (which suggests that this might appropriately have been the first point) those who "do theology" in this fashion must be doing it with their lives as well as with their minds. Theology is not so much a matter of the classroom (though it can also be that) as of the arena of human need, immersed in the stuff of politics, engaged in the struggle with the oppressed, being open to personal risks for the sake of those whom the world counts as nothing. The key word here, a word always in danger of being co-opted and defused, is *praxis*. Thinking must be engaged thinking; it must come out of *doing* and not just cogitating. As Gustavo Gutiérrez has put it, "All the political theologies, the theologies of hope, of revolution, and of liberation, are not worth one act of genuine solidarity with exploited social classes."[3] Whatever authentic theology emerges for our day will spring from genuine acts of solidarity with the exploited.

This is the stuff of a new theology; it will be out of this sort of mix that we will do our most important thinking and acting in the future, if we are to be faithful both to the oppressed of our world and to the God who (as a rereading of Scripture reminds us) has already indicated the divine faithfulness toward them by taking sides with them and entering into their struggle.

Recognizing the Threats

Such a prospect is threatening. It may be more threatening to some than to others, but in varying degrees it is threatening to all. Why? Because it calls into question the implicitly held assumptions by which we govern our lives—or think we do. Even more threatening may be the discovery that the assumptions we think are normative for our lives are only a facade to hide from public (or private) scrutiny the truly normative assumptions.

At the Detroit conference referred to above, I was part of the group that overtly, at least, seemed most threatened—the white male theologians. Every other group had reason to mistrust us: To them we were the epitome of the oppressive power structure, as seen through the eyes of women, blacks, Chicanos, native Americans, Asian-Americans, Appalachians, and so on. Even if we weren't oppressing people personally (and delegates were occasionally, though not uniformly, willing to offer that concession) we were clearly part of the group that tended to benefit most by the oppression of others.

But it is important to realize that this was by no means a reality only for white male theologians. All the groups discovered other groups to whom they were beholden only in terms of guilt or threat. The "oppressors" in one situation had reason to feel "oppressed" in other situations; the "oppressed" could always find someone who looked upon them as "oppressors."

Granting all that, it is still the case that certain groups will feel threatened by liberation theology. For it is an undeniable fact that many of the structures of society that benefit middle class people are structures that destroy other people. Their backs and lives are broken producing the food we eat. They will never be able to stand as long as our feet are on their necks. Their exploitation seems to be necessary for our comfort.

Unless we are callously insensitive, we cannot help being threatened by the discovery that our survival is purchased at the cost or the demise of others. And if we would like to "do something" about it, to change the world so that such conditions do not continue, we are further threatened when it turns out that all the things we are prepared to "do" are looked upon as cheap palliatives, as foredoomed-to-failure cosmetic attempts to beautify an ugly monster, as trivial evasions of the real problem. Our concepts of "help," of "charity," of "doing good," are interpreted as ways in which we can salve our consciences without changing our lives, our status, or our comfort. We may feel better, but *nothing has changed*. The conditions that brought about the evils we attempt to remedy with a little aid or a little emergency help are still the same conditions; their evil consequences may have been alleviated for a moment or two, but *nothing has changed*.

And surely it is the insistent call for radical change that is most threatening—"radical" in the sense of going to the *radix*, the root, of things. Consequently: if an economic system based on competition can finally only grind down and destroy, then the system must go; it will not be enough to have those on top grind with a smile on their faces instead of a sneer, or give an occasional charitable loaf of bread to those to whom they deny the possibility of earning enough loaves to feed their families adequately. And yet, if it is said that "the system must go," that becomes a genuine threat, because with the disappearance of the system would go our securities, our status, our luxuries, possibly our necessities, perhaps even our lives.

Refusing the Evasions

In the light of such a threat, most of us look for ways to evade the validity of such an analysis. And there are a number of ways to evade a position as threatening as that of liberation theology:

1. A threatening position can sometimes be disposed of simply *by calling it a "fad" and those who espouse it "naive."* This is not to say that positions can be exempted from hard-nosed analysis, but in the case of liberation theology the put-

down has often been a substitute for the analysis. Concern for liberation is dismissed as this year's theological kick, similar to previous flurries over "the secular city," "the death of God," "the theology of play," or whatever; those who take it seriously are naive souls who will jump on any bandwagon; for them the present one will do until the next one comes along, at which point they will desert liberation for something else.

These are cheap shots. We can be sure that the phenomenon of "liberation theology" (by whatever name) will not disappear until oppression has disappeared, and that, unfortunately, will not be for a long, long time. Concern for liberation does not arise from theologians looking for new intellectual toys; it arises from the reality of grinding poverty, the distended stomachs of starving children, the brutality of political repression, and from a recognition that the Christian gospel announces the possibility of liberation from just such evils. And even if liberation should come this side of the eschaton, we will need to ride herd on the new situation so that the oppressed, having finally gotten power, do not merely imitate those whom they have replaced. The "fad theory" of liberation theology needs to be countered by pointing out that the *real* fad these days is calling every position but one's own a fad.

2. A threatening position can sometimes be disposed of *by co-opting it*. Third World theologians are legitimately nervous as they look at what North Americans are doing with their terms. As Hugo Assmann has put it:

Perhaps the first important contribution Christians can make to the process of liberation is not to add to the process of diluting the revolutionary implications that circumstances have dictated it should contain.[4]

It will be in the short-run self-interest of most people in power to try to co-opt such a movement by broadening the term "liberation" enough to defuse it of any revolutionary power. This can be done by talking, for example, about "inner liberation," liberation of the soul, liberation of the insecure, liberation from guilt, and so on, until the word "liberation" has no more political content left than simply changing-things-a-little-bit-but-not-too-much. Although white middle-class people also need certain kinds of liberation (a theme to which we shall return), there is a danger of claiming this too readily and too quickly and hence too conveniently, so that liberation from too many cocktails is somehow equated with liberation from starving to death.

To be sure, liberation theology speaks of various kinds of liberation—from sin and guilt as well as from oppressive social structures—but there is the further fact (which the co-opters usually want to hide) that personal sin and guilt cannot be privatized, but become imbedded in social structures and achieve a kind of objective reality in them. This means that it is not enough to suggest, as those who benefit from the status quo want to insist, that freeing individuals from their own hangups will automatically lead to a just society. The just society will have to incorporate just social structures, and those are not going to come into being until a lot of unjust social structures are torn down. Their tearing down is going to involve challenges to the forms of capitalism, racism, classism, imperialism, and sexism that have become imbedded in the very nature of our society.[5]

3. A threatening position can sometimes be disposed of by *keeping it at a safe distance*. We can examine oppression far away—the denial of civil rights to Spanish-speaking poor people in Santiago, Chile, for example—and never have to confront the denial of civil rights to Spanish-speaking poor in the central valley of California. We can even be romantic about urging "revolution" upon rural guerrillas in Colombia, and still remain exceedingly uptight whenever there is the slightest sign of "unrest" in Harlem or Watts. We need at this point to hear the voice of Dom Helder Camara, archbishop of Recife, Brazil:

> Instead of planning to go to the Third World to try and arouse violence there, stay at home in order to help your rich countries to discover that they too are in need of a cultural revolution which will produce a new hierarchy of values, a new world vision, a global strategy of development, the revolution of mankind.[6]

Those who follow Dom Helder's first suggestion ("stay at home") do not frequently follow his second (create a "revolution" at home). We examine manifestations of injustice at a safe distance by keeping our own engagement at a minimum— theorizing, or talking, or writing prefaces to books, so that we never have to take sides in a conscious fashion. (It is necessary to add "in a conscious fashion," because the presumed posture of neutrality is always a vote for the status quo.) Even when we bewail the denial of civil rights in Santiago, we are usually unwilling to face the fact that the military junta denying those rights is in power largely because American political, economic, and business interests gave covert support to the overthrow of a previous regime, and give overt support to the dictatorial regime now in power. To put it more strongly: American tax dollars, *our* tax dollars, sponsor the torture of Chilean priests.

4. A threatening position can sometimes be disposed of *by describing it in emotionally discrediting terms*. In the United States, this means disposing of liberation theology by applying Marxist or communist tags to it. It would be foolish to pretend that there is not a lot of Marxist analysis in the way the liberation theologians look at the world. But the important question is not, "Is liberation theology's analysis tinged with a Marxist hue?" The important question is, "Is the analysis true? Does it make sense of what it is describing? Do we understand the world better when we look at it in that way?" The descriptive power of an analysis to illumine the world of oppressed people is at stake, not how much the analysis is or is not Marxist.

Americans should also bear in mind that Marxism does not have a corner on descriptive analysis. The fact that "Marxists say it" must not preclude to others the right to reach similar conclusions, perhaps by very different routes. The cry for social justice considerably antedates Karl Marx; the promise of "liberty for the oppressed" was not only enunciated by Jesus, but borrowed by him from the book of Isaiah. Christians cannot be asked to disavow or be suspicious of a position of their own simply because close to two millennia later Karl Marx happened to offer his own version of the same truth.

Furthermore, it is descriptively inadequate to characterize

liberation theology in simplistic terms as Marxist. Some liberation theologians rely heavily on Marxist analysis; others do not. Some prefer to be called Marxist Christians, or Christian Marxists; others do not. For almost all of them the mix varies. Rather than weigh nicely the components of that mix, it would be more useful to start with a recognition of the strong engagement of liberation theology with the biblical story and the way in which the Scriptures help to corroborate or challenge a given sociological analysis, both in providing their own tools for analysis and by indicating a source of power by means of which those gripped by the biblical message can be enlisted in the struggle for change.[7] Not all liberation theologians subscribe to a "surplus-value" theory, but almost all of them would affirm the Exodus story or Jeremiah 22:13-16 or Isaiah 61:1-4 or Luke 4:16-30 or Matthew 25:31-46 or a host of other passages as basic resources for dealing with the world.

There are, of course, other ways to evade the challenge of liberation theology.[8] But the above are sufficient to indicate that there are always ways to evade a challenge, particularly a threatening one.

Next Steps for North Americans

Suppose, however, that one were to try to respond. How could those of us in North America begin to take seriously the challenge of the liberation theology of Latin America? Where would we go from here? What would constitute a "theology in the Americas"?

Such concerns must be explored by those who take this book seriously. What follows is only a initial set of reflections that must be clarified and verified for each reader as he or she participates in the process itself.

Perhaps the primary need is to *reconceive the question*. The task is not to take Latin American theology and "apply" it to North America, or even to look for ways to find out the "meaning" of liberation theology for North America. Rather "the goal is to contribute to a new theology that emerges from the historical, social, and religious context of the North American experience."

Theology is not a set of timeless truths, no matter how much the goal of achieving such truths may have been sought by theologians in the past. It is rather a certain kind of reflection on what is going on in very specific situations—Palestine, Rome, Constantinople, Geneva, Canterbury, Copenhagen, Hell's Kitchen, Alabama, Johannesburg, Santiago, Tokyo, Recife, Nairobi, New York, or wherever. A common heritage may be drawn upon to explain or challenge what is going on in such places. But what is going on in these places will also explain or challenge that common heritage. There is a two-way street. The specific *context* will determine the specific *content* of the emerging theology. Things will need to be emphasized in a certain way in Santiago that will need to be emphasized in a different way in San Francisco. So the real question will not be: How can we "transfer" the position of Christians in Santiago to San Francisco? It will be: Observing how Christians in Santiago try to live and think authentically in *their* situation, how can we find ways to live and think authentically in *our* situation? Certain social, political, economic, and ecclesiastical dynamics contribute to how Chilean Christians see their task. Certain other social, political, economic, and ecclesiastical dynamics—very different, perhaps—will contribute to how United States Christians see their task. So the theological task is not to imitate some other situation, but to be authentically responsible in one's own situation.

This is a tall order. Here are a few considerations that might help us begin to deal with it:

1. "Theology in the Americas" must be a combination of *particularity and global vision*. We must continue to stress the need for particularity, taking with utmost seriousness the context in which theology is done. Blacks are going to have to do black theology together; women are going to have to develop feminist theology together; Chicanos are going to have to discover theological insights specifically related to their own situation; "academic" theologians are going to have to confront together the pitfalls of traditional academic theology. All this is necessary, and it will probably constitute the next step for such groups.

But sooner or later (and at least sooner, if not concurrently) such varied contextual situations will need to be related *to one another,* for none of them ultimately exists in isolation. As Detroit made clear, each group helps to deliver other groups from parochialism. Furthermore, the final Christian vision does not point to a tightly circumscribed context for some only, but to a context that is inclusive of all. Each struggle for liberation is finally related to all other struggles for liberation; differing initial agendas may help to establish self-identity and self-worth, but all agendas, if authentic, will gradually converge. The convergence must not be too rapid or some groups will be engulfed and co-opted by others. But the convergence must not be too slow, or the groups will be manipulated into competitive stances. And nothing could make the holders of power happier than to keep those without power fighting among themselves so that they cannot join forces against the common enemy that must be displaced.

The development of a North American theology, in other words, will need to go through several stages of particularization: North American blacks, Chicanos, Asian-Americans, Appalachians, women, white males, and so on, clearly have some agendas of their own. But coalitions must emerge in the process. And to the degree that common concerns and goals emerge for North Americans, those will, in turn, need to be related to theologies emerging out of Latin America, Africa, Asia, and Europe. For conclusions that North Americans begin to reach about domestic problems will need reassessment in the light of global problems. The Christian gospel is not concerned only about the emancipation of the oppressed in North America, but about the emancipation of the oppressed in every part of the world. The dialectic between particularity and global vision will be an ongoing one.

2. One way to keep the dialectic alive will be to recognize that *global problems must be examined in the perspective of particular situations.* The clearest example of the need for different approaches to the same problem is the issue of power. The problem of power for Third World peoples, and for minority peoples elsewhere, is very clear: They do not have enough power and they must find ways to get more; otherwise their oppression will continue unchallenged. Their theologies must deal with that need and seek to satisfy it. But the problem of

power for those in the First World is very different: The United States, for example, has too much power, and it is imperative that ways be found to see that such power is shared. The problem is the same—power—but the problem must be approached in very different ways. One who has no power cannot be asked to share it; one who has too much power must not be asked to acquire more.

3. *The new theology must be grounded in a community.* If one's final loyalty is to North America or the United States, there is no reason to work for the sharing of power; indeed, the impulse would be to make that power strong enough to resist all threats. And while institutional Christianity is frequently little more than a pale reflection of its surroundings, there do exist within the church networks, remnants—what might be called "God's underground"—which can furnish the sustenance and nurture necessary to empower people to stand against the popular currents of the culture.

The fact that the community is a global community is particularly important in this context. For it is commitment to a global community that can potentially free one from the parochialism that a local context alone may nurture. One can be open to challenges to one's own perspective when they come from others within the same global community. I may have difficulty internalizing what the reality of my affluence does to people in other parts of the world; but members of the global community can point this out to me, in the context of the faith we share in common, in ways that I have to take more seriously than if I am simply the object of a diatribe from those with whom I share very little.

Allegiance to such a community can help to liberate us from other parochialisms as well. If one is middle-class, it is difficult to avoid doing theology without taking middle-class values for granted. If one's upbringing has conditioned one to believe that capitalism is the best system for the most people, a radical challenge to capitalism is difficult to internalize. To see one's communal commitment in global terms is to be at least a little closer to escape from such ideological entrapment. North American Christians might even begin to be able to understand why many Christians elsewhere are socialists.

4. If one is to contextualize theology, it will be necessary

to ask not only about Latin American oppression, but about *North American oppression* as well, and even the possible "oppression" of the "oppressors." This must not be done so quickly or glibly that it falls prey to the co-optation cited earlier. But middle-class readers of this essay need to recognize that there are certain kinds of oppression, for example, from which they too need to be liberated, such as: *a)* bondage to middle-class values with their high emphasis on success-orientation, an implicit assumption that financial security is the *sine qua non* of a full life, and so on; *b)* bondage to what in 1976 was described as "bicentennialism," the need to believe that "American is great because America is good" (as former President Eisenhower put it), that criticism of the United States is never justified, and that support should be given to a Ronald Reagan when he virtually suggests going to war over Panama or sending troops to Africa to protect American interests; *c)* bondage to the status quo, interpreted to mean that more of the same is always good, that change is always a threat, and that evil is never due to the basic structure of society but only to a few individuals who have temporarily exploited it.

Such oppressions are powerful obstacles to the achievement of justice and freedom both domestically and globally. They are destructive not only to those who are immediately subservient to them, but destructive in their impact on the lives of those who have no control over them. Vietnam is only one symbol among others of this truth. So a "theology in the Americas" must acknowledge the importance of liberation from such oppressions as these.

5. What are *the most appropriate tools* with which to work for these ends? In Latin America, as we have observed, Marxist analysis has been a particularly relevant tool for Christians and has provided a point of contact with members of the working class, many of whom are already Marxist. In North America, however, the very mention of Marx is liable to end the discussion before it gets under way. What is one to do?

Some groups have responded that one must simply bite this particular linguistic bullet, and chapters of "Christians for Socialism" are springing up in various parts of the country.

Their members contend that the degree of change needed is of such magnitude that there is no way of avoiding "scandal," threat, and challenge, so the reality might as well be faced head on: Capitalism is no longer compatible with Christianity, if it ever was, and a full-scale change of direction is needed. While this position is likely to be a minority position for some time, its forthrightness is very attractive.

There are others who argue that it is better not to draw on explicitly Marxist categories. Rosemary Ruether suggests that Christians in the United States will get a more significant hearing by drawing on the terms and experience of the special American heritage, so that the emotive power of the American past need not be surrendered to right-wing reactionaries. There *is* an "American past" that can be invoked in the name of a freedom that is not freedom for the few, and although this is still a minority report on that past, the appeal can be made with telling effect. Those concerned with the contextualization of "theology in the Americas" can thus appeal to such themes as "liberty and justice *for all*" as a part of an overall heritage that challenges the present reality, which is liberty and justice for *some*.

A Short Digression for "Professional" Theologians

There is indeed need for an indigenous "North American theology," based neither on overdependence upon recent Latin American theology nor upon slightly less recent European theology. But it may be that certain liberation themes can be introduced more successfully if the ties with European theology are not cut too quickly. I realize that some Latin Americans would interpret this as a retreat from radical theology into the comforting arms of a bourgeois mentality. But some interesting things happened to European theologians in their encounters with the need for radical change from which some lessons, both pro and con, might be learned by the rest of us.

The fact that Dietrich Bonhoeffer, for example, came out of a bourgeois background gives added importance to the fact that he began to move beyond that background as a result of a new solidarity with the oppressed. Commenting in 1942 on what he had learned during the previous decade, Bonhoeffer wrote to a select group of friends from similar backgrounds:

> There remains an experience of incomparable value. We have for once learnt to see the great events of world history from below, from the perspective of the outcast, the suspects, the maltreated, the powerless, the oppressed, the reviled—in short from the perspective of those who suffer. . . . We have to learn that personal suffering is a more effective key, a more rewarding principle for exploring the world in thought and action than personal good fortune.[9]

Paul Tillich was deeply involved in "religious socialism" in the years just after World War I. A number of his writings from that period are available (in Tillich, *Political Expectations* [New York: Harper & Row, 1971]), and more are shortly to appear under the editorship of Franklin Sherman. It is important for those already familiar with Tillich's thought to trace again this early part of his own pilgrimage and to reflect on why he did not pursue the socialist option more vigorously in his later life.[10]

Similar concerns can be explored in the pilgrimage of Karl Barth, who became a socialist during his youthful pastorate at Safenwil, Switzerland, and always insisted on a close alignment between theology and politics, giving support to socialist regimes in Eastern Europe after World War II, at a time when his contemporaries were trumpeting an anticommunist line.[11]

Most significant in this discussion has been Jürgen Moltmann, whose theology of hope has had undeniable influence in many parts of the world where liberation theologies have come into being, and who has himself opted for a theological position that has a more radical political side to it than that of most of his European counterparts.[12]

The task is not to take ready-made theologies from Europe and graft a few liberation themes onto them. But there were some important liberation concerns expressed in the lives and thoughts of such theologians, and one can learn from their mistakes as well as their successes.

A similar exercise is worth undertaking in discerning a slow but clear "tilt to the left" in the various papal encyclicals, conciliar documents, synodical reports, and other Roman Catholic writings of the last fifteen years.[13] There are similar documents in the history of the World Council of Churches, most notably the report of the conference on Church and Society held in Geneva in 1966 ("Christians in the Social and Technical Revolutions of our Time") as well as reports of subsequent World Council conferences and assemblies.[14]

It is not being suggested that there are clear continuities between such theologies and contemporary theologies of liberation. But there are at least connections; and those who stand in the heritage of such movements have a responsibility to scrutinize them carefully before too freely casting them aside.[15]

Can "Oppressors" Do Theology Today?

It may seem as though we have managed to blunt the radical concern that must characterize a new theology and have successfully co-opted it in ways that remove its threatening character.

It is always possible for this to happen. Attention must always be directed to the danger. And there is no doubt that this chapter would have been written very differently had the writer been a black or a woman or a Chicano. So let us conclude by focusing on a problem that lies behind all of these pages: Can theology today be done by those who are not oppressed? Can those who are relatively comfortable, whose daily existence is not seriously threatened, play any role in developing a "theology in the Americas"?

Notes, then, for those whom the world usually denominates "oppressors," by one of them:

1. Surely *our first task is to listen*. Those in the saddle usually insist on issuing directions for the caravan. Those with the goods and the know-how usually feel that others want only to learn from them in order to become like them. It is time to listen for awhile, to let others speak, to acknowledge that the impetus for change may well originate in quarters other than our own, and that we had better not be writing agendas for the oppressed.

One of Elie Wiesel's characters comments, "When a Jew says he is suffering, one must believe him, and when he is afraid, one must assume his fear is justified. In neither case does one have the right to doubt his word. Even if one cannot help him, one must at least believe him."[16]

This provides an excellent starting point for a new theology: When we hear the cry, "I'm hurting," we must take it seriously. And when we discover that the cry really means, "You are hurting me," we must hear it with utmost seriousness. If others say that we are hurting them, our initial assumption must be that they are correct. Even if it should turn out that they are not correct, it is important for us to know how we were being perceived. Those living in a nation with 6 percent of the world's population who are nevertheless consuming 40 percent of the world's resources had better take seriously the cry of "the wretched of the earth."

2. We must *interpret what we hear.* Consciousness-raising, conscientization, is not limited only to peasants trained by the methods of Paulo Freire. Others can be "conscienticized" as well, not least of all ourselves. I was encouraged, at the conclusion of a recent course on "liberation theology," at how many students said in effect, "I never knew the world was that way. . . . I never realized before that people don't necessarily appreciate receiving foreign aid from us. . . . I didn't understand how much Americans are feared and hated in the Third World. . . . I always thought other countries wanted to be like us."

Of course, nothing is changed until lives begin to change as well as attitudes. But those who have come to see the world in a different way can help interpret to others why it looks that way and why we are so reluctant to see it that way. Most North American students believe that all is well in Chile, until they are exposed to first-hand Chilean accounts that have not been filtered through the State Department or the public relations officer of a large corporation with a vested interest in keeping the Chilean junta in power. Those who hear something different must share and interpret what they hear.

This creates a special responsibility to speak to constituencies that will listen to us. If middle-class Christians become aware that they themselves bear responsibility for the fact that their brothers and sisters are hurting, then they must use whatever levers of power they possess, however feeble, to introduce the possibility of change, and do this in a responsible fashion. For white middle-class Christians to advocate a violent revolution in middle America today is as futile as it is irresponsible. But we may need to point out why other Christians in other places could feel that violent revolution is their only hope, and that other options appear closed off to them because the United States is backing the most reactionary elements in their own countries. Although electoral politics no longer seems a very direct route to increased justice for the dispossessed, it can at least be a means of containing the spread of injustice—and that is quite a lot, if one is a potential victim of the spreading injustice.

3. All of this must lead toward a position in which we develop an increasing ability *to see the world through eyes other than our own.*[17] To us, the judicial system looks just; to members of minority groups it is frequently a monument to injustice. To us, police protection is usually beneficial; to members of minority groups it can be a source of terror. To us, democracy "works"; to members of minority groups it appears to spawn petty fascists who occasionally accumulate and abuse an alarming amount of power. No radical challenge to the status quo is likely to come from us when only our own interests are at stake; the system pays off too well to us. But to be enabled, through the resources of "God's underground," to see that system *in terms of what it does to others,* to be forced toward what Bonhoeffer called "the view from below," is at least to be started on the way to disengagement from uncritical allegiance to it.

How will the possibility of such changes become more widespread? This could begin to happen in a couple of ways. North Americans might be subjected to a kind of social science analysis that would convince us, in the most hard-nosed pragmatic way, that it is in our own best interest to share some of our power and resources with the Third World, to divest ourselves of our life-and-death control over the destinies of others, realizing that if we do not, we, who are in reality a small minority of the human family, will one day have such power and control taken from us, forcibly if necessary, since outrage against us will finally pass the boiling point. A time might come, in other words, when altruism and long-range self-interest coincided.

That would be an argument, and an important one, in the courts of power. But there would be another stance as well for the Christian remnant to propose and seek to embody—a recognition that Christian faith also talks about the fact that servanthood, voluntarily assumed, can be a vehicle for justice (cf. Isaiah 42), and that self-denial, curiously and paradoxically, can be a way to fulfillment. That will not be the message to those presently destitute and powerless; it will be an important ingredient in any witness the Christian community offers to those already too powerful.

The "Abrahamic Venture"

All of which will surely sound naive. Who indeed is likely to make "one act of genuine solidarity with exploited social classes" (to quote Gustavo Gutiérrez again), when he or she already has comfort and security? Who is going to engage in the "self-emptying" that such a decision would involve?

Here is where we must finally go beyond social analysis, no matter how acute, and noble words, no matter how finely honed. For this is a matter of willingness to subject oneself, at risk, to the power of the gospel—a gospel that emphasizes turning around, "conversion," a fresh start, a letting-go, and a recognition that this finally comes by grace—not to be attained but only received. Simply to wait passively for grace to come will mean an ongoing consenting to present injustice; but to give up hope in its coming at all will mean consigning ourselves to despair and thereby also settling for injustice.

Our true hope surely lies in aligning ourselves with what Dom Helder Camara has called "the Abrahamic minorities," those groups here and there who have taken the risk of trying to embody the power of justice and love, those, like Abraham, who "hope against hope," willing to venture forth not knowing where they are going, taking their cue from the fact that "the protests of the poor are the voice of God."[18] At the time Abraham went forth, he had no assurance that his choice to leave security had been a wise one. Only later, in retrospect, was it clear that Abraham was all the time under the providence of God. Nor will any advance assurances be guaranteed to Abraham's children. But something of the Abrahamic quality will have to invest the lives of those who take on the task of liberation today. The degree of our ability to respond will not finally rest on the soundness of our analysis, though that is important, but on the extent of our willingness to risk our security on behalf of the insecurities of others.

NOTES

1. For a full development of the methodology and themes of liberation theology see the essay by Philip Berryman in Sergio Torres and John Eagleson, eds., *Theology in the Americas* (Maryknoll, N.Y.: Orbis Books, 1976).

2. For making this point in an earlier published report on the conference, I was accused by Fr. Andrew Greeley, in one of his typically acerbic columns, of being a "Nazi." The point about mutual self-correction seems important enough to repeat, however, and I am willing to leave any judgments about my Nazi mentality to readers who may be less than fully captivated by Fr. Greeley's frantic prose.

3. Gustavo Gutiérrez, *A Theology of Liberation,* trans. Caridad Inda and John Eagleson (Maryknoll, N.Y.: Orbis Books, 1973), p. 308.

4. Hugo Assmann, *Theology for a Nomad Church,* trans. Paul Burns (Maryknoll, N.Y.: Orbis Books, 1976), p. 129.

5. It is encouraging that groups that were formerly unimpressed by this fact, the so-called "conservative evangelicals," are beginning to include this social dimension in their analysis. See especially Jim Wallis, *Agenda for Biblical People* (New York: Harper and Row, 1976).

6. Helder Camara, *Church and Colonialism,* trans. William McSweeney (Denville, N.J.: Dimension Books, 1969), p. 111. The same point is made more stridently by Ivan Illich in *The Church, Change, and Development* (New York: Herder and Herder, 1970), pp. 45-53.

7. An excellent tool for exploring the biblical analysis is José Porfirio Miranda, *Marx and the Bible,* trans. John Eagleson (Maryknoll, N.Y.: Orbis Books, 1974).

8. I have extended the discussion in *Is Faith Obsolete*? (Philadelphia: Westminster, 1974), pp. 125-29.

9. Dietrich Bonhoeffer, *Letters and Papers from Prison,* expanded edition (New York: Macmillan, 1971), "After Ten Years," p. 17. On the whole issue of the substantive contribution of Bonhoeffer's theology to the theology of liberation, see the fascinating essay by Julio de

Santa Ana, "The Influence of Bonhoeffer on the Theology of Liberation," *Ecumenical Review,* April 1976, pp. 188-97. This is a treatment of Bonhoeffer's impact on the Protestant ISAL group in Latin America. On the other side, Gustavo Gutiérrez has noted that while Bonhoeffer was concerned about ministry to the "nonbeliever," the real task in Latin America today is ministry to the "non-person."

10. Much help is given in the definitive biography of Tillich: Pauck and Pauck, *Paul Tillich: His Life and Thought,* vol. 1 (New York: Harper & Row, 1976), esp. chap. 3.

11. The roots of Barth's position are helpfully explored in George Hunsinger, ed., *Karl Barth and Radical Politics* (Philadelphia: Westminster, 1976).

12. Moltmann has been both appreciated and attacked by Latin Americans. Cf. *inter alia,* Rubem Alves, *A Theology of Human Hope* (Washington, D.C.: Corpus Books, 1969); Hugo Assmann, *Opresión-Liberación: Desafío a los cristianos* (Montevideo: Tierra Nueva, 1971); Assmann, *Theology for a Nomad Church* (Maryknoll, New York: Orbis Books, 1976); José Míguez Bonino, *Doing Theology in a Revolutionary Situation* (Philadelphia: Fortress Press, 1975). Moltmann has responded to comments about him in the latter book in, "On Latin American Liberation Theology: An Open Letter to José Míguez Bonino," in *Christianity and Crisis,* March 29, 1976, pp. 57-63, reprinted in this volume.

13. A convenient collection of these documents is found in *The Gospel of Peace and Justice: Catholic Social Teaching since Pope John,* presented by Joseph Gremillion (Maryknoll, New York: Orbis Books, 1976).

14. Paul Bock, *In Search of a Responsible World Society* (Philadelphia: Westminster, 1974), offers a brief historical treatment of these and other themes in recent World Council history, updating the pioneer work by Fr. Edward Duff, S.J., *The Social Thought of the World Council of Churches* (New York: Association Press, 1956).

15. As an exercise to test this proposal, I suggest reading the following Roman Catholic documents in their chronological order to see if one cannot be "radicalized" in the process: *Gaudium et Spes* (1965), *Populorum Progressio* (1967), the Medellín documents on "Peace" and "Justice" (1968), *Octogesima Adveniens* (1971), and the declaration of "Christians for Socialism" (1972).

16. Elie Wiesel, *The Oath* (New York: Random House, 1973), p. 214.

17. I have developed some of the implications of this concern and the need to move beyond it in more detail in "Who Is This Jesus Christ Who Frees and Unites?" *The Ecumenical Review,* January 1976, pp. 6-21.

18. Helder Camara, *The Desert Is Fertile,* trans. Dinah Livingstone (Maryknoll, New York: Orbis Books, 1974), p. 13.

Birth Pangs:
Liberation Theology
in North America

Frederick Herzog

Many North American Christians have difficulty identifying
with two fundamental emphases of liberation theology: God's
commitment to the poor; and praxis comes first, then theology.
The reason for the difficulty, Frederick Herzog explains, is that
"systematic theology [has] systematically ignored the poor as
its hermeneutical starting point," and "all of us have been
brainwashed by the model of theological education we grew up
with. It was theory first, then application." Herzog, who
teaches theology at Duke University Divinity School, complains that North American theological schools "are enclaves of
self-perpetuating intellectual elites reversing the order of God's
priorities. Thought gives rise to thought—world without end. In
the New Testament it is the opposite. Praxis gives rise to
thought, action/reflection including acknowledgment of the
claims of the poor." Herzog's article originally appeared in the
December 15, 1976 issue of *The Christian Century*, and is reprinted by permission of the Christian Century Foundation.

Once considered exotic and fanciful, liberation theologies now
have a good chance of becoming the way ahead for theology in
the next century—if only they can manage to be true both to the
aspirations of the oppressed and to the reality of the beyond in
their midst ["Third World Theology, Fourth World Liberation," *The Christian Century*, May 19, 1976, p. 477].

    With all the myths still surrounding liberation theologies, it
is important that those of us involved in these efforts attempt to

state with some clarity the dynamics of the process in the United States. A fad it is not. Even *Time* sensed that: "If anything, liberation theology may well be just too demanding to become a fad" (September 1, 1975).

North American liberation theologies are not, of course, identical to those of Latin America. The Latins are confronted with poverty on a vaster scale. They have had to cope with liberation more concretely when socialists acceded to power. The present formulations on our part of the American continent are at best only beginnings. Could we think of them as birth pangs, agonies heralding a new life?

At least we have progressed to the point that U.S. Christians are no longer saying: "Liberation theologies are only for the Third World." We are also past the time when liberation theologies in the U.S. were concealed, like an unwanted pregnancy. Recently conflicts have arisen as some liberal theologians have sought to abort the liberation theology effort (cf. "Protestant Liberalism Reaffirmed," by Deane William Ferm, *The Christian Century,* April 28, 1976, p. 411). No matter—in the crucible of conflict and affliction a new vision of theology may be formed. Some say that liberation theology is merely a thematic theology. Not so: it is one of the few unrelenting efforts to think hard about the theological task as a whole.

A fruitful debate has begun in the south, though much of it is still in the "oral tradition" stage. One characteristic of the liberation theology effort is that it is hammered out in oral communication. Especially from oral exchange we know which elementary presuppositions need to be challenged. Leroy T. Howe, editor of the *Perkins Journal,* has graciously made some of that dialogue accessible in print, stating among other things that liberation theology cannot make good on its claim to relevance in the southern situation by "looking in more kindly fashion on the poor" (*Perkins Journal,* Summer 1976).

The Objective Claims of the Poor

Whether in the south or in the country as a whole, we will not be able to understand what is going on unless we acknowledge the premise of liberation theology in this regard. To put it somewhat rashly: liberation theology in the U.S. did not emerge because some people were looking in more kindly fashion on the poor, but because the poor were looking in more unkindly fashion on some people. In a new encounter with the Bible, the poor crossed the threshold of the theological consciousness. God's claim in the poor Christ was felt anew. The experience was not triggered by the kindly sentiments of do-gooder white theologians. Rather, "objective" claims made on us by God and by the poor on the margins of society turned us around. Unless this "objective" event is acknowledged, one does not get one step further in understanding liberation theologies in the U.S. The human condition is obviously characterized by a goodly number of dimensions. The relationship between the poor and the rich is one dimension among others, but one that has been widely overlooked in Protestant theology.

Are we expected to provide warrants for this dimension? Is that not like asking Christopher Columbus to provide warrants for the existence of the New World? For a long time countless people believed that the world was flat. There are still those who do. The only thing one can say is: take a look for yourself. What we are arguing is that the poor are part of the human condition—and if in theology we overlook them, we will not encounter God. We can no longer theologize apart from the global social context. Liberation theology is created for us by the world's poor and the God of the poor.

Why Begin Again with the Bible?

The discovery of the poor would probably be less offensive were it not coupled to a recovery of the Bible.

But why *now* should one want to begin again with the Bible, in an ecumenical age whose major thrust now appears to be from many quarters the recovery of *tradition*, a common Christian history? Return to *sola scriptura* seems regressive in an ecumenical age for whom Scripture is primary but whose available resources for theological interpretation are more encompassing than *mere* Scripture [Leroy T. Howe].

This is the kingpin of all the arguments against liberation theology in the United States. The counterargument is that all of us have been brainwashed by the model of theological education we grew up with. It was theory first, then practice. First, courses in church history, systematic theology, etc.; then, somewhere down the pike, application. What some of us learned in a new action/reflection encounter with the New Testament and its poor is that praxis comes first, and that theology is built into it as a second step. The New Testament writings grow out of a particular praxis. Theology today has to arrange itself accordingly.

To begin again with the Bible means to begin again with praxis. The model of theological education today is still much more the philosophical academy than Christian praxis. Theological schools are enclaves of self-perpetuating intellectual elites reversing the order of God's priorities. Thought gives rise to thought—world without end. In the New Testament it is the opposite. Praxis gives rise to thought, action/reflection including acknowledgment of the claims of the poor.

To call this a return to *sola scriptura* is a misnomer. We're not going to the Bible for proof texts. We're not appealing to a heteronomous authority. Rather, the New Testament Scriptures claim us in the empowerment of Christian praxis. In its beginnings Christianity ushered in a whole new world of brainpower. As compared with biblical praxis, theological education as we know it today is an anachronism. Most theology still tries to interpret the world in terms of abstract theory, an ideal pattern at a safe distance from history. It does not really think. It dreams—in the ivory tower. Hard theological thinking happens only as the mind pierces the granite of history and carves out the truth in toil and sweat in the midst of conflict. Exactly in this way it differs from pragmatic how-to concerns of practical theology courses. Theological education today is flooded with practical concerns but lacks brainpower.

In praxis empowered by the New Testament, it is not we who create theology, but the God of the poor. This is the way Christianity began. This is the way it still begins, making us immerse ourselves in history. So long as the fundamental necessity of praxis is not conceded, there is little hope for appreciation of the thinking which liberation theology tries to engender.

For those unfamiliar with the word "praxis," it should be pointed out that it does not mean sheer activism. Praxis seeks to get at the interaction of deed and thought, the holistic embodiment of meaning. David Tracy has offered us an unsurpassably clear characterization: "Such *praxis*, of course, is not to be identified with practice. Rather *praxis* is correctly understood as the critical relationship between theory and practice whereby each is dialectically influenced and transformed by the other" *(Blessed Rage for Order: The New Pluralism in Theology* [Seabury, 1975], p. 243). The New Testament is that witness in the Christian tradition where dialectical influence and transformation are whole. Wholeness is its warrant.

Playing Chess Without the King

There are several kinds of liberation theology developing in the U.S. at present. Among white males involved in the process, we find at least two distinct types of theology—the one empowered by biblical praxis, the other determined by secular priorities. It is a truism to say that the process of liberation is not exclusively tied to the church. Liberation is tied to multiple causes, in modernity the Enlightenment foremost among them. Thus countless claims on liberation are also made on secular grounds—great! There is no reason, however, to force biblical praxis into straitjackets of secular liberation priorities. If they agree, fine. If not, so be it. But in an overreligionized society like the United States, people get nervous when they cannot maintain the fusion of religion and culture. Since much of Christianity does not jibe with secular liberation, some of it is compelled to conform.

Examples are legion. A recent instance is a book edited by Glenn R. Bucher, *Straight/White/Male* (Fortress, 1976), the moral of which is reflected in the demand that "the Bible will have to be re-edited. Passages that reinforce the oppression of women and gays must be revised, reinterpreted, or eliminated altogether" (p. 66). Only one with a superfundamentalist hangover can still hanker for the Bible as literal authority for all occasions, if only in re-edited form. Its authors never expected to provide literalistic guidelines for the 20th century. But they did want to communicate the power of God (cf. I Cor. 4:20). The whole notion of authority has to be rethought in terms of praxis-empowerment.

The New Testament witnesses communicate the power of God in the Lord Jesus Christ, King of kings (Rev. 17:14). In the church we dare not give the lie to the specific Christian liberation experience. Much that is promulgated today as Christian liberation is playing chess without a king, an exercise in futility. The Bucher book claims: "Straight white males cannot define for others what liberation should mean—the power of definition is a form of oppression" (p. 124). But in the church, defining God in Christ on our own secular or subjective terms is also a form of oppression. Christianity cannot *be* without the Lord Jesus Christ. We won't get on with liberation in the church unless we let "the beyond" in our midst define itself again. Beginning with the New Testament, the Christian community has had a theological way of looking at liberation, not an arbitrary secular way. In the south this is our fundamental spiritual experience.

The tenor of present liberation-theology reflection is often excoriated as too political or sociological. In the south, we have had a completely different orientation. The first concern is a recovery of *God* as justice. This emphasis coincides with the best of Latin American liberation theology. Says Gustavo Gutierrez: "An authentic theology is always a spiritual theology." Liberation theology is also an act of prayer, of worship and of contemplation, but in the midst of politics and economics where all of us live. It seeks to evoke a dynamic evangelism and mission that embody God's justice. Its motto is struggle and *contemplation*.

The Schleiermacher Cul-de-Sac

Quite a number of white male theologians, while not buying into the more secular demands of liberation, still want to retain the liberal starting point of theology developed by Friedrich Schleiermacher as they seek to tie into the liberation process. Most recently this approach has been perfected by Peter C.

Hodgson (in *New Birth of Freedom: A Theology of Bondage and Liberation* [Fortress, 1976]): "Schleiermacher offered a phenomenological description of religious experience formally similar to what we are proposing . . ." (p. 122). However, it is this very Schleiermacherian approach which tunes out commitment to God's praxis as starting point of theology.

The bias of the approach is that the white male theologian already knows—before he turns to God's praxis—what the essence of Christianity is. So what he first has to do is to develop the intellectual framework for making sense of the Christian faith. The theological argument thus begins by showing that theological doctrines "correspond to something essential in human being and experience" (Hodgson, p. 121). "Human being and experience" are here phenomenologically described as universally available without class determination. That is, there's no serious reflection on the difference between the rich and the poor.

A careful study of Schleiermacher shows that he was explicating the human being and experience of the rising Prussian bourgeoisie. The liberal theologian thus usually defines as religiously possible what is possible for the bourgeois human being and experience. Over the years I have walked in Schleiermacher's footsteps from the Herrnhuter dissenters to the Halle establishment to his king's Berlin. I am no longer surprised that toward the end of his life he could declare:

> Since the peace of Tilsit we have made tremendous progress, without revolution, without houses of parliament, even without freedom of the press. But always the people with the king, and the king with the people. Wouldn't one be out of one's mind to think that we would make more progress with a revolution? For my part, I'm very sure always to be on the side of the king when I'm on the side of the intellectual leaders of the nation [*Friedrich Daniel Ernst Schleiermacher,* by Friedrich Wilhelm Kantzenbach (Rowohlt, 1967), p. 145].

I know very well that Schleiermacher at crucial points of his career showed courageous independence of political judgment. My question is: to which class was he loyal? Which class interests was he expounding when he interpreted religion as the universal feeling of absolute dependence? If we copy his approach, will we not inevitably have to be loyal to the same class?

I'm not excoriating Schleiermacher, but rather our inability in our situation to think as creatively as Schleiermacher in his day. Liberation theology, as I understand it, makes a radical break with Protestant liberalism's feeling of absolute dependence on Schleiermacher. It is important to see that Roman Catholics as well still orient themselves in this approach. We can learn much from David Tracy's *Blessed Rage for Order.* But his Schleiermacherian commitment to the ''community of the church'' and the academic ''community of inquiry'' refined in a revisionist method of correlation inevitably relegates the explicit discussion of praxis to the end of the book. God's commitment to the poor nowhere appears as part of the model of systematic theology determining the whole enterprise. In view of the approaches taken by white male theologians, Roman Catholics as well as Protestants, liberation theology in the U.S. is unfortunately forced to develop a model all its own, painful though it is to go it alone. There's nothing to be gained from Schleiermacher anymore. In our day his approach has reached a dead end.

Karl Marx as Watershed

As we all know, Latin American liberation theologians are deeply engaged with Marxism. Recently at Maryknoll, just for the record, I asked Gustavo Gutierrez: ''Why do you use Marx in your theology?''

''Because the people use him,'' he shot back. That's a crucial point. We can't say anything similar about the North American poor, at least not in the south. Our struggle took a different route. The black/white confrontation initially led us to face the horror of racism as the hermeneutical starting point of theology. In the south, theology has a focus strikingly similar to politics. We would have been out of our minds—to use the Schleiermacher phrase—had we failed to pay attention to politicians like Jimmy Carter, whose politics developed out of the same nitty-gritty: "To an amazing degree the lives of both black and white Southerners have been centered around the church. The 'Bible Belt' designation is substantiated in fact" (*Why Not the Best?* by Jimmy Carter [Bantam Books, 1976], p. 125).

I wish the constant carping on our use of the Bible could stop right here and now. Why do we use the Bible in our theology? Because the people use it. This does not mean that we have closed our eyes to Karl Marx. But we want all the world to know that our use of Marx in theology at this time is a matter of cerebration. In our neck of the woods there are no Marxist poor to identify with. Anyone who says otherwise is telling a tall tale.

What we are doing in North America by using Marx in theology is expounding the revolutionary significance of the poor for theology—a task "dangerous" enough. There's a brutal clash in theology on this point. And yet the clash need not be. There is simply the catch-up need to acknowledge the historical watershed position of Marx. When Schleiermacher was still taking sides with the intellectual leaders of the nation, Karl Marx was being readied for the discovery of the "proletariat." It did not enter Schleiermacher's ken that the uneducated classes were an issue for theory as well as praxis. The cultured despisers of religion remained his theological orientation point throughout his life. In a sense, Protestant theology has had blinders on ever since. Whatever may have happened in Christian ethics, systematic theology systematically ignored the poor at its hermeneutical starting point. So ideological smokescreens more and more clouded the vision of the theologian. The whole focus on religion as the chief concern of systematic theology became part of the concealment syndrome of the ruling classes.

It is here that we are most at the beginnings. Through the young Reinhold Niebuhr, especially his *Moral Man and Immoral Society* (1932), Marx impinged on a significant segment of American Protestant thought. However strong the influence might have been, the impact remained primarily in the field of ethics. Systematic theology kept chiefly on the Schleiermacher track and paid little attention to the point Marx tried to make.

Now that can change. For liberation theology in the U.S., Marx initially is important in at least two respects: as demystification and as social analysis. There is still the terrifying abuse of God by society as well as the abuse of God by theology itself in legitimating the abuse by society.

A recent cartoon with two executives at a manager's desk reflects the blasphemy as one tells the other: "Before God made profits, he made production, and before production, he made capital. So be it" (*Time*, August 16, 1976). Taking the Lord's name in vain ain't funny. God's name here is taken in vain not in the abstract but in the socioeconomic and sociopolitical matrix where all of us live. Marx radically questions the idolatry implied. Without Marx's theory, we will continue to take God's name in vain in economics and politics. All we are saying now in liberation theology is this: in the United States we've finally got to take Reinhold Niebuhr's pioneering step seriously in theology as well as in social ethics.

There can be no systematic theology in North America today without the analysis of Marx. It has become a question of giving an adequate rationale for what Protestant theology is all about in the global village. Theology that does not take the world's poor into account from the word "go" isn't Christian theology. According to David Tracy, the Christian theologian "believes that the Christian faith is at heart none other than the most adequate articulation of the basic faith of secularity itself" (*Blessed Rage for Order*, p. 10). The justice articulated by the secularity in Marx is the justice that churches are still hiding behind the smokescreen of religion. Christianity is all about justice because God is justice. We get a "handle" on the historical process when we understand its momentum toward justice.

Thinking the Historical Process

This is an issue of uncompromising scholarship. The reasons for taking the Lord's name in vain are the primal occasions for *theological* scholarship. Playing footsie with God's justice is what theology is called to guard against. What de-deifies God dehumanizes humanity. It is the practical atheism of the West, exposed by Marx, that dehumanizes humankind. How to come to terms with practical atheism in the United States? Black theology, native American theology and feminist theology have given us the first clues. Without Marx's analysis, however, we will never see—and battle—the *practical* atheism in economics and politics.

I am not blind to what has been developed from Karl Marx's theories in communist countries. But *abusus non tollit usum* (the abuse does not undo the proper use)—a good rule of scholarship. Karl Marx saw something in his day that theologians were blind to. It was not just a matter of not closing one's eyes to the horrors of poverty among the working class. It was especially a matter of paying attention to the historical process—climaxing in industrialization, with its reserve armies of the poor—as a process subject to science and disciplined thinking. I also know the myth of science, and no less the myth of science in Karl Marx. Even so, we today have to try to think through the class contextualization of theology. The particular circumstances are, of course, different. But how else are we going to come to grips, for example, with the continuing presence of the Indian reservation in our midst? The average life expectancy of the native American is 44 years; the unemployment rate is 50 per cent on the average, ranging up to 80 per cent on some reservations.

Christ-centered tautologies don't help us here. Pious sectarian withdrawal from history is unthinkable for the theologian. John B. Cobb makes a crucial point in this regard: "Since the actual decisions about the course of history are made on other grounds and on the basis of a situation that is not Christ-centered, one cuts oneself off from all that" (*Occasional Papers,* United Methodist Board of Higher Education and Ministry, 1:12, August 9, 1976, p. 6). This is the issue: liberation theology seeks to understand why the actual decisions about the course of history are made on grounds other than Christ-centered faith *and* tries to connect the faith with the actual course of history.

Making Praxis Come Alive

It is a misunderstanding, however, when Cobb assumes that the first priority of liberation theology in the U.S. is to mobilize rank-and-file Christians. As though we were generals in search of armies! The more immediate priority is to engender understanding of the impossibility of Christian theology apart from praxis. Cobb is to the point when he states that theology today is sadly unthinking. It is not thinking through what the process of history actually is like. And it is unable to do so because it shuns praxis like the plague.

Making praxis come alive for theology will, of course, mean to tie into North American struggles over the course of history. But whether we turn to Michael Harrington, John Kenneth Galbraith or Peter L. Berger (to mention only a few examples), the thread of thought will always lead back to Marx's watershed position in the "discovery" of the poor. All this cannot go on without Christian criticism of Marxism and other secular perspectives. But the basic watershed datum is nonnegotiable. It is nonnegotiable because of the struggle of real people—warm, suffering, dying people.

In reordering the theological spectrum, liberation theology thus says: (1) biblical praxis-empowerment comes first and (2) social analysis follows. Thus Christian theology emerges. This may be a new way of doing theology.

In many instances theology is still doing the national henchman's job of legitimating injustice, however subtly. Thus the "religious" problem in North America today is not that religion does not give us the right answers but that theology does not give us the right neighbors.

Against the hedonism infecting even theology in our society we are saying: the undisciplined life is not worth living. Much more is at stake than mouthing a few Marxist phrases. We are caught up in an awesome struggle over the character of human personhood. That is what the actual course of history is all about. Creating the new human being for the just society is God's work. Our response will require sacrifice, self-denial and much secular asceticism. But in the agonizing struggle over the new piety, the new chastity and the new social order, we just may be surprised—by justice.

Human Rights and the Mission of the Church

Richard A. McCormick, S.J.

There is tension, even polarization, in the missionary enterprise between those who emphasize evangelization of individuals and those who emphasize liberation of people from the structures of society that oppress and exploit them, and thus deny them their human rights. "What is the Church's proper mission in the sphere of the defense and promotion of human rights?" asks Jesuit theologian Richard A. McCormick. He says the connecting link between evangelization and liberation in all forms is "human dignity as we know it from the Christ-event and the Church's commission to spread this good news." In response to those who stress the salvation of individuals and neglect the need for systemic change, he maintains that "enslaving structures are, pure and simply, unevangelical structures; they factually deny what the Gospel affirms." Therefore, he concludes, "Unless the Church at all levels is an outstanding promoter of the rights of human beings in word and deed, her proclamation will be literally falsified." McCormick is the Rose F. Kennedy Professor of Christian Ethics in the Kennedy Institute for the Study of Bioethics at Georgetown University in Washington, D.C. In 1969 he was named "Outstanding Theologian of the Year" by the Catholic Theological Society of America, of which he is a past president. This article is part of a longer essay that appeared originally under the title "Notes on Moral Theology" in the March 1976 (vol. 37, no. 1) issue of *Theological Studies,* published quarterly in Baltimore for the Theological Faculties of the Society of Jesus in the United States.

There is an undercurrent of concern today about the formulation of the Church's proper mission in the sphere of the defense and promotion of human rights. Two extremes are possible in stating this mission: simple identification of the Church's mission with human liberation and development, or a dualism that unduly separates the two.

In the past there may have been at least verbal leanings toward the latter extreme. Pius XI wrote to Fr. M. D. Roland-Gosselin: "It is necessary never to lose sight of the fact that the objective of the Church is to evangelize not to civilize. If it civilizes, it is for the sake of evangelization."[1] Pius XII in an address (March 9, 1956) stated: "Its divine Founder, Jesus Christ, has not given it [the Church] any mandate or fixed any end of the cultural order. The goal which Christ assigns to it is religious. . . . The Church can never lose sight of the strictly religious, supernatural goal. . . ."[2] Vatican II itself noted: "Christ, to be sure, gave His Church no proper mission in the political, economic, or social order. The purpose which He set before her is a religious one."[3]

Terms such as "proper mission" and "strictly religious" cry out for clarification; for they are capable of yielding a very dualistic meaning which ends up restricting the mission of the Church to instruction in the faith, liturgy, preaching, and sacraments—in brief, a kind of "sanctuary Christianity." In this view those directly concerned in one way or another with righting unjust social structures would not be involved in the Church's "proper mission" or with something "religious."

Pope Paul once again struggled (I believe the word is not inaccurate) with the formulation of these matters in his opening address to the fourth Synod of Bishops in September 1974. While speaking of the "specific finality" of evangelization, he made the following suggestion to the assembled bishops: "It will be necessary to define more accurately the relationship between evangelization properly so-called and the whole human effort toward development for which the Church's help is rightly expected, even though this is not her specific task."[4] Now if it is necessary to define this relationship more accurately, clearly such a definition seems not yet to have been achieved. He warns against forgetting the priority of the message of salvation and thus reducing "their own action to mere sociological or political activity, and the message of the Church to a man-centered and temporal message." His final statement about evangelization and human progress is that "there is no opposition or separation, therefore, but a complementary relationship between evangelization and human progress. While distinct and subordinate, one to the other, each calls for the other by reason of their convergence toward the same end: the salvation of man."

Here one is tempted to ask: If human progress and liberation converge toward the salvation of man, why are they not the proper mission of the Church?

In his report to the Synod, Archbishop Joseph L. Bernardin stated that no one (from the region he represented) questions the integral relationship between evangelization and human liberation; however, there was a difference in the emphasis to be given to this relationship. In developed countries "the need for the Church to deal with the themes of justice and peace is felt as a demand of the gospel. . . ."[5] Speaking for the bishops of South America, Bishop Eduardo Pironio referred frequently to "complete liberation in Christ," "liberation of the whole man."[6] He referred to a "dualism between faith and life," but cautioned against a "superficial identification between evangelization and human advancement" (which he saw as a real danger in South America).

After these preparatory statements, the Synod issued (Oct. 23, 1974) its statement "On Human Rights and Reconciliation."[7] This statement is extremely interesting. It refers to the fact that the "integral development of persons," the "complete liberation of man," makes clearer in man the divine image. "Hence she [the Church] believes firmly that the promotion of human rights is *required by the gospel* and is *central to her ministry*."[8] Then, speaking of the relationship between evangelization and liberation, the document first notes that the Church as evangelizer must conform to Christ, who was sent "to announce glad tidings to the poor, to give prisoners their freedom, the blind their sight, to set the oppressed free" (Lk 4:18). Faithful to this mission the Church "can draw from the gospel . . . ever new incentives to . . . eliminate the social consequences of sin which are translated into unjust social and political structures."[9] Thus, for the Synod, correction of unjust social and political structures is *part* of evangelization, though evangelization does not stop there but leads to "full communion with God and with men."

Pope Paul felt compelled ("We could not allow false directions to be followed") to return to this subject at the close of the Synod. After noting that human liberation had been rightly emphasized as part of that love Christians owe their brethren, he warned that the "totality of salvation is not to be confused with one or other aspect of liberation. . . . Hence human advancement, social progress, etc. are not to be excessively emphasized on a temporal level to the detriment of the essential meaning which evangelization has for the Church of Christ: the announcement of the good news."[10] Obviously, the Pontiff felt that this or that aspect of liberation was being confused with the totality of salvation and that there was excessive emphasis on the temporal aspects of social progress.

I have cited these documents extensively because they manifest a very human and understandable groping toward a balanced formulation of the Church's mission in the social sphere. One can sense in this movement from "no proper mission" to "required by the gospel and central to her mission" a kind of consciousness-in-transition. Where is that consciousness now? It is hard to say, but perhaps it could be put as follows: elimination of the social consequences of sin is essential to the Church's evangelizing mission but does not exhaust this mission—and therefore should not be "excessively emphasized." As noted, this matter is of more than speculative interest. It has everything to do with how ministry is conceived, implemented, and supported at all levels. For instance, unless I am mistaken, the phrase "genuinely priestly work"—taken exclusively to mean preaching and administration of the sacraments—must be seen as a relic.

Here attention should be called to a long and very detailed document issued by the Pontifical Commission on Justice and Peace.[11] The document reviews the Church's teaching on human rights from the time of Pope Leo XIII to the present and shows how these rights, rooted in the dignity of the person, receive new light and depth through the Incarnation which so luminously affirmed this dignity *(imago Dei)*. At one point the document notes that "although the Church with her religious role has no proper mission in the political, social, or economic order, she is far from looking on religion as purely private. . . ." A bit later the study states that to imitate Christ and to be his true continuation in the world "the Church as a whole, like every Christian community, is called to work for the dignity and rights of man, both individually and collectively; to protect and promote the dignity of the human person; and to denounce and oppose every sort of human oppression."

One has to wonder whether the borrowed phrase "no proper mission" is really appropriate. If it is integral to the Church's mission to protect and promote human rights, and if these rights are violated precisely by unjust political, economic, and social structures, does not the Church have a proper mission, at least in some sense, in the political, economic, and social order? Otherwise, what does it mean to say that the "Church . . . is called to work for the dignity and rights of men," that this is integral to her mission? Indeed, at one point the study refers to "a continuously political community. . . ." Again we read: "To take part in the process of liberating the whole man, as seen in the light of the gospel, is an indispensable element in any genuine pastoral mission of effective and authentic proclamation."[12] Now if this liberation is from every form of slavery (sin and selfishness and their effects in the social sphere), as the document insists, then it seems that the Church does indeed have a proper mission in the social, political, and economic areas. I realize that the word "proper" (as in the phrase "proper mission") can be understood to mean "exclusively the Church's," "hers and no one else's," etc. But this is not the way the term is generally understood and will be understood.

Much of the concern over formulating the Church's proper mission in the social sphere stems from the emergence of the theology of liberation. The literature on liberation theology is already out of control.[13] Only a few recent entries can be touched here and they will be reviewed uniquely from the perspective of the Church's mission. The purpose, therefore, is neither to defend nor to attack liberation theology. There are already sufficient combatants in that arena. Among the attackers, e.g., Andrew Greeley and Michael Novak are, if not *facile principes,* very upward-mobile contenders.[14]

Francis P. Fiorenza presents a useful comparison between political theology and liberation theology.[15] He uses Metz, Moltmann, and Sölle as examples of the latter. Fiorenza finds three common elements in the political theologians. "The contemporary situation is secularized, the existential response is inadequate, and a political (public) theology is not a theology of politics, but a hermeneutical task . . ." The inadequacy of the existential response refers to the fact that a theology of transcendental subjectivity privatizes the Christian message and confirms the withdrawal of religion from societal life. The "hermeneutical task" refers to the discovery of those principles of the Christian message that reveal its meaning for the life of all people, not just the individual.

By contrast, the situation of the liberation theologians of Latin America is remarkably different. It is not one of secularization and consequent privatization of faith, as in Europe. Thus, Gutierrez criticizes Metz for predicating of the world what describes only parts of it, and not Latin America. The Church still has power in Latin America and the question is: how is it to be used in the service of society? Secondly, liberation theologians are at one in criticizing "developmentalism," namely, the attempt to achieve social advances within existing structures without altering these structures. Thirdly, where political theology concentrates on the proper hermeneutic, liberation theology is "concerned with the interpretations of the Christian symbols of faith."

Here Fiorenza notes that "at the center of all the deliberations by the liberation theologians stands the question of the Church and its mission."[16] The heart of this mission is to be a sign of universal salvation. The Church realizes this mission in so far as it signifies and proclaims that salvation. How does it do this? In many ways, but "its confrontation with the oppression and injustice of its concrete situation is an integral part of its mission to be the sign of salvation."

Fiorenza concludes that the critics of liberation theology (e.g., Richard Neuhaus, who warns that Gutierrez ultimately equates the mission of the Church with revolutionary struggle) have misunderstood it; for even though liberation theologians insist on a direct, immediate relationship between faith and political action, they also argue that if faith is to develop norms and criteria for political action and options, it can do so only on the basis of a concrete historical and societal analysis. A very thoughtful article.

René Coste reviews many of the key books on liberation theology, including several that are highly critical (e.g., uncritical acceptance of the terms "praxis" and "history," tendency to identify the kingdom of God and political liberation, uncritical use of Marxist categories, selective use of scriptural texts for prefixed theses, etc.).[17] Coste then gives his own evaluation: liberation theology is fecund, yet quite discussible. Among the discussible aspects Coste includes the fact that this theology is "insufficiently clear" on the mission of the Church. That is, he believes the Church ought to have a liberating political impact "on the condition that it remain faithful to its specific mission, which is a mission of salvation and not a mission directly political." Otherwise, Coste is convinced, the Church will fall into a new form of social messianism.

A pastoral session met in Paris (Sept. 13-15, 1974) to discuss the social apostolate. It included many bishops, representatives of lay movements, priests, religious, and some theologians. Following this lively discussion, the Permanent Council of the French Episcopate proposed its own reflections under title of *Les libérations des hommes et le salut en Jésus Christ.*[18] The document attempts to relate liberation movements to salvation, that is, it searches for the specificity of the Church's mission. The episcopal document first cautions against either dissociating or confusing liberation and Christian salvation. Some oppose these dualistically, some identify them uncritically. Such errors are analogous to deviations of the past wherein either the divinity or humanity was isolated in Christ's salvific activity. The relationship, the document states, "cannot be expressed either in terms of a radical rupture or in those of a continuity without breaking points."

How, then, is the relationship to be understood? The French episcopal analysis begins by describing salvation. "In so far as he is savior, Jesus introduces us to the life of the Trinity and associates us with the work of the Father in which he is incessantly at work. In Jesus Christ salvation is already given, the kingdom of God is already present in the gift that inaugurates communion with God.''[19] But this salvation cannot be conceived in a ''spiritualistic'' way; rather, by grace it is the transfiguration of everything human. It should not be seen as a salvation to be realized in the future and elsewhere, but rather as the mysterious growth of the kingdom already present, even though not fully revealed and realized. For this reason, the document argues, ''the essential link between salvation and liberation consists in this meeting between man who aspires to freedom and fights to be himself, and the God of the Alliance, who is present in the heart of history to lead it to its final term. Thus man does not reach God by leaving the world, but by inserting himself in it and collaborating with the Creator's plan.''[20]

In conclusion, the French document insists, on the one hand, on the irreducibility and radicality of salvation. On the other, it asserts that ''Christians would be unfaithful to their mission of evangelizing if they did not mobilize effectively to work with all their brothers, believers and nonbelievers, for the liberation of men, of each person and all persons.'' But the means it uses are proper to itself: ''announcing the good news, service of the word of God, communication of the riches of the paschal mystery through the sacraments and prayer.''

It is highly doubtful that liberationists from Latin America would rest satisfied with such a formulation. Segundo Galilea, writing in the Mexico City monthly *Servir,* has a good summary of what liberation theology is all about. He notes that the appeal of the Medellín *Conclusions* ''was meant to remind the Church of its proper sociopolitical role, which it had quite forgotten in recent decades.''[21] He sees this theology as an attempt to move beyond dualism, yet to preserve both the autonomy of the sociopolitical and the transcendence of salvation.

Even though liberation theology is no monolith, Galilea sees three presuppositions in it: (1) the condition of underdevelopment and unjust dependence; (2) a Christian interpretation of this as a ''situation of sin''; (3) the pressure on the conscience of Christians to commit themselves to remedying the situation. On the basis of these three themes, liberation theology's ''fundamental objective is to clarify the intrinsic relation there is in

God's plan between sociopolitical, economic, and cultural liberation and the eschatological salvation by Jesus Christ.''

Galilea acknowledges the criticisms that this theology has encountered. He argues, however, that it must not be seen as a single, uniform school, but as a pluralistic current. Furthermore, one must carefully distinguish in this current the truly theological literature from the abundant documentation on the sociopolitical liberation theme. Failure to make the distinction has hurt liberation theology.

In his presentation to the 1974 Synod of Bishops, Peruvian Bishop Germán Schmitz asked the Synod to "declare the word 'liberation' and its integral meaning *an* essential—if not *the* essential—element in the notion of salvation."[22] For him, this integral meaning includes positive liberation (freedom for full communion with God and neighbor) and negative liberation (the break with sin in the heart of man and in the unjust structures of society "that keep people from thinking and acting as children of God and brothers in Christ"). The Bishop does not say so, but if liberation is "an integral part of God's salvific plan," it would seem to follow that the Church has a "proper role" in all aspects of liberation.

If this is so, the Church must get involved in politics to some extent. Dom Helder Camara, Archbishop of Olinda and Recife, addressed this subject in the Synod bluntly and stirringly.[23] He acknowledged the risk to the Church in being considered political and subversive, but added: "The time has come now for the Church to stop worrying about the accusation of getting into politics. 'Politics' is simply a synonym for working for the common good, i.e., advancing the dignity of the human person and the concrete conditions that insure that dignity."

A pamphlet published by Mons. Miguel Obando, Archbishop of Managua (Nicaragua), faces the same problem, "getting into politics."[24] The Church simply has to get into politics in the sense of seeing to it "that the subject and object of the economy is man." She ought not to be in politics if this means speaking for or against a given political system that is simply trying to translate into effective and productive terms the laws of economics. Economic structures, the Archbishop points out, will either be constructive for man's dignity or they will not. "If they are not, then the Church, to safeguard the very value of man, who is willy-nilly caught up in and dependent on economic activity, must take steps to combat those structures. That is its mission. A mission that the entire Church must fulfill— hierarchy, lay people, and religious, each according to the nature and function of his particular vocation in the Church." Thus the Church must speak and act concerning the justice and injustice of given situations, but it can do so freely "precisely because it refuses to be captured by any one faction or party." This is a far cry from those approaches that speak of the relation of the Church to the economic and political spheres through means "proper to herself."

In the foregoing sampling of a huge literature, the center of concern has been the relation of salvation to human liberation in all its forms (economic, political, racial, sexual, etc). This relationship obviously determines the basic meaning of evangelization and its appropriate methods. One senses a tension throughout this literature, almost a foreknowledge of the fact that the attempt to formulate the matter is, given the mysterious depth of our salvation in Christ and its "already" but "not yet" character, doomed to failure. When the transcendence of salvation is emphasized, its immanent claims seem to be minimized. When the immanent claims (liberation) are urged, there is the ever-present danger of collapsing salvation into a particular socioeconomic policy. Thus the literature represents a series of *sic et non* statements, with the *sics* getting much stronger emphasis in the Latin American version of liberation theology than elsewhere.

When this literature is viewed from the perspective of the Church's mission, the following emphases would represent, I believe, the thrust or direction of thought:

    (1) a move away from statements asserting that the Church has "no proper mission in the political, economic or social order."

    (2) This move is made, above all, in terms of human rights.

    (3) These rights are founded on the dignity of man.

    (4) This dignity is stated in and sharply illumined by the

gospel—a dignity rooted in what man already is in Christ. (This represents a slight de-emphasis in the vocabulary associated with the natural-law presentation of rights, though by no means its denial.)

(5) Therefore, to preach the gospel, the Church must be concerned with rights.

(6) Rights are at stake in many ways, but especially in unjust and oppressive social structures.

(7) Therefore the Church is necessarily concerned with such structures.

(8) Since these structures are affected, shaped, and often controlled by social, economic, and political factors, the Church is, in her concern for rights, necessarily concerned with these factors, though she must remain beyond any merely partisan or ideological approaches.

(9) This concern is not preparatory to evangelization but is an essential part of it, even though such concern for and promotion of rights does not exhaust the notion of salvation.

If one were to attempt to bring these emphases together into a theological synthesis, the connecting link between evangelization and liberation in all forms would be: human dignity as we know it from the Christ-event and the Church's commission to spread this good news. Man *is* redeemed in Christ. He shares the unspeakable life of God's love, His sonship—mysteriously and inchoatively, but nonetheless really. His life must be a free and deepening embrace of this reality. The Church, the extension of Christ's presence, is in the business of spreading this great good news.

However, if the person as person truly *is* what we say he is (and not merely an imprisoned spirit who will be this in a hereafter if he behaves), then to tell him this (evangelization) is to do all those things that remind him of his true dignity; for if the person *is* someone of dignity, he must be treated as such. To deny him his rights or to tolerate this deprivation is to tell him in a practical way that he is not worth these rights, that he is not dignified. We are reminded of our true worth and dignity by being treated in accordance with this dignity. (It is axiomatic

that we expand and become capable of love by being loved).
Hence the Church's proclamation is necessarily action. She
does not civilize in order to evangelize (a kind of *removens
prohibens*), if one may for the moment use the phraseology of
Pius XI to depart from it. She civilizes because that is an essential aspect of evangelizing. It is the most concrete and effective,
indeed the indispensable, way of communicating to human beings their real worth—namely, the good news. For if the
Church proclaims to people what they truly are here and now,
and yet tolerates a variety of injustices visited upon them, she
literally does not mean what she says. Proclamation of the gospel is by inner necessity concern for those to whom the gospel is
proclaimed; for that gospel is about the kingdom already aborn-
ing. In this sense it is true to say, as has long been admitted, that
the Church's ethical action is *anticipation* of the kingdom and,
as such, proclamation of it.

The power of sin and selfishness remains and it becomes
concrete in the social structures that oppress and enslave.
These structures are a daily reminder to people of their worth-
lessness. If it is not important that the person have equality of
opportunity, reasonable security, religious freedom, sufficient
food, medical care, etc., if it is of no moment that persons in
some countries are desperately poor while others are com-
fortably affluent, then clearly man's real present dignity is of
little moment. Enslaving structures are, purely and simply, unevangelical structures; they factually deny what the gospel
affirms.

That is why the Church at all levels must be involved in
liberation (one can choose his own word). It is the human way,
and therefore the only way, of communicating dignity and therefore of proclaiming. That is why the Church of the past has been
involved in orphanages, the redemption of captives, the care of
the sick, and all kinds of social concerns. And that is why, it
would seem, we must eventually say that she has a proper mission in the political, economic, and social order; for it is these
orders that tell persons in our day in a very concrete way what
they are. And that is what the Church is about. If she renounces
this mission, she renounces proclamation of the good news; and
this she cannot do.

This is not to say that salvation is reducible to e.g., economic liberation or that the Church has a special economic competence. Nor is it to say that one can leap from eschatology into practical economics and politics with a ready-made evangelical solution, ignoring the hard word of social ethics and spurning the achievements of a tradition of civil liberties. It is to say only that the Church's concern in evangelization is people and that if people are being countereducated by economic, social and political structures (counter = told of their real lack of worth and dignity), then she must speak and act. In this sense liberation is absolutely essential to evangelization. However this matter is to be formulated, one thing is clear: unless the Church, at all levels, is an outstanding promoter of the rights of human beings in word and deed, her proclamation will be literally falsified.

NOTES

1. *Semaines sociales de France* (Versailles, 1936) pp. 461-462, as cited in Abbott, *The Documents of Vatican II.* p. 264, n. 192.

2. *Acta apostolicae sedis* 48 (1956) 212.

3. *Gaudium et spes,* no. 42 (Abbott, *The Documents of Vatican II,* p. 241).

4. *Catholic Mind* 73 (1975) 6.

5. *Ibid.,* p. 20.

6. *Ibid.,* p. 35.

7. *Ibid.,* pp. 50-52.

8. *Ibid.,* p. 51; emphasis added.

9. *Ibid.,* p. 56.

10. *Ibid.,* p. 63.

11. "The Church and Human Rights," *L'Osservatore romano* (English edition) 1975, Oct. 23, pp. 6-8, Oct. 30, pp. 8-9, Nov. 6, pp. 6-8, Nov. 13, pp. 9-10.

12. *Ibid.,* Nov. 6.

13. For a bibliography cf. Francis P. Fiorenza, "Latin American Liberation Theology," *Interpretation* 28 (1974) 441-57; Egidio Vigano Cattaneo, "Fe y liberación," *Estudios teológicos* 2 (1975) 139-215; "Latin American Liberation Theology," *Theology Digest* 23 (1975) 241-50.

14. Michael Novak, "Theology of Liberation," *National Catholic Reporter,* Nov. 21, 1975, p. 12; Andrew Greeley, "Liberation without Freedom?" *Catholic Chronicle* (Toledo), Nov. 28, 1975, p. 5 (a syndicated column, found in many diocesan papers).

15. Francis P. Fiorenza, "Political Theology and Liberation The-

ology: An Inquiry into their Fundamental Meaning," in *Liberation, Revolution, and Freedom,* ed. Thomas M. McFadden (New York, 1975) pp. 3-29.

16. *Ibid.,* p. 21.

17. René Coste, "Foi et société: 'Liberation et salut,'" *Esprit et vie* 85 (1975) 577-88. The article is marked "a suivre."

18. Paris, 1975, pp. 1-107, I am using Coste's summary and also "Liberazione degli uomini e salvezza in Gesù Cristo," *Civiltà* cattolica 126 (1975) 3-12.

19. *Les libérations des hommes et le salut en Jésus Christ,* p. 33.

20. *Ibid.,* p. 36.

21. Segundo Galilea, "Liberation Theology Began with Medellín," *Ladoc,* May 1975, pp. 1-6.

22. Germán Schmitz, "Let's Officialize the Word 'Liberation,' " *ibid.,* pp. 7-8.

23. Helder Camara, "The Gospel and Liberation," *Ladoc,* Sept.–Oct. 1975, pp. 30-34.

24. Miguel Obando, "Should the Church Be in Politics?" *Ladoc,* June 1975, pp. 29-31.

Liberation
and Conformity

Jim Wallis

"Evangelicalism has become rich, fat, patriotic, and very comfortable with the present order of things," says Jim Wallis,
editor of *Sojourners,* the Washington, D.C., journal of those
sometimes described as "the evangelical left." Scornful of "the
capitalist captivity of the churches," Wallis contends "it was the
trust in the legitimacy of the system that gave rise to the political and economic conformity which has bankrupted evangelical
ethics." It is, therefore, very difficult, he says, "to grant the
integrity of evangelical critiques of liberation theology from an
evangelical theology which has spent much of its energy justifying the privilege of the powerful and the poverty of the poor."
Wallis warns, however, against Christian conformity to any regime, because "biblical politics are invariably alien to the politics of the established regime *and* will also question the politics
of the new regime that any revolution will eventually establish
for itself." Those who hope in the gospel alone, he urges, will
"establish an eternal revolutionary posture in the world . . .
never being satisfied to rest false hopes in the powers and idols
and systems of the world that continually claim to be our salvation." This article is reprinted from the September 1976 issue of
Sojourners.

Liberation is God's intention. Liberation from all the spiritual, structural, and ideological shackles which bind and
oppress—is the promise of God's salvation in history. The God
of the Bible is about the creation of a new peoplehood who
begin to experience the reconciliation, the justice, the healing,
the wholeness, the fellowship that God wills to restore to men

51

and women and to the entire creation. If liberation is so close to the heart and purpose of God, liberation must clearly be on the agenda of the people of God.

In addressing the question of liberation, the church faces a double danger. First, there is the constant tendency in the churches to withdraw to the private religiosity that spiritualizes liberation into personal piety, removes the gospel message from its concrete historical situation, and retreats into the contradictory religious experience that seems to deny the world while being totally conformed to its dominant values, structures, and ideological assumptions.

The other danger is to reduce the meaning of liberation to a particular political option, to equate it with movements and systems, and to replace one set of idols with another.

Both of these dangers are clearly evident in the present discussions and controversies surrounding the emergence of "liberation theology," a movement born out of the experience of oppression especially in Latin America and elsewhere in the Third World.

This new way of "doing theology" has put forward a clear and prophetic challenge to the capitalist captivity of the churches in the rich nations. In unmasking the idolatries of North American and European theology, however, it must be said that liberation theologians run the danger of establishing new idolatries and falling into new ideological captivities which may, ultimately, be as difficult to escape as the ones which presently bind the life and paralyze the witness of the affluent churches.

The familiar piety of American evangelicalism has been shaken to its foundations in recent times. Harsh revelations, come by way of such events as the civil rights movement, Vietnam, and Watergate, have uncovered the racism, violence, and economic greed at the heart of the American spirit and system. Religion that was merely private and not public seemed empty after such shattering experiences. A gospel given solely for the sake of our eternal salvation and not for the sake of the world seemed painfully inadequate. The old evangelical advice to keep your personal life morally upright and trust the government and the economy for the rest was no longer enough.

It was the trust in the legitimacy of the system that gave rise to the political and economic conformity which has bankrupted evangelical ethics. Belief in the system is always required of those who seek a place in it. So, as established evangelical leaders and institutions have struggled to extricate themselves from the cultural backwaters of fundamentalism and carve out for themselves a place of cultural and intellectual respectability, they have had to pay the price of success. Evangelicalism has become rich, fat, patriotic, and very comfortable with the present order of things.

It is therefore difficult to grant the integrity of evangelical critiques of liberation theology from an evangelical theology which has spent much of its energy justifying the privilege of the powerful and the poverty of the poor. It is very hard to accept the scathing attacks on the violence of liberation movements from evangelicals who have defended every American military, political, and commercial aggression for decades. Denunciations of the abuses of socialism ring quite hollow when being offered by the affluent and loyal beneficiaries of American capitalism, clinging to a system that is morally dead and ought to die, justifying a way of structuring the world that can only be preserved by the use of the superior firepower of the rich against the poor. Clearly, the proponents of liberation theology have more to say to evangelicals than most evangelicals have to say to them.

More liberal brands of American religion have been advocating social reform for some time, almost to the point of suggesting that the gospel is intended to change election results, laws and institutional policies more than to change people's lives. Social action agencies have sought to persuade the government to do a better job, tried hard to make the system work, and, most importantly, advised us on how to make our Christianity more politically realistic. The unspoken hope seems to be that our reforms, programs, agencies, and institutional pressure shall overcome.

Here too, the legitimacy of the system has been an article of faith and a reason for trust. Liberal religion and liberal capitalism have enjoyed a close friendship and mutually advantageous alliance for years, both financially and ideologically.

The desires for cultural respectability and political recognition have taken their toll in this segment of the church as well.

In particular, the influence of the "Christian realism" formulations in liberal theological ethics have resulted in a far too eager willingness to meet the system on its own terms. The efforts to develop a "responsible theology of power" have predominated over the desire to bring the presence of the kingdom into the midst of current historical realities with explosive and disruptive power.

Realpolitic has come to replace prophetic witness as religious social activists have been willing to operate within the structural realities and official parameters of public policy rather than to openly challenge basic assumptions. The results have been similar to the evangelical bankruptcy—a paralyzing conformity, a numbing affluence, and a prophetic impotence.

Much of this is changing now, and the emergence of liberation theology is part of this change. From both evangelical and liberal religion, many are openly challenging the church's misplaced trust in the system itself. But what happens when Christians cease to believe in the basic values and structures of their society and culture and rather repudiate them?

Chances are that many will begin to look for another system in which to place their trust, another ideological explanation of things that is more worthy of their allegiance. This transferring of trust from one system to another, this shifting of faith from one ideological consensus to another, is common in the churches. It has been a persistent practice ever since the time when Emperor Constantine wedded the church to the Roman regime and thereby converted the church to the world.

The identification of the church with the regime, either with the established regime or with the new regime that is seeking to replace the old, is Constantinianism. It has manifested itself in many different forms and circumstances. As more Christians become influenced by liberation theology, finding themselves increasingly rejecting the values and institutions of capitalism, they will also be drawn to the Marxist analysis and praxis that is so central to the movement.

That more Christians will come to view the world through Marxist eyes is therefore predictable. It will even be predictable among the so-called "young evangelicals" who, for the most part, have a zeal for social change that is not yet matched by a developed socioeconomic analysis that will cause them to see the impossibility of making capitalism work for justice and peace.

Now that the "new socialist society" is replacing the capitalist system in the minds of many as the hope for the future, growing numbers of Christians will join the movement and seek to provide a convincing religious rationale and justification for what is defined as historically inevitable. They will join for many of the same reasons that their predecessors put their faith in capitalism, when, at its inception, it too seemed to be the hope of the future.

The reasons for the new Christian alliance with Marxism (which is much further advanced in Europe and elsewhere than here) will be understandable: an acute sense of political injustice, a sharpened social analysis which perceives the essential corruption of the present system, and a compassion for those who suffer from the existing order of things.

Unfortunately, it has been the conformity to the inevitabilities of history that has been such a common and debilitating failing in the history of the church. The distinctive and decisive witness to the Word of God, and the uniquely crucial role that can be played by the gathered community of God's people, can become obscured or completely lost in that process of conformity.

There is another possibility. Those who study the biblical witness seriously will discover that their alienation from the present system can be understood as the *normal* existence for the people of God. They will find that biblical politics are invariably alien to the politics of the established regime *and* will also question the politics of the new regime that any revolution will eventually establish for itself. They will see that to break free from one system only through an allegiance to another is no break at all.

Ideology does not ultimately liberate but rather captivates, and no idolatry can ever deliver liberation from itself. We begin to understand that we have been programmed for idolatry, for putting our trust in systems, governments, revolutions, declarations of independence, and new socialist orders.

To place our faith solely and completely in the efficacy of

the Word of God, to hope in the gospel alone, is to establish an eternal revolutionary posture in the world which unceasingly and in every circumstance perpetually seeks justice, liberation, and peace, never being satisfied to rest false hopes in the powers and idols and systems of the world that continually claim to be our salvation.

Biblical politics takes, as their starting point, the manner of God in Jesus Christ. Biblical politics thus exemplify the political authority of the Incarnation. Jesus rejected the political realism of the Sadducees and the revolutionary violence of the Zealots out of their mutual subservience to the politics of power, which is common characteristic of both established regimes and the revolutionary forces which seek to replace them. The subordination of persons to causes and ideological necessities has always been alien to the gospel.

The new order which Jesus called the kingdom of God created a new peoplehood centered around a new way of living more than a new system or political program. That new way of living, and its radical meaning in relationship to money, power, race, violence, and our relationships to one another is intended to bring revolution to any society and bring revolution to any revolution.

An Open Letter to José Miguez Bonino

Jürgen Moltmann

In his book *Doing Theology in a Revolutionary Situation* (Fortress Press, 1975), José Miguez Bonino—the noted Methodist theologian from Buenos Aires, Argentina—described Jürgen Moltmann's critique of liberation theology as failing "to grasp the basic challenge of Latin American theological thought" (p. 146).

Moltmann, who teaches theology at the University of Tübingen, Germany, responded with an "open letter" in which he charges that Latin American theologians criticize European and American theologians, but then turn around and do their own writing "in the framework of European history," and frequently end up saying things already said by those whom they are criticizing. For instance, Moltmann maintains that Gustavo Gutiérrez in *A Theology of Liberation* "has written an invaluable contribution to European theology. But where is Latin America in it all?" Similarly, Moltmann expresses reservations about the way Marxism is used by Latin American theologians without adequately relating it to the history of their own people. "Orthopraxis," he says, "is a dangerous word if by it is meant that the practice of life should be dogmatized and made uniform." The goal of "a world society in which human beings no longer live against but with each other" should be common to all, but recognizing that orthopraxis will have a different face in different situations, "should it not be possible to acknowledge and with all criticism also to appreciate each other mutually?" asks Moltmann. His open letter was first published in *Christianity and Crisis*, March 29, 1976.

Dear Friend: I have read through your book *Doing Theology in a Revolutionary Situation* in one sitting, and I am as deeply moved by it as I am disturbed. I have learned something from it about the history and the present situation of Latin America. The "theology of liberation" has become more understandable for me as seen in the context in which it lives. But I have learned even more about the history of Europe as it appears to the eyes of a Latin American and about the effect European "political theology" has on others in another situation.

After Hugo Assmann's announcement at the Geneva conference of 1973 that "incommunication" was to take the place of dialogue with European theologians because they are Europeans, my readiness to deal with his criticism, as you can understand, was somewhat diminished. But you want to sharpen the criticism of Metz and me in order to carry the dialogue forward (p. 146), not to break it off. That is an invitation.

I believe that European theologians would misunderstand Latin Americans if they were to remain silent any longer. Confrontations can shatter a dialogue, but they can also lead the participants out of a superficial friendliness into a deeper community. After you, Rubem Alves, Juan Segundo, Gustavo Gutiérrez and Hugo Assmann have made crystal clear what you find dissatisfying in us and what in our theology seems so irrelevant for your situation and then also for our own situation. I would like to begin to clarify what we find dissatisfying in you and what we actually are expecting from you.

(1) The "theology of liberation" wants to be an indigenous theology that frees itself from the European tradition and North Atlantic theology in order to give its full attention to the unmistakable experiences and tasks of Latin America. That is a necessary historical process of liberation, as can be observed also in Africa and Asia. The sooner it is accomplished, the more European theologians will be able to learn from others.

But the destruction of European theological imperialism should not lead to the provincialization of theology. If that were to happen, we in Europe would be able to abandon the rest of the world and Christianity as a whole and occupy ourselves with our own concerns and traditions. The destruction of that

imperialism can lead in a meaningful way only to the construction of a common world-theology at the expense of the one-
sided "West-theology." The tendencies toward a narrow pro-
vincialism with blinders are already strong enough among us.
They should not be strengthened by an "incommunication"
policy from outside.

Persons who know their own historical and socioeconomic
borders are eager to experience that which is different and
strange as it encounters them beyond their borders. *African
theology* confronted us with something really new, for the African modes of thought have been entirely unfamiliar to us ever
since Aristotle. *Japanese theology,* done in the Buddhist context, forces Western activists again and again to fundamental
reorientations of their interests and thought forms. In *North
American Black theology* we have encountered new forms of
communication through the language and music of an oppressed
community.

But up to now scarcely anything comparable has come out
of Latin America. We hear severe criticism of Western theology
and of theology in general—and then we are told something
about Karl Marx and Friedrich Engels, as if they were Latin
American discoveries. Nothing against Marx and Engels, but
the one was born in Trier and the other in Barmen, and both
occupy an important vantage point in European history. And
they are not just a disadvantage but an advantage to this history.
They will not be totally unknown to European theologians.
Later on I want to try to clarify this phenomenon of ideological
re-import.

"Where Is Latin America in It All?"

One gets a quite ambiguous impression as regards the Latin
American theological criticism of European theology: One is
first criticized intensely, and then, to one's surprise, finds that
in the end the critics confirm with their own words exactly the
same thing that one had said oneself. Rubem Alves in his *A
Theology of Human Hope* criticizes the "theology of hope" as
too transcendental in the definition of divine promise and too
negative in the judgment of the present. Over against this he

wants to emphasize the future as coming out of the pregnancy of
the historical present, as Leibniz and Bloch had maintained.
But because he cannot present the future of history as the virgin
birth of the present, in the end he must ask about the "father"
who has begat the child and has engendered the present with
hope. Therefore he speaks of the divine promise and of the
language of freedom and ends at the point where the "theology
of hope" already was.

Juan Segundo ("The Choice Between Capitalism and
Socialism as the Theological Crux," *Concilium,* Oct. 1974)
lodges against "political theology" the criticism that by means
of its eschatological hope it would simply relativize all absolute
experiences and ideologies and would validate only non-binding
anticipations, analogies and designs directed at the wholly other
eschatological future. In this respect he has indeed read only
half, for Bonhoeffer and Barth had already spoken constantly of
the stimulation and intensification of historical hopes through
the eschatological hope, not to speak of Metz and me. But he is
right, of course, in maintaining that in his messianic actions
Jesus did not "deabsolutize" but rather—according to our experiences, an activity that is a bit "unwise"—"absolutized."
To be sure, the individual event of liberation or salvation does
not gain in this way a "causal character" for the Kingdom of
God—even Pelagius never would have said that—but rather
the Kingdom attains a causal character for the experienced
event of liberation, for all messianic activity realizes the possibilities that have been made possible through the inbreaking of
the messianic time (Lk. 4:18ff.). To this extent the messianic
kingdom is the subject of its historical realization and not vice
versa. But precisely this "absolutizes" the relative or brings the
unconditioned into the conditioned.

If Segundo had remained with this point, one would have
had to accept it self-critically. However, at the end of his article
he relativizes his own conception by speaking of a "fragile,
partial causality that not infrequently errs and must be initiated
anew" and by saying that in history "it is the eschatological
kingdom is the subject of its historical realization and not vice
way." In this way he has only replaced the critical expressions
"anticipation," "design" and "analogy" by the expression

"fragment." That is truly not a "radical criticism of even the most progressive European theologies," as he suspects, since they have all used the expression "fragment" in this context—and in my opinion much too often.

You have the same problems in *Doing Theology in a Revolutionary Situation*. Your Barthianism always lets you distinguish neatly between what God does and what human beings do. But at the same time, you reproach Barth, the Europeans and thus, in the same breath, also yourself for not overcoming this dualism through a new, historical-dialectical way of thinking.

Over against me and European theology you would like to "materialize" the kingdom of God from an historical perspective and block the retreat to a neutral "critical function" in theology. Good, one says to oneself, this is a new orientation that we, consciously or unconsciously, have not seen clearly enough. But then one reads your summary of your own thoughts and, behold, everything you have criticized in the "political theology" of Metz and Moltmann is again in place.

You present the positive relationship between the kingdom of God and human undertaking in history as calling, invitation and impulse to engagement. Our concrete historical options should "correspond" to the Kingdom (true to Barth). You describe the critical connection of the judgment of God to the whole of our human efforts (true to Luther). Finally, you speak of the "utopian function" of Christian eschatology, of Christian faith as stimulus and challenge for revolutionary action, and of the eschatological faith that makes meaningful the investment of life for the building up of a temporal, imperfect order, and of the resurrection of the dead as the triumph of God's love and of God's solidarity with all human beings in which the imperfect is perfected (true to Moltmann). One can also read all of this in Bonhoeffer, Barth, Gollwitzer, Metz and other Europeans. One is, therefore, inclined to agree fervently with you, but then ask what sense your criticism has after all.

Gustavo Gutiérrez' *A Theology of Liberation* is often viewed by Latin American and European theologians as the first theology in the Latin American perspective. The reader is expectant; one would like to discover Latin America in this book. As magnificent as the book is otherwise, in this respect the reader is disappointed. Gutiérrez presents the process of liberation in Latin America as the continuation and culmination of the European history of freedom. One gets a glimpse into this history of freedom by being enlightened about Kant and Hegel, Rousseau and Feuerbach, Marx and Freud. The "secularization process" is portrayed in detail through the work of Gogarten, Bonhoeffer, Cox and Metz. This is all worked through independently and offers many new insights—but precisely only in the framework of Europe's history, scarcely in the history of Latin America. Gutiérrez has written an invaluable contribution to European theology. But where is Latin America in it all?

It is not easy to interpret these impressions, for they are truly not meant as remonstrances or counter-criticism. Presumably we Europeans have a wrong expectation. Latin American theologians become interesting in Europe and the United States only when they offer something new, which is then, as you and Assmann complain, made fashionable as a "consumer good" in order to overcome one's own boredom. That is paternalistic—to act as if the young should entertain and cheer up the old. It can easily lead to Oedipal reactions when those who profess to be "young" want to get free from those who consider themselves "old."

Is it true that in the relationship of the Europeans to the Latin American theologians there is still at work unconsciously the relationship between motherland and colonial land, mother church and daughter church? It would really be more meaningful to work in concert at a new construction of theology rather than in a rivalry to try to pass each other by on the "left" or the "right" or in the "middle" and in the process step on each other's toes.

Turning toward the People

(2) The second problem, to which I have already referred, has to do with the use of Marxism by Latin American theologians. We are speaking now not about how often, with the joy of missionary discovery, it is introduced and interpreted to those Europeans who live in the land of Marx and Engels but rather

about the way it is employed theologically. First let us consider the reception of Marxism in Latin America from an historical perspective.

You and Gutiérrez have described impressively the various historical epochs of your continent. After the phase of conquest and colonization for God and the King of Spain in the age of European imperialism, there followed the phase of national liberation from Spain and Portugal in the 19th century—partly as a consequence of the developing civil nationalism in Europe. Today we see the initial phases of the social and political liberation of the people from Western economic imperialism and from subjection to class rule by military dictatorship. That is, the proletarian revolution has begun, but again in the train of socialistic movements and their theories in Europe.

The history of Latin America, in contradistinction to that of Africa and Asia, is obviously more persistently defined by the European history of rule and revolution. Even now the necessary socialistic revolution of the proletariat remains in this framework. Whereas China, which was only briefly and never completely ruled by the West, found quite early through Mao its own Chinese way to socialism, there are still scarcely any beginnings of a peculiarly Latin American way to socialism. At any rate this is what one would conclude from the writings of the liberation theologians.

To be sure, they recommend that theologians in the whole world turn to a Marxist class analysis in order to stand in the concrete history of their people. But they do not carry through this class analysis with respect to the history of their own people; they only quote a few basic concepts of Marx. And they do this in such a general way that one learns only something about the fruits of the theologians' reading and scarcely anything about the struggle of the Latin American people. In them one reads more about the sociological theories of others, namely Western Socialists, than about the history or the life and suffering of the Latin American people. One is called upon to opt, in a moral alternative, for the oppressed against the oppressors and to accept Marxism as the right prophecy of the situation.

Now it is simply not the case that European theologians

prefer to remain politically neutral and to theorize only on the universal plane, as they have been accused. But it is one thing to be involved in an incisive analysis of the historical situation of the people and quite another thing to make declamations of seminar-Marxism as a world view. Whoever assumes that sociology can be a substitute for a deficient contact with the working and suffering people (J.B. Metz, *Stimmen der Zeit,* 192, 1974, p. 809)—which is not meant to be imputed to anyone—practices a sociology about the people but does not tell the history of the people as his/her own history. Marxism and sociology do not yet bring a theologian into the people but, at least at first, only into the company of Marxists and sociologists.

On the other hand, moral appeals and biblical language about the poor also do not bring the theologian where he/ she belongs. Theology as pure theology, and even theology that has been extended and broadened to Marxism and socialism, remains in its own circle. The true radical change that is neces- sary is still ahead of both the "political theologians" in the European context and the "liberation theologians" in the Latin American context. In my opinion they can enter in a thoroughly mutual way into this change, namely a radical turn toward the people.

It is also not a particularly impressive indication of solid socio-political analysis or of good judgment when, in the discus- sion of the actual function of "political theology" and of the words that Metz and I myself use, it is maintained that "in Europe, for instance, they immediately are integrated into the developmentalist, technological, liberal ideology adopted by the Common Market and its orbit in relation to the Third World" (Bonino, p. 80). As the sociologists of knowledge make clear, such suspicion of ideology can be advanced in any context and at any time, but in this case the author unfortunately adduces not the slightest shade of evidence. The conclusion that "Or- thopraxis, rather than orthodoxy, becomes the criterion for theology" (p. 81) is a literal quote from Metz, who was just charged with propounding the ideology of the Common Market. And that "theology has to stop explaining the world and to start transforming it" (p. 81) stood already in 1964 in the *Theology of*

Hope (p. 74) of the no less suspect Moltmann. Both sentences, however, could well be true; therefore I have no desire to enter into a dispute about them.

Assessing the Historical Situation

(3) The most decisive difference between the Latin American theology of liberation and political theology in Western Europe lies in the assessment of the various historical situations. I believe that there is an extensive unanimity about what is necessary in terms of world politics. But the various countries, societies and cultures do not live synchronously at the same point in history. Therefore, according to each concrete situation, there are diverse ways to realize what is generally good for all.

Many Latin American theologians believe that they are living in a "revolutionary situation." Others make a more skeptical judgment of their situation and speak, as does Rubem Alves, of a "pre-revolutionary situation." One cannot say much about this from a European vantage point. But it is clear that there are two issues involved when, on the one hand—in view of the ever more harsh economic imperialism of the North Atlantic nations and of the brutal military dictatorships it supports—one speaks of the *necessity* of a socialistic revolution and when, on the other hand—in view of the awakening of the people—one speaks of the *possibility* of such a revolution. The necessity of a speedy and radical transformation of the socio-economic conditions can be understood by everyone as indisputable. But what use is the best revolutionary theory when the historical subject of the revolution is not at hand or is not yet ready? The subject of revolutionary liberation can only be the oppressed, exploited people themselves.

The intellectuals and the students are certainly not the subject. They can at most throw the revolutionary sparks into the dried-up and parched woods. But if the people are not "burning" and do not rise up, the most beautiful sparks are of no use. The sparks then become sectarian candles around which elite circles gather ceremoniously in order to confirm themselves.

One is justified in speaking of a revolutionary situation only when the common misery is generally experienced, when it is unbearable, when the one necessary thing is recognized, and when the potential to realize what is necessary is at hand and ready.

If we take these indicators and apply them to the situation *in* Europe, then we cannot speak realistically of a "revolutionary" or "pre-revolutionary" situation. There was, it is true, a time in the sixties during the student revolt, the anti-Viet Nam War movement and "socialism with a human face" when one could point to such a situation and to concrete alternatives to the existing system. But it became clear that the most beautiful revolutionary theories found no basis in the people and therefore remained without a subject.

The elite cadre of ideologists developed a "socialism for the people," but the "socialism of the people" did not see the light of day. The reactions of the people were therefore rather hostile. The people had quite a realistic view of the privileges of the students who were able to demonstrate during working hours, and were thus not interested in their slogans. The so-called leftist theoreticians did not suffer from a manifest loss of reality, as they were reproached by the conservative theologians, but rather from a lack of contact with the people.

It is understandable in our country that the people are not interested in an ideological imperialism. Obviously there are conditions in which long trains wait only on the locomotives to lead them to the destination. But there are also times in which the locomotive departs so quickly that the couplings are torn apart and with the train remains motionless on the track. Then, for better or for worse, the locomotive must come back and couple itself to the train again.

To say it without images, it seems more important to maintain a connection with the people than to travel alone into the paradise of the future. It is more important to live and to work in and with the people than to relish the classless society in the correct theories. Of course this sounds like a compromise, but it is not, for a concrete step is of more worth than the most beautiful idea of possibilities.

Democratic Socialism

The concept I consider the most realistic and at the same time pregnant with future in Europe is *democratic socialism*. It corresponds to the tradition of the German worker movement. Besides Marx there is also Lasalle; that is, besides the economic liberation from exploitation there is also the struggle for the universal right to vote and to participate in governance, the struggle for political liberation. It also corresponds to the European history of freedom. Without the French civil revolution there would have been no socialist revolution. From the historical perspective the reverse is also true: without socialism, no democracy.

In the European countries—and here we include also the United States—one cannot develop socialism at the cost of democracy. No one would be ready to sacrifice the freedoms that have already been won, freedom of the press, freedom to vote, right to express one's opinions, freedom to strike, freedom of movement, right to trial, etc., however imperfect and one-sided they may be. At least no one would be ready to give up these freedoms and rights for new dreams.

But many are ready to transfer these democratic rights and freedoms over to economic conditions and to struggle with the unions for the democratization of the economy. The direct leap from feudalism to socialism is not possible in Western Europe. In Western Europe Russian socialism continues to have the scent of czarism. There are also Eastern European countries that have not experienced a civil revolution but have simply passed over this stage of historical development. In the West their socialism has the appearance of Prussian military socialism or feudal bureaucratic socialism, in any case a state socialism without a democratized state.

There are countries that, while maintaining intact the whole apparatus of state control, change over from a rightist dictatorship to a leftist dictatorship. Portugal has been standing on the threshold of this danger and perhaps Peru also. This way makes no sense for us. Whoever has tasted a bit of political freedom no longer believes the theories by which a dictatorship, be it rightist or leftist, tries to justify itself. For such a person the real situation is plain.

Socialism without democracy, economic justice without realization of human rights are not hopes among our people. Democratic socialism must advance on both fields at once, on the way of the democratization of political institutions and on the way of the socialization of economic conditions. It will engage itself in the midst of the positive issues and of the real potentialities at hand. Working with the trade unions to give everyone the right to participate in decisions, it will divide economic power and distribute it in such a way that the people will have control over it. It will try to change its political organizations from ideological parties into people's parties, for it is more important to represent the interests of the little people, the mass of the employed and the unemployed, than to chase after the phantom of pure theory.

Whether this democratic way to socialism will be successful and whether it could work in a liberating way for the countries of the Third World is something that remains to be seen. Guarantees cannot be given, and no one would maintain that this would be the only right and infallible orthopraxis. But we should take this direction in our situation since the reverse way—from socialism to democracy—has produced such few satisfying results among us.

This certainly does not preclude others in their own situation from taking another course and under certain conditions seeking to overcome class rule and dictatorship of the right by a temporary leftist dictatorship, a protective and transitional dictatorship for the building up of socialism and democracy. In specific emergency situations this probably cannot be excluded as ultima ratio, even though the price is always rather high. But in any case it should be assumed that the one way from democracy to democratic socialism and the other way from socialism to social democracy do not mutually exclude each other but rather converge.

I am aware that with this statement I am laying myself open to the charge of being a "convergence theoretician," a term that stimulates a neurosis about one's profile on both sides of divided Germany. But I do not think that I am thereby withholding anything from the freedom and the humanity of the people. In the end the only thing that is at stake in socialism and democracy is that the people become the subject of their own history of freedom and that human beings attain their unhindered humanity.

The Common Goal

Orthopraxis is a dangerous word if by it is meant that the practice of life should be dogmatized and made uniform. In the different political situations and in the different historical times in which we actually live the right thing and the timely thing that must be done appear differently. But the goal can only be one and common to all. The goal lies in a world society in which human beings no longer live against but with each other. The Latin American orthopraxis will have a different face than the Western European orthopraxis. But of crucial importance within the difference is the common prospect. Should it not be possible to acknowledge and with all criticism also to appreciate each other mutually?

I would like to close this letter with comments on two incidents that are deeply troubling to me at the moment.

(1) In December 1974 32 leading Protestant church officials greeted the power grab of the military junta in Chile as "God's answer to the prayers of all believers who see in Marxism a satanic power." This declaration is so atrocious that it cannot be passed over in painful silence. Whoever expects the "fulfillment of his prayers" from the terror of tyranny does not pray in the name of the crucified Messiah of the people. The God of Jesus Christ does not answer the prayers of those who believe in him through the execution of more than 10,000 poor people. With this declaration the "believers" who were referred to and their alleged "Protestant church officials" expose themselves as adherents of a murderous political religion that has nothing in common with Christianity.

The God of the Chilean military junta is the political idol Moloch. Whoever brings his/her thank-offering to him separates him/herself from every Christian community. That is religious fascism. "Satanic powers" can only be overcome by the risen

Christ, not through another satan. By declaring Marxism to be a "satanic power" one makes out of Christ an anticommunist satan. Christianity throughout the whole world will have to repent for the perverse declaration of those 32 "Protestant church officials" in Chile. It will have to turn away from such apostasy and toward new obedience.

(2) In January 1975 the Socialist Government of Yugoslavia discontinued the world-renowned journal *Praxis* and dismissed from the university eight Belgrade teachers, all members of the *Praxis* circle. *Praxis* was the last center of democratic socialism in Europe in which Eastern and Western socialists could work together. Ernst Bloch and Jürgen Habermas were Western co-editors. The self-governance of workers and democratic socialism obviously became dangerous to Moscow's state socialism, even in Yugoslavia. With this one of the few European lights that burn for Socialists and democrats in common is extinguished. Dogmatism and bureaucratism rule. Nothing could be more opportune for the technocrats of capitalism. Now the managers and the rulers of the people can be counted among them and of their kind, and they will divide the purse between themselves.

Today our hope can point to only a few positive "signs of the times." The signs of destruction are increasing. Our hope can no longer afford to be childish and enthusiastic. In common resistance against evil and the flunkies that serve death it must become mature and steady. However we analyze our situation, hope is faithfulness to the resurrection and therefore perseverance in the cross. One learns this among the people, in the community of the poor, among those who are heavy laden and hungering after righteousness.

In the community of the "people of the beatitudes" I greet you.

An Open Letter to
North American Christians

In September 1976, the National Council of Churches' Division of Overseas Ministries received "An Open Letter to North American Christians," signed by eight Protestant leaders in Latin America, along with five others who could not reveal their names for fear of reprisals. Timed to the then-current U.S. presidential election campaign, the letter is a plea to North Americans to realize what the oppressive power of their nation is doing to Central and South America—turning it into "one gigantic prison, and in some regions one vast cemetery," as North American business and government interests operate in collusion with Latin American oligarchies to provide enormous profits for the few, and repression, malnutrition, misery and death for the many. After describing the desperate conditions of their people, the Latin Americans propose, "If in the past you felt it to be your apostolic duty to send us missionaries and economic resources, today the frontier of your witness and Christian solidarity is within your own country." Pressure on United States authorities, the letter says, can be used either to influence the government "toward paths of greater justice and brotherhood or to accentuating a colonialist and oppressive policy over our peoples." The Governing Board of the National Council of Churches, in October 1976, voted to send the open letter to the presidential candidates and to reply to the Latin American church leaders. In its brief reply, the Governing Board affirmed, "You have raised . . . the authentic and key issues impacting the relations between our nations and peoples." It also acknowledged that "you are asking us to look at the more global and systemic nature of the impact of our nation and society on our brothers and sisters in Latin America." The letter and reply are reprinted here as they appeared in the October 18, 1976 issue of *Christianity and Crisis*.

Our brothers and sisters: It is very significant and symptomatic that in these days we Latin Americans are following

71

with such intense interest and concern the political process that the people of the United States are living in this time. We do it with as much interest or even more than we normally dedicate to our own electoral conflicts, which in many cases have represented nothing more than gigantic and barefaced frauds.

Can you comprehend the reason for our preoccupation? Can you account for our avid interest in the declarations made by a Carter, a Church, a Reagan or a Ford regarding various matters, particularly insofar as they touch on international policy and relations with Latin America? Simply, this phenomenon is due to that fact that we—with the exception of Cuba—are trapped in the same system. We all move within one economic-political-military complex in which one finds committed [the] fabulous interests of [the] financial groups that dominate the life of your country and the creole oligarchies of our Latin American nations. Both groups, more allied today than ever, have held back time after time the great transformations that our people need and desperately demand.

If we still had some doubt regarding this sad and painful "Pan-American" reality, the scandalous intervention of the United States in the installation and maintenance of military regimes in Guatemala, Nicaragua, Brazil, Paraguay, Bolivia, etc.; the revelation of the activities of ITT and other North American businesses in Chile; the resounding case of Watergate; the discoveries [regarding the activities of] the CIA and other agencies of penetration and espionage in our countries; the shameful Panamanian enclave with its military training centers that our Christian and Latin American consciences cannot tolerate any longer; the sometimes subtle and other times brazen domination and colonization practiced by Rockefeller and many others of low reputation in our continent, now [articulated by Kissinger in a scientific and Machiavellian fashion], which has eliminated one at a time all possibilities of economic independence and authentic development in our rich but excessively bled nations; all this and much more has been opening our eyes to a reality that has cost a great deal for you as well as for us to recognize and accept. This sorrowful reality has demolished the image of "the great democracy of the North," which we have been taught to admire as the "mecca" and the "model" since we were children in our schools and churches and through the mass media.

Today we Latin Americans are discovering that, apart from our own weaknesses and sins, not a few of our misfortunes, miseries and frustrations flow from and are perpetuated within a system that produces substantial benefits for your country but goes on swallowing us more and more in oppression, in impotence, in death. In a few words: Your precious "American Way of Life"—the opulence of your magnates, your economic and military dominion—feeds in no small proportion on the blood that gushes, according to one of our most brilliant essayists, "from the open viens of Latin America."

The problem becomes more acute day by day, minute by minute, because in the presence of the rapid awakening of extensive sectors of our peoples, tyrannical regimes like those of Somoza in Nicaragua, Stroessner in Paraguay, Pinochet in Chile (and the list becomes constantly more extensive), which represent and serve the interests of your large corporations associated with powerful local interests, are intensifying repression and terror to a degree rarely equalled.

It is no longer sufficient to keep the large mass of indigenous peoples and workers of our nations marginated and exploited. Now it is necessary to subject to systematic persecution, to scientifically perfected torture, union leaders, political and student leaders, priests and pastors, intellectuals and artists, journalists and other professionals—all who attempt to denounce the injustice and the falsehood or who are in solidarity with the poor and the oppressed. Now it is necessary to commit silent genocide, killing with hunger, with malnutrition, with tuberculosis the children of working families without resources, because unemployment also is being made into a political weapon.

The prisons of Latin America no longer suffice to hold so many prisoners detained for indeterminate times and without the possibilities of defense. The few countries that still enjoy some margin of liberty and security have already stretched their capacity to receive exiles and refugees of all nationalities, professions and ages. Paramilitary and parapolice organizations multiply in a fearful manner, and the streets of many towns and cities of the continent appear to be sown daily with cadavers.

All this, our brothers and sisters, is carried out in the name of "democracy," in the name of "Western Christian civilization," on the backs of our people, and with the benediction and the support of your government, of your armed forces, without which our dictators could not maintain themselves in power for much time.

Friends and fellow Christians, it is time that you realize that our continent is becoming one gigantic prison, and in some regions one vast cemetery; that human rights, the grand guidelines of the Gospel, are becoming a dead letter, without force. And all this in order to maintain a system, a structure of dependency, that benefits the mighty privileged persons of your land and of our land at the expense of the poor millions who are increasing throughout the width and breadth of the continent.

For this reason this open letter seeks to be the lamentation or the outcry of those who now have no voice in our America, because they are buried in the volcanos, the rivers or the cemeteries; because they are rotting in prisons or concentration camps; or because they languish in incredible conditions of malnutrition and misery. This letter seeks to be an anguished, fervent call to your conscience and to your responsibility as Christians.

If in the past you felt it to be your apostolic duty to send us missionaries and economic resources, today the frontier of your witness and Christian solidarity is within your own country. The conscious, intelligent and responsible use of your vote, the appeal to your representatives in the Congress, and the application of pressure by various means on your authorities can contribute to changing the course of our governments toward paths of greater justice and brotherhood or to accentuating a colonialist and oppressive policy over our peoples. In this sense you must ask yourselves if you will or will not be "your brother's keeper" in these lands of America, from which the blood of millions of Abels is clamoring to heaven.

We, between tears and groans, are interceding for you in order that you may respond with faithfulness to the historic responsibility that as citizens of one of the great contemporary powers and as disciples of Jesus Christ it falls on you to assume.

May the true piety, about which the prophet Isaiah speaks

to us in the name of God, ". . . to loose the fetters of injustice, to untie the knots of the yoke, to snap every yoke and set free those who have been crushed . . . and never evading a duty to your brother" (58:6–7) become reality in your lives and in the lives of your churches.

Signed by: Sergio Arce, Moderator, Presbyterian Church of Cuba and Rector, the Evangelical Theological Seminary, Matanzas, Cuba; Plutarco Bonilla, Rector, Latin American Biblical Seminary, Costa Rica; Augusto Cotto, Rector, Baptist Seminary of México; Secundino Morales, Pastor, Methodist Church of Panamá, former Superintendent; Tapani Ojasti, General Coordinator, Lutheran Church in Costa Rica; Jacinto Ordoñez, Executive Secretary, Latin American Association of Theological Schools and former Bishop, Methodist Church of Panamá; Antonio Ramos, Bishop, Episcopal Church of Costa Rica; Saul Trinidad, Director, Extension Program of Costa Rican Methodist Church and Pastor, Peruvian Evangelical Church; and five women and men whose names have not been included in order to protect them in the dangerous situations in which they live and work.

*   *   *

The Governing Board of the National Council of Churches of Christ in the USA is deeply moved by the appeal to our consciences made in the "Open Letter to North American Christians." Some of you who have signed the letter have done so at great personal risk. Nevertheless, we recognize that as leaders of your respective Christian communities in Latin America you have been moved by your responsibility under God to address yourselves to those concerns that affect us mutually.

We feel that what you have raised are the authentic and key issues impacting the relations between our nations and peoples. These matters have been brought before us on other occasions and from many sources in the past, but seldom have they been presented with such forcefulness and timeliness. Equally important is the fact that these are issues that . . . are applicable [not only] in our inter-American relations but in our relations with other parts of the world as well.

In a variety of ways our churches have attempted to speak

to particular problems relevant to the concerns of your "Open Letter." Among these have been: (1) the defense of basic human rights under repressive regimes; (2) the relation of US foreign assistance and human rights; (3) Panamanian sovereignty and a new canal treaty; (4) the social responsibility of the investment of Gulf & Western in the Dominican Republic and of General Motors and IBM in Chile.

Now, however, you are asking us to look at the more global and systemic nature of the impact of our nation and society on our brothers and sisters in Latin America.

The challenge that has been laid before us is to act as well as to make statements. You have shown us some of the dimensions of that challenge when you state:

> If in the past you felt it to be your apostolic duty to send us missionaries and economic resources, today the frontier of your witness and Christian solidarity is within your own country. The conscious, intelligent and responsible use of your vote, the appeal to your representatives in the Congress, and the application of pressure by various means on your authorities can contribute to changing the course of our governments toward paths of greater justice and brotherhood or to accentuating a colonialist and oppressive policy over our peoples.

We are hopeful that we can accept this understanding of our Christian mission with all its implications.

As a first step in our response to you we are urging all member denominations of the National Council of Churches of Christ in the USA to make use of all their available means of communication to share your "Open Letter to North American Christians" with all members of their constituencies; and further, we are requesting that the denominations recommend to every parish and congregation of their communion that they study and meditate upon the significance of this letter during the current election campaign and beyond.

We pray that you will be strengthened in your faith and in your commitment to God's Word and to God's people.

Evangelization and Liberation

Pope Paul VI

In the autumn of 1974 about 220 representatives from each of the Roman Catholic National Episcopal Conferences met in Rome for a month at the third Synod of Bishops since the Second Vatican Council. After two years of preparation, the bishops discussed evangelization. The theme was a complementary follow-up to the 1971 synodal topic, "Justice in the World," when they stated that participation in the process of transforming the world is "a constitutive element of the preaching of the Gospel" (cf. *Mission Trends No. 2*, pp. 253-259). The 1974 final statement, quickly composed and short, affirmed the "intimate connection between evangelization and liberation" (cf. *Ibid.*, pp. 259-267).

But the most fecund summaries of the bishops' lengthy discussions were placed in Pope Paul's hands, and to him it was left to refine, enlarge, deepen and in many ways personalize the theme. Thus his exhortation, *Evangelization in the Modern World*, promulgated on December 8, 1975.

From Christ the Evangelizer to the evangelized and evangelizing Church shapes the outline of Pope Paul's reflections. After explaining his definition of evangelization ("bringing the Good News into all strata of humanity, and through its influence transforming humanity from within and making it new"), Pope Paul continues to describe the content and methods, its beneficiaries and workers, and concludes by confessing the Holy Spirit as the principal agent and goal. Of the eighty paragraphs of the pastorally accented statement, we share a few which explicitly deal with the Good News as a message of liberation, a profound relation between evangelization and human advancement/development/liberation.

Giovanni Battista Montini was born in Concesio, Italy, 1897. He was chaplain to Catholic students at the University of Rome, developed a weekly newspaper to develop a Catholic intellectual elite, and founded an association of Italian university graduates. In 1932 he entered Vatican service in the Secretariat of State, and remained there until Pope Pius XII appointed him Archbishop of Milan in 1954. He succeeded Pope John XXIII as Paul VI in June 1963.

He presided over the last three sessions of the Second Vatican Council, the single objective of which he summed up ten years later in hindsight, "to make the Church of the 20th century ever better fitted for proclaiming the Gospel to the people of the 20th century." To Pope Paul this effort was a "daily preoccupation (cf. 2 Cor 11:28)" and "a fundamental commitment of our pontificate," until his death on August 6, 1978.

The extracts presented here are from the translation issued by the Publications Office of the U.S. Catholic Conference, 1312 Massachusetts Ave, N.W., Washington, D.C. 20005. Other related papal statements and Bishops' Synods' conclusions are found in Joseph Gremillion's *The Gospel of Peace and Justice: Catholic Social Teaching since Pope John* (Maryknoll, N.Y.: Orbis Books, 1976).

18. Evangelizing means bringing the Good News into all the strata of humanity, and through its influence transforming humanity from within and making it new: "Now I am making the whole of creation new."[1] But there is no new humanity if there are not first of all new persons renewed by Baptism[2] and by lives lived according to the Gospel.[3] The purpose of evangelization is therefore precisely this interior change, and if it had to be expressed in one sentence the best way of stating it would be to say that the Church evangelizes when she seeks to convert,[4] solely through the divine power of the message she proclaims, both the personal and collective consciences of people, the activities in which they engage, and the lives and concrete milieux which are theirs.

19. Strata of humanity which are transformed: for the

Church it is a question not only of preaching the Gospel in ever wider geographic areas or to ever greater numbers of people, but also of affecting and as it were upsetting, through the power of the Gospel, mankind's criteria of judgment, determining values, points of interest, lines of thought, sources of inspiration and models of life, which are in contrast with the Word of God and the plan of salvation.

30. . . . . Peoples engaged with all their energy in the effort and struggle to overcome everything which condemns them to remain on the margin of life: famine, chronic disease, illiteracy, poverty, injustices in international relations and especially in commercial exchanges, situations of economic and cultural neo-colonialism sometimes as cruel as the old political colonialism. The Church, as the bishops repeated, has the duty to proclaim the liberation of millions of human beings, many of whom are her own children—the duty of assisting the birth of this liberation, of giving witness to it, of ensuring that it is complete. This is not foreign to evangelization.

31. Between evangelization and human advancement— development and liberation—there are in fact profound links. These include links of an anthropological order, because the man who is to be evangelized is not an abstract being but is subject to social and economic questions. They also include links in the theological order, since one cannot dissociate the plan of creation from the plan of redemption. The latter plan touches the very concrete situations of injustice to be combatted and of justice to be restored. They include links of the eminently evangelical order, which is that of charity; how in fact can one proclaim the new commandment without promoting in justice and in peace the true, authentic advancement of man? We ourself have taken care to point this out, by recalling that it is impossible to accept "that in evangelization one could or should ignore the importance of the problems so much discussed today, concerning justice, liberation, development and peace in the world. This would be to forget the lesson which comes to us from the Gospel concerning love of our neighbor who is suffering and in need."[5]

32. We must not ignore the fact that many, even generous Christians who are sensitive to the dramatic questions involved in the problem of liberation, in their wish to commit the Church

to the liberation effort are frequently tempted to reduce her mission to the dimensions of a simply temporal project. They would reduce her aims to a man-centered goal; the salvation of which she, as the messenger, would be reduced to material well-being. Her activity, forgetful of all spiritual and religious preoccupation, would become initiatives of the political or social order. But if this were so, the Church would lose her fundamental meaning. Her message of liberation would no longer have any originality and would easily be open to monopolization and manipulation by ideological systems and political parties. She would have no more authority to proclaim freedom as in the name of God. This is why we have wished to emphasize, in the same address at the opening of the Synod, "the need to restate clearly the specifically religious finality of evangelization. This latter would lose its reason for existence if it were to diverge from the religious axis that guides it: the Kingdom of God, before anything else, in its fully theological meaning. . . ."[6]

33. With regard to the liberation which evangelization proclaims and strives to put into practice one should rather say this:

—it cannot be contained in the simple and restricted dimension of economics, politics, social or cultural life; it must envisage the whole man, in all his aspects, right up to and including his openness to the absolute, even the divine Absolute;

—it is therefore attached to a certain concept of man, to a view of man which it can never sacrifice to the needs of any strategy, practice or short-term efficiency.

34. Hence, when preaching liberation and associating herself with those who are working and suffering for it, the Church is certainly not willing to restrict her mission only to the religious field and dissociate herself from man's temporal problems. Nevertheless she reaffirms the primacy of her spiritual vocation and refuses to replace the proclamation of the kingdom by the proclamation of forms of human liberation; she even states that her contribution to liberation is incomplete if she neglects to proclaim salvation in Jesus Christ.

35. The Church links human liberation and salvation in Jesus Christ, but she never identifies them, because she knows through revelation, historical experience and the reflection of

faith that not every notion of liberation is necessarily consistent and compatible with an evangelical vision of man, of things and of events; she knows too that in order that God's kingdom should come it is not enough to establish liberation and to create well-being and development.

And what is more, the Church has the firm conviction that all temporal liberation, all political liberation—even if it endeavors to find its justification in such or such a page of the Old or New Testament, even if it claims for its ideological postulates and its norms of action theological data and conclusions, even if it pretends to be today's theology—carries within itself the germ of its own negation and fails to reach the ideal that it proposes for itself, whenever its profound motives are not those of justice in charity, whenever its zeal lacks a truly spiritual dimension and whenever its final goal is not salvation and happiness in God.

36. The Church considers it to be undoubtedly important to build up structures which are more human, more just, more respectful of the rights of the person and less oppressive and less enslaving, but she is conscious that the best structures and the most idealized systems soon become inhuman if the inhuman inclinations of the human heart are not made wholesome, if those who live in these structures or who rule them do not undergo a conversion of heart and of outlook.

37. The Church cannot accept violence, especially the force of arms—which is uncontrollable once it is let loose—and indiscriminate death as the path to liberation, because she knows that violence always provokes violence and irresistibly engenders new forms of oppression and enslavement which are often harder to bear than those from which they claimed to bring freedom. We said this clearly during our journey in Colombia: "We exhort you not to place your trust in violence and revolution: that is contrary to the Christian spirit, and it can also delay instead of advancing that social uplifting to which you lawfully aspire."[7] "We must say and reaffirm that violence is not in accord with the Gospel, that it is not Christian; and that sudden or violent changes of structures would be deceitful, ineffective of themselves, and certainly not in conformity with the dignity of the people."[8]

38. Having said this, we rejoice that the Church is becom-

ing ever more conscious of the proper manner and strictly evangelical means that she possesses in order to collaborate in the liberation of many. And what is she doing? She is trying more and more to encourage large numbers of Christians to devote themselves to the liberation of men. She is providing these Christian "liberators" with the inspiration of faith, the motivation of fraternal love, a social teaching which the true Christian cannot ignore and which he must make the foundation of his wisdom and of his experience in order to translate it concretely into forms of action, participation and commitment. All this must characterize the spirit of a committed Christian, without confusion with tactical attitudes or with the service of a political system. The Church strives always to insert the Christian struggle for liberation into the universal plan of salvation which she herself proclaims. . . .

39. The necessity of ensuring fundamental human rights cannot be separated from this just liberation which is bound up with evangelization and which endeavors to secure structures safeguarding human freedoms. Among these fundamental human rights, religious liberty occupies a place of primary importance. We recently spoke of the relevance of this matter, emphasizing "how many Christians still today, because they are Christians, because they are Catholics, live oppressed by systematic persecution! The drama of fidelity to Christ and of the freedom of religion continues, even if it is disguised by categorical declarations in favor of the rights of the person and of life in society!"[9]

NOTES

1. Rev 21:5; cf. 2 Cor 5:17; Gal 6:15.
2. Cf. Rom 6:4.
3. Cf. Eph 4:23-24; Col 3:9-10.
4. Cf. Rom 1:16; I Cor 1:18, 2:4.
5. Pope Paul, Address for the opening of the Third Assembly of the Synod of Bishops, Sept. 27, 1974.
6. *Ibid*.
7. Pope Paul VI, Address to the *Campesinos* of Colombia, August 23, 1968.
8. Pope Paul VI, Address for the closing of the Third Assembly of the Synod of Bishops, October 26, 1974.
9. Address given on October 15, 1975.

This Land Is Home to Me

A Pastoral Letter on Powerlessness in Appalachia

by the Catholic Bishops of the Region

In February 1975, twenty-four Roman Catholic bishops of the mountainous "Appalachia" region of the eastern United States—one of the most economically depressed areas of the nation—issued a pastoral letter. It is the result of three years of dialogue by priests, and sisters, and many lay groups—church workers, union people, poor people, country people, city people—with their bishops. The document is political theology in blank verse, based on the theme of Psalm 72—"The mountains shall bring peace to the people, and to the hills justice." One observer says the letter "marks a milestone in the development of more people-centered forms of ministry"; it is a call to Catholics in the region to involve themselves in the problems of the poor and the powerless. It gives no answers, but proposes steps, principles, and a process—to challenge the rich, the powerful, and the system. One theme throughout the letter is the church as the church of the poor, because "the poor are special in the eyes of the Lord." Bishop Walter Sullivan of Richmond, Virginia, a leading drafter of the statement, says, "The pastoral letter is a special example of the bishops' attempting to listen and to dialogue with the people of the region before issuing a pastoral statement. The church has begun to focus more on the depth of its listening rather than the degree to which it is being heard by others. . . . This whole role of learning rather than teaching was, in many ways, a new stance and a new form of presence for our church. . . . We began to discover a new way of 'being-church' in Appalachia, and we began to 'be with' the people of Appalachia as sisters and brothers rather than as do-gooders or messiahs." The excerpts presented here represent less than a tenth of the full statement, found in *Redemption Denied: An Appalachian Reader,* edited by Edward Guinan and published in 1976 by Appalachian Documentation (ADOC), 1335 N. Street, N.W., Washington, D.C. 20005.

Many of our Catholic people,
especially church workers,
have asked us to respond
to the cries of powerlessness
from the region called Appalachia.
We have listened to these cries
and now we lend our own voice.

The cries come now from Appalachia,
but they are echoed
—across the land
—across the earth
in the suffering of too many peoples.
Together these many sufferings
form a single cry.

The living God hears this cry
and he tells us,
what long ago
on a different mountain,
he told his servant Moses that,

—he had heard the cry of his people.
—he would deliver them out of the hands of oppression.
—he would give them a rich and broad land.

But before we turn
to this message from the Lord,
we must hear first
the cry of Appalachia's poor.

Their cry is a strong message,
not because we have made it that way,
but because the truth of Appalachia
is harsh.
In repeating this message
we do not put ourselves
in judgment of others.
The truth of Appalachia
is judgment upon us all,
making hard demands on us bishops,
as well as on others.

We know that there will be other opinions
about the truth of Appalachia,
other views than those of the poor.
But we must remind ourselves
that the poor are special
in the eyes of the Lord.

*   *   *

We dare to speak,
and speak strongly,
first,
because we trust our people
and we know
that those who belong to the Lord
truly wish to do his will;
and second,
because we believe
that the cry of the poor
is also a message of hope,
a promise from the Lord,
for he has told us,
The truth will make you free (John 8:32)

*   *   *

There is a saying in the region
that coal is king.

That's not exactly right.
The kings are those who control big coal,
and the profit and power
which come with it.
Many of these kings
don't live in the region.

*   *   *

The way of life
which these corporate giants create
is called by some
"technological rationalization."
Its forces contain the promise
of a world where
—poverty is eliminated
—health cared for
—education available for all
—dignity guaranteed
—and old age secure.
Too often, however,
its forces become perverted,
hostile to the dignity of the death
and of its people.
Its destructive growth patterns
—pollute the air
—foul the water
—rape the land.

The driving force
behind this perversion is
"Maximization of Profit,"
a principle which too often converts itself
into an idolatrous power.

This power overwhelms the good intentions
of noble people.
It forces them to compete brutally
with one another.

It pushes people into
"conspicuous consumption"
and ''planned obsolescence.''
It delivers up control
to a tiny minority
whose values then shape
our social structures.

*   *   *

Thus,
there must be no doubt,
that we, who must speak the message
of him who summoned Moses
and who opened his mouth
in Jesus of Nazareth,
and who keeps the Spirit alive
on behalf of justice
for so many centuries,
can only become
advocates of the poor.

*   *   *

We must choose life.
We must choose justice.
We must choose the Living God.

*   *   *

We have no easy answers,
so this is but a first step.
It must not be the last step.
Hopefully, this letter,
itself a product of dialogue,
will start a process,
wherein the Catholic community
can join together with all people of good will
throughout the region

to reflect on and act for
a more just society.

While we have no answers,
we have some principles
to guide the process.
Our searching must carefully balance
the following three elements:

1.—closeness to the people;
2.—careful use of scientific resources;
3.—a steeping in the presence of the Spirit.

In regard to the first element, we must
continually take time and invest creativity
into listening to our people,
especially the poor.
For it is they who,
out of their frustrations, dreams, and struggles,
must lead the way for all of us.

* * *

Throughout this whole process
of listening to the people,
the goal which underlies our concern
is fundamental in the justice struggle,
namely, citizen control,
or community control.
The people themselves
must shape their own destiny.
Despite the theme of powerlessness,
we know that Appalachia
is already rich here
in the cooperative power
of its own people.

* * *

We note with joy
the renewal zeal
for the presence of the Spirit
in prayer and meditation
among our Catholic people.

We know that if this renewed presence
can mature into a convergence
with the thirst for justice,
a new Pentecost will truly be upon us.

* * *

We would like to know in what way
the church might cooperate
with other major institutions
of the region,
provided they are open
to the voice of the poor.

* * *

We commend where they exist,
and recommend where they do not,
Centers of Popular Culture,
in every parish,
or in areas where there are no parishes,
as a sign of the church's concern,
linked to the broader action centers
places where the poor feel welcome,
spaces for people to come and share
at all levels,
so that if a new society is to be born,
it will emerge from the grass roots.

* * *

As a counter-force
to the unaccountable power

of the multinational corporations,
there must arise a corresponding
multinational labor movement,
rooted in a vision of justice,
rising above corruption
and narrowness,
with a universal concern
—for all workers
—for all consumers
—for all people.

*   *   *

Dear sisters and brothers,
we urge all of you
not to stop living,
to be a part of the rebirth of utopias,
to recover and defend the struggling dream
of Appalachia itself.
For it is the weak things of this world,
which seem like folly,
that the Spirit takes up
and makes its own.
The dream of the mountains' struggle,
the dream of simplicity
and of justice,
like so many other repressed visions,
is, we believe,
the voice of the Lord among us.

In taking them up,
hopefully the church
might once again
be known as

—a center of the Spirit,
—a place where poetry dares to speak,
—where the song reigns unchallenged,
—where art flourishes,

—where nature is welcome,
—where little people and little needs come first,
—where justice speaks loudly,
—where in a wilderness of idolatrous destruction
the great voice of God still cries out
for Life.

The Lord Appears,
The Mighty Scurry
for Cover/
Psalm 76

Daniel Berrigan, S.J.

Daniel Berrigan says that "the vision of humankind, the simple, truthful sense of who we are offered by the psalms, is in principle denied by the spirit and drift of the world today." The psalms, he says, are "a source of sanity in an insane time"— they speak up "for soul, for survival." In this reflection on Psalm 76, Berrigan professes that "God is impelled to take sides," but only "in order that sides need not be taken forever." Prophet, poet, priest—and now psalmist—Daniel Berrigan lives in New York City, and is vice-chairman of the American Fellowship of Reconciliation. This selection is from his book *Uncommon Prayer: A Book of Psalms* (Seabury Press, 1978), and is used by permission.

A terror to the great ones
is our God

How they dread him
this breaker of arrows

Armed to the teeth, the warmakers flee like chaff
He wrests their ill-gotten lands, their blood drenched
borders

And the valiant sleep;
   spears, swords at side
   inert, gunmetal cold

The Lord appears;
   chariot, charioteer, they fall
   broken like stones

   The Lord appears
   the mighty
   scurry for cover
   judgment at hand!

   [*The lowly stand firm*
   he beckons them to his side]

   The Lord appears;
   princes, satraps
      whimper like infants

A terror to the great of the earth
   is our God.

Unfortunately for all sides, in the Bible God is impelled to take sides. Or so it seems. He stands against the warriors, kings, killers, architects of violence, pharaohs, slave masters. And from the first pages, he stands with Abel, Noah, Abraham (but also Isaac the near victim), Jacob; and later with David (reservedly), Moses, the exiles, the desert remnant.

In time, his preferences grow reasonably clear, consistent. They grow more than clear in the case of Jesus—blindingly self-evident. This young rabbi claims a privileged place in the line of prophets. He steps calmly into that place and promptly pays for it with his blood. And God, the great Absenter, Abstainer, albeit tardily, is with him; in a stupendous intervention, the dead man walks again.

We have to insist—in a century ridden with division, hatred, distrust—that in so acting, Jesus and God his father were doing something more profitable to us, more significant, than merely taking sides. (What an abstract notion that is, after all, stale, fraught with jealousy, ego. Can we not offer something better to our times, to the people of the mid-70s, castaways, survivors?)

I think we can. I think we can be confident that in announcing his vocation

> He has sent me to proclaim good news to the poor, release for prisoners, recovery of sight for the blind, to let the broken victims go free. . . .

In this, he is not excluding the jailer, the rich, the high and mighty of this world. Indeed, he stands for all, speaks for all, suffers for all, overleaps death for all. Either this is true, or, it seems to me, he does these things in vain, finally, for no one. For the warlike as for the meek, for the valiant as for the pusillanimous, for the mighty as for the lowly. Finally, for sinners. . . .

In saying this, we are not attempting to make him into a graham cracker for every deadened taste. No, he stands somewhere, he is visible to the moral sense, he speaks aloud, outrages the conventional. If he takes sides, if he excoriates the hypocrites, it is to unwind the infection veiled in swath upon swath of deceit, respectability. He unmasks conflict, he exposes long festering hatreds. It is in this sense that he seems to take sides for the present, for the unfinished, poisoned, broken present, in order that sides need not be taken forever.

Remember "the surgeon with the wounded hands." Remember, "In order to be healed, our sickness must get worse."

As I reflect on these things, a message is sent to me. Five friends have been arrested for pouring their own blood on the river portico of the Pentagon. Others are arrested at the same hour for digging a symbolic grave on the lawn.

A Catholic bishop in Rhodesia is sentenced to ten years for opposing the racist policies of that country.

A Korean bishop is imprisoned for protesting the denial of civil rights to citizens. And so on and so on.

Are these resisters worthy of their tradition? Of the Gospel?

The lowly stand firm
he beckons them to his side

Their lives are offered for the healing of the nations. They are taking sides now, that sides need not be taken forever.

The False Consciousness
of "Consciousness Raising"

Peter L. Berger

Peter L. Berger believes there are some "highly questionable" assumptions behind the practice of consciousness-raising, a concept developed by Brazilian Paulo Freire. The problem, according to Berger, is that in current practice " 'consciousness-raising' is a project of higher-class individuals directed at a lower-class population. . . . A crucial assumption is that lower-class people do not understand their own situation, that they are in need of enlightenment on the matter, and that this service can be provided by selected higher-class individuals." Berger charges that this is "elitist" and "paternalistic," a kind of "cognitive imperialism." He proposes a very different approach that begins with "an injunction to be skeptical of any outsider's claim to superior knowledge of an insider's world." He concludes that there can be no such thing as "consciousness-raising," because "all of us are, in principle, equally endowed when it comes to having consciousness." Dr. Berger is Professor of Sociology at Rutgers University. This article, excerpted from his book *Pyramids of Sacrifice: Political Ethics and Social Change* (Basic Books, 1974), is reprinted from the January 1975 issue of *Worldview*, which is published in New York by the Council on Religion and International Affairs.

In the early 1960's, before the military coup, Paulo Freire and his collaborators experimented with a new method of literacy education in the Northeast of Brazil. The basic idea was simple: Teaching literacy was not to be an isolated activity but part of a larger broadening of the intellectual horizons of the previously illiterate. An important aspect was political. The illiterate were to learn reading and writing at the hand of topics (Freire called these "generative themes") that concerned their everyday experience. For the impoverished rural proletariat of the Northeast this was to a high degree an experience of deprivation, exploitation, and oppression. The educational purpose was to combine "alphabetization" with inculcating an awareness of the facts of oppression, as well as an understanding of the forces (economic, political, social-structural) that supposedly caused these facts. This political awareness, rather than literacy for its own sake, was what Freire was primarily interested in. His method was thus, in essence, one of political activity. After 1964, not surprisingly, the military regime put a stop to the program, forcing Freire to leave the country.

From a purely pedagogical viewpoint, Freire's method has shown itself to be very successful. It has demonstrated that adults of average intelligence can be taught literacy in about six weeks. The clue to success is in the motivation. People learning to read and write around topics that relate directly to their everyday experience will do so more easily than if they use texts having nothing to do with their own lives. The learning process is further stimulated if results are directly related to actions desired by the learner—in this instance, political actions designed to alleviate his overall condition.

Freire called his method *concientizaçao*—literally, "making conscious." This name has caught on internationally—as *concientización* in Spanish-speaking Latin America, as *Bewusstmachung* in the West German Left, and (a very apt translation) as "consciousness raising" in the United States. In most current usage of the term the original educational context has been left behind. Rather, "consciousness raising" is the method by which any oppressed group is taught to understand its condition and (in a unity of theory and praxis) to be activated politically for the revolutionary transformation of this condition. In its Left context, "consciousness raising" is the cognitive preparation for revolutionary action.

Even if one has great sympathy with Freire's original intentions, and also concedes that there are situations in the world calling for revolution and requiring something like revolutionary consciousness, the concept of "consciousness raising," as currently used, implies some highly questionable assumptions. To wit, it implies philosophical error and political irony.

Whose consciousness is supposed to be raised, and *who* is supposed to do the raising? The answer is clear wherever the term is used in political rhetoric: It is the consciousness of "the masses" that must be raised, and it is the "vanguard" that will do the job. But who are these people? "The masses" are, of course, whatever sociological category has been assigned the role of the revolutionary proletariat by the ideologists of the putative revolution—industrial workers (in countries where this particular assignment seems plausible), peasants, landless rural laborers, even white-collar "wage slaves" or students. The "vanguard" consists of the ideologists—typically intellectuals, who may be defined for our purposes as individuals whose major preoccupation is the production and distribution of theories. Such people have usually gone through a long period of formal education and usually come from the upper middle or upper classes of their societies. It may therefore be said: "Consciousness raising" is a project of higher-class individuals directed at a lower-class population. Moreover, the consciousness at issue is the consciousness that the lower-class population has of *its own situation*. Thus a crucial assumption is that lower-class people do not understand their own situation, that they are in need of enlightenment on the matter, and that this service can be provided by selected higher-class individuals.

Concretizing the concept in this way reveals that it is not necessarily linked to the political Left. In the United States, for example, a left-wing ideologist may be convinced that he understands the real interests of the working class much better than most workers do. But a right-wing politician or a middle-of-the-road liberal social worker may be animated by precisely the same conviction in dealing with other clienteles. "They don't understand what is good for them" is the clue formula for all "consciousness raising," of whatever ideological or political coloration—and "we do understand" is the inevitable corollary. Put differently, the concept allocates different cognitive levels to "them" and to "us"—and it assigns to "us" the task of raising "them" to the higher level.

One philosophical assumption lies in what we might call the hierarchical view of consciousness. There is something medieval about this, rooted perhaps in the old Scholastic notion of the "chain of being"—the mind of God is at one end, that of the dumb animals at the other, and in between are we humans, carefully stratified in terms of proximity to either pole. The divine pole is hardly visible in the universe of discourse under consideration, but the animal pole certainly is. Even Freire himself, a man reputed to be personally unpretentious, says about the consciousness of peasants (in his rather unfortunate essay "Cultural Action"): "This level of consciousness . . . corresponds to such a dehumanized reality that existence in it, for men, means living like animals. It is often impossible for such men to recognize the differences between themselves and, say, horses." One may wonder about the ethnographic data on which such an assertion is based. But there is no ambiguity about the implications for the "consciousness raising" program: Someone, whose consciousness is on a less than human level, is raised to the level of humanity by someone else—who, by definition, is more human already.

There is, of course, an affinity between "consciousness raising" and the Marxist concept of "false consciousness." There, too, the intellectual identified with the "vanguard" lays claim to a cognitively privileged status: He and only he has reality by the shortest possible hair. The cognitively superior individual is, by virtue of his consciousness, at a higher level of freedom, and thus of humanity. It cannot be our task here to pursue these conceptions to their roots, but it is possible to make some fairly simple observations.

If the hierarchical view of consciousness simply referred to levels of information on specific topics, there would be no quarrel with it. One might stipulate (even if one sometimes wonders) that bourgeois intellectuals as a group know more about economics than peasants as a group. If the process of imparting information from the first group to the second is called "consciousness raising," there would be nothing more wrong with the term than a certain maladroitness in choice of words. But the term, of course, is not that innocent. It implies the aforementioned cognitive and indeed ontological hierarchy. For that, however, there is no evidence whatever—at least not for anyone who has not performed an act of faith. Intellectuals may be superior to peasants in their information and perspectives on *specific topics*. If one wishes to extend this superiority to information and perspectives *in general*, plausibility disappears, for peasants very clearly have far superior information and perspectives on *other topics*—such as plant and animal life, soil conditions, the weather, and a multitude of manual skills and material artifacts (not to mention the intricacies of kinship and the true significance of dreams).

It is *not* possible to claim intrinsic superiority for either the intellectual's or the peasant's body of information. Furthermore, even if it were possible, superiority of information is not *human* superiority. To assume the contrary exhibits the most obviously self-serving myopia of those who have invested their lives in gathering and organizing information, and who then claim that this activity, more than any other, defines what is truly human. The peasant who has even a vestigial relationship to the mythology of his tradition can easily turn the tables in this argument: It is the soil that gives life, he may say, and to be human is to adhere to the soil.

The philosophical error implied by the concept of "consciousness raising" is closely related to its political irony. Those who employ the concept usually see themselves as genuine democrats, close to the throbbing life of "the masses," and emphatically "antiélitist." In the same essay in which Freire tells us that peasants cannot distinguish themselves from horses (on the very next page, no less), he denounces the allegedly reformist activities of the higher classes: "The more representatives of the élites engage in paternalistic action, the more generous they consider themselves. The practice of this false generosity . . . requires men's misery, their alienation, their docility, their resignation, their silence." It is hard to imagine a more "élitist" program (and, for that matter, a more "paternalistic" one) than one based on the assumption that a certain group of people is dehumanized to the point of animality, is unable either to perceive this condition or rescue itself from it, and requires the (presumably selfless) assistance of others for both the perception and the rescue operation. The "paternalistic'' social worker perhaps has a slight moral advantage over the revolutionary intellectual, because he at least does not delude himself that *his* consciousness embodies the true will of ''the masses.''

The critique of the concept of ''consciousness raising'' is important because it may serve as an introduction to a very different approach to the relationship of theory and policy. Such an approach begins with a *postulate of the equality of all empirically available worlds of consciousness*.

Every human being lives in a world. That is, he is conscious of reality in terms of specific cognitive structures that give cohesion and meaning to the ongoing flux of his experiences. No individual has a world identical with that of any other, but human groups do live together in shared worlds, and indeed society would not be possible otherwise. Thus the world of a middle-class intellectual differs greatly from that of a peasant, and so do the consciousnesses of these two social types. It is possible to argue that the one consciousness is superior, or on a higher level, than the other in terms of specific contents. In other words, people know different things, and one body of knowledge may be more useful in a given situation than another. It is also possible to make moral judgments concerning different worlds and consciousnesses. For instance, one might propose that the intellectual's consciousness is superior in compassion but that the peasant's is on a higher level of personal integration (peasants, that is, tend to be callously indifferent to the suffering of outsiders, while intellectuals are a notoriously neurotic lot). Such moral evaluations, however, are debatable. How is one to decide on the weight of these two traits, compassion and integrity, in a hierarchy of consciousness? One thing is clear: No objective, scientific analysis of empirical data will help in making a decision.

Moral judgments apart, every human world must be deemed, in principle, as being equal to every other human world in its access to reality. Perhaps one might want to modify this proposition with respect to very young children or mentally deficient individuals. The proposition nevertheless holds for any world that gives meaning to the lives of any collectivity of adults. In the nineteenth century, in sharp opposition to the

Hegelian metaphysics of progress, the historian Leopold von Ranke insisted that "every age is immediate to God." Thus Western civilization could not view itself as the pinnacle of human history—nor, in principle, could any other civilization or era. *Mutatis mutandis*, the same proposition may be made against any attempt to order different human worlds hierarchically: "Every consciousness is immediate to reality."

On the level of meaning, every "inhabitant" of a world has an immediate access to it which is superior to that of any "noninhabitant." Thus the peasant knows his world far better than any outsider ever can. Now this does *not* mean that the outsider may not have information and perspectives bearing on the peasant's world which are not in the peasant's possession. Such information and perspectives may be transmitted, conceivably to the peasant's benefit. What is involved in this kind of transmission is the "exportation" of the cognitive contents from one world to another. What *may* be involved, moreover, is that eventually one world swallows up the other. Empirically, this will mean that the "inhabitants" of one world impose their particular modes of perception, evaluation, and action on those who previously had organized their relationship to reality differently. This kind of "cognitive imperialism," as one might call it, is a crucially important component of modernization. The process may be welcomed or deplored. But it is not very helpful to call it "consciousness raising." A better term would be *conversion*, and a very good way of understanding anyone claiming to raise the consciousness of other people is to see him as a *missionary*.

If one society "converts" the other to its order of priorities, there will be a shift in the contents of consciousness. People will become attentive to one set of data (such as the data of science and technology), and they will "forget" another set (such as the data obtained from mystical exercises or from other forms of "irrational" intuition). Again, the term "consciousness raising" is misleading when applied to this change. It immediately implies a value judgment. To designate a rearrangement of cognitive contents more objectively, one may call it a *trade-off*. There will probably be different opinions as to who made the better bargain. Put simply, no one is "more conscious" than anyone else; different individuals are conscious of different things. Therefore there is no such phenomenon as *concientização*, unless one is reviving someone who's just been hit over the head.

The moral implication of this critique of the concept of "consciousness raising" is exceedingly simple: It is tantamount to a lesson in humility. The political implication is essentially an injunction to be skeptical of any outsider's claim to superior knowledge of an insider's world. What people say about their own social reality must always be taken with great seriousness—not only because this is morally right, but because failure to do so may lead to great and sometimes catastrophic practical consequences. The area of development policy is full of cases in which costly disaster could have been avoided if the policy-makers had paid less attention to alleged experts brought in from the outside—and correspondingly more attention to what the insiders in question had to say.

All this has to do with what we might call "cognitive respect." It is an attitude based on the postulate of the equality of worlds of consciousness. The term leads to another—that of "cognitive participation." One of the most-quoted maxims of sociology is the statement by W.I. Thomas: "If people define a situation as real, it is real in its consequence." All action in society depends upon specific "definitions of the situation." A crucial question, therefore, is: "Who does the defining?" Every "definition of the situation" implies specific theoretical presuppositions, a frame of reference, and in the last resort a view of reality. Once a situation has been defined in certain terms a number of practical options are foreclosed. It is a very limited notion of participation to let an •elite define a situation in complete disregard of the ways in which this situation is *already defined* by those who live in it—and then to allow the latter a voice in the decisions made on the basis of the preordained definition.

An individual, by virtue of his power or his status, can say to a group of people that what they need right now is to repair the roofs of their houses, and he can then ask them to vote on different methods of doing this job. It is quite possible, however, that this group of people is perfectly satisfied with their roofs, and greatly concerned with their ancestral shrines. Does the individual with the power and the status allow them to propose a different order of priorities—different not only in terms of perceptions but of values? If he does, whatever one calls the resultant process, it will be participation of a more fundamental and ample sort.

Two issues having large significance for the methodology of the social sciences are also relevant to understanding any human situation. These are the issues of "ethnocentrism" and "value-freedom."

"Ethnocentrism" is a pejorative term, coined in the early years of this century by William Graham Sumner. Since then it has acquired wide usage also outside the social sciences. The term refers, of course, to an attitude that is narrowly bound by the cultural or social biases of an individual. It has long been a truism of social-science training that this attitude is bad for the scientist; largely in conjunction with the diffusion of liberal ideals of tolerance, it is now widely assumed that the attitude is bad for anyone. The good social scientist, and by extension the good liberal citizen, will constantly seek to overcome his "ethnocentric" prejudices in dealing with people or situations outside his own sociocultural background.

In the area of development the label of "ethnocentrism" is commonly used to denigrate the imposition of Western perspectives and Western values on non-Western situations. For example, for a long time American political scientists tended to view the political side of development as a progressive approximation to Western institutions of representative democracy—the closer a society could be placed to the latter, the more developed it was pronounced to be. This viewpoint has been criticized in recent years (vigorously so from within the discipline of American political science) as an ideological expression of "ethnocentrism." Of all social scientists it is probably the anthropologists who have for the longest time and with the strongest emphasis placed the battle against "ethnocentrism" at the heart of professional training. The anthropologist must rigorously discipline himself to suspend his sociocultural bias and to immerse himself, in complete openness, in the alien situation he is studying.

As far as development is concerned, however, the injunction against "ethnocentrism" has recently taken another turn: It is no longer just a methodological caveat against the imposition of Western frames of reference, but is, in addition, a moral attack on Western values as such. The difference between these two variants of anti-"ethnocentrism" must be clarified.

Consider an extreme example. Suppose an anthropologist is studying a cannibalistic society. In order to understand this society he must try to suspend or control his own horror and moral outrage, at least for the duration of the study. Unless he does this he will be incapable of accomplishing the art of understanding. He knows that he could participate in a cannibalistic ritual only by fighting down intense nausea, and that he would be plagued with terrible guilt feelings afterwards—but he must refrain from projecting such nausea or guilt onto the actual participants. Needless to say, this does *not* mean the anthropologist must cultivate moral approval of the practice, recommend it to others, or enthusiastically join in it. But now suppose that the same anthropologist is called upon to contribute to the formation of development policy in this particular society. Suppose further that the nationalist leadership of that society is quite willing to build cannibalism into the development plan (perhaps for the purposes of population control?). Is the anthropologist meekly to assent to this, in the name of anti-"ethnocentrism"? Is he perhaps even to express a sense of inferiority about his Western soft-heartedness, and admiration for the robustness of the other society's moral code?

Actually, the example is not that extreme. The Third World today is blessed with a number of development strategies that calmly include (implicitly or explicitly) the sacrifice of large numbers of human beings, be it by direct violence or by policies that deliberately refrain from alleviating suffering. Criticisms of these strategies are routinely turned back by negative reference to Western "ethnocentrism." If the strategies are by right-wing regimes, the critics are labeled "bleeding-heart Western liberals." If it is left-wing regimes that are engaged in the "cannibalism," the critics are denounced for their "Western bourgeois morality." In both instances the anti-"ethnocentric" proposition will be that "there is a different attitude to the value of individual life in society X." This proposition is put forth not only as an empirically valid description but as a moral justification.

Some basic confusions are involved in this expansion of the notion of "ethnocentrism." Most basically there is no ready nexus between methodology and morality: To accept a fact as empirically existent is by no means to accept it as morally right. Within the moral universe of discourse, furthermore, it is not consistent to apply Western values to one set of facts and denounce such application as "ethnocentric" in relation to other facts. For example, one cannot quiver with moral indignation at exploitation of the peasantry in society Y but reject as "ethnocentric" Western bias any indignation about mass executions in society Z. If "ethnocentrism" is bad in the realm of moral judgment, the only proper attitude toward *both* situations is moral acceptance of the fact that these people just happen to have different values.

Western civilization has produced historically unprecedented values concerning human rights, human dignity, and human freedom. These values are today at the heart of *all* politically relevant ideologies of development and liberation. If it is "ethnocentric" to adhere to these values, we would suggest that one be "ethnocentric" with enthusiasm. The currently fashionable denigration of Western values is as intellectually confused as it is morally distasteful. To hold values, however, means to engage in moral judgments. If one believes that human beings are entitled to certain fundamental rights simply by virtue of being human (a Western value *par excellence*), then one is morally constrained to condemn situations in which these rights are denied. If, on the other hand, such moral judgments are deemed impermissible, then they will be impermissible in all cases—and, logically, the only political attitude possible will be one devoid of any morality. Such an attitude, we would contend, is tantamount to dehumanization.

"Cognitive respect," then, means that one takes with utmost seriousness the way in which others define reality. It does *not* mean that one makes no moral distinctions among these definitions. Similarly, "cognitive participation" means that one tries to safeguard the right of others to codefine those aspects of reality that are relevant to policy. It does *not* mean that one accords the same moral weight (and, if one has the power, the same political support) to the definition of the cannibals and of those who would do away with cannibalism. Put simply: To understand is *not* to choose, but to accept as facts the choices of others. To act politically *is* to choose—and that means, whether one sees this or not, to choose between moral alternatives. Such choice, when there is power behind it, inevitably means *imposing* some of one's values upon others.

The intrinsic relations among theory, policy, and morality may be further clarified by a consideration of the concept of "value-freeness." This concept was coined in Germany by Max Weber at about the same time that Sumner was teaching his American students not to be "ethnocentric," and there was a similar intention behind it. The ideal of "value-freeness" is that the scientific observer of human affairs should subdue his own values for the sake of understanding. It is virtually identical with the notion that science should be objective.

In Weber's time there was an intense controversy over this matter, most of it centering on the question of whether "value-freeness" was possible in the first place. In American social science there has been a reiteration of the controversy in recent years, most of it based on misinterpretations of Weber and most of it marked by a lack of methodological sophistication. One interesting aspect of the recent debates is that the *same* people who have rejected "value-freeness" as an ideal for social scientists have also been exhorting the latter to divest themselves of their Western "ethnocentrism"—a rather remarkable contradiction. This cannot be the place to review either controversy, but a few basic clarifications might be useful.

"Value-freeness" is an ideal for theoretical understanding. It does *not* imply (and was never intended by Weber to imply) that the social scientist who aspires to it is himself free of values, is unaware of the values operative in the situation he is studying, or has the notion that one can engage in policies devoid of value consequences. To the extent that all these implications have been falsely deduced from the term, it is perhaps poorly chosen. In essence "value-freeness" means that one tries to perceive social reality apart from one's hopes and fears.

This does not mean that one has no hopes or fears, nor does it mean that one refrains from acting to realize what one hopes for or to avert what one fears.

The value-free analysis of situations pertinent to development means that one tries to understand, even if that understanding is contrary to one's wishes. It especially means that one tries to gain a detached view of the probable consequences of one's favorite policies—including the probable unintended consequences. It also means that one carefully observes the interaction between values and facts, regardless of whether one adheres to the values in question. In all this "value-freeness" pertains to the theoretical attitude; it cannot pertain to action. One may aspire to value-free science; value-free policy is an absurdity.

The recent controversy about "value-freeness" has to a large extent been an exercise in shadowboxing. The real debate has been about something else—to wit, the question of who is served politically by the social scientist, and who *should* be served. In the United States revelations about Project Camelot and utilization of the social sciences in "counterinsurgency" research have brought this question into sharp focus. But it is a moral rather than a methodological question, and it would be helpful if it were dealt with as such. It is a moral, not a methodological, principle that a social scientist is responsible for the political uses to which his findings are put. If, in a given situation, one says that social scientists should support the revolution rather than support those trying to suppress it, one is making a moral judgment rather than taking a philosophical position on the possibilities of scientific understanding.

In the area of development a social scientist may be propelled by his values in different directions. He may want to advocate socialism, to search for capitalist alternatives, perhaps to find methods that will resist modernization and preserve traditional ways of life. Given favorable circumstances, he may want to engage in any number of actions that will foster these value commitments. However, his greatest usefulness qua social scientist is going to be the calmer business of clarification. Probably the most useful statements he can make will be in an "if/then" form: "*If* your development policy is based on such-

and-such values, *then* these are some of the likely consequences." Or: "*If* you take action A, *then* you are implicitly choosing value B over the alternative value C." Or: "*If* you take this action, *then* you should be aware of these particular side effects that you did not originally intend or foresee." Such statements are, if you will, value-neutral—but they are not value-blind. Nor do they preclude the addendum: "This is all I can tell you as a social scientist—but here is what I believe you ought to do, given that both you and I adhere to value C." Or: "If you do this—give me a gun, I want to join you." Or, for that matter: "I regret that, for reasons of conscience, I must herewith submit my resignation—and I've already given a copy of my report to the opposition."

"Cognitive respect," therefore, is a category very close to that of "value-freeness." It is, as it were, a theoretical virtue. "Cognitive participation," however, is a political rather than theoretical category. As such, it cannot be divorced from considerations of value, since politics is never value-free. Thus one will seeks ways to *deny* participation, cognitive as well as active, to those who would define reality in terms of cannibalism, or of racial hatred, or of the right of one group to enslave another. It will be helpful if, in doing this, one is clear about the clash of both values and power—that is, if one does *not* delude oneself that the values one is seeking to impose are really "their" values as well.

A critique of the concept of "consciousness raising" leads to the proposition that there can be no such thing, because all of us are, in principle, equally endowed when it comes to having consciousness.

Any approach to the problems of development (and, indeed, to the politics of social change in general) that claims to be moral in intent will have to face up to some of the questions we have discussed. In addition to the "merely technical" (value-neutral if not value-blind) accounting of the probable costs of different policy models, there must be added a moral accounting. Needless to say, this cannot be an exercise in pure science; from the beginning it will entail value considerations and at least the possibility of moral judgment.

We will all be further ahead if we replace the self-deceptive concept of "consciousness raising" with a more candid acknowledgment that we are faced with the problem of differing information and differing values. From this new beginning all parties involved can truly participate in shaping both the theory and practice of development.

II: Black Experience

The New Context
of Black Theology
in the United States

Gayraud S. Wilmore

While still concerned with racist oppression, Gayraud S. Wilmore observes that recent statements and activities of black theologians "seem to point in the direction of a less exclusive introspective obsession with the American race problem than was characteristic of the earliest development of Black Theology. The black-white dichotomy shows signs of breaking up, yielding to a widening perspective on human oppression which recognizes the importance of the class and cultural analyses of other theologians—especially the Latin Americans." Wilmore credits the Detroit conference on "Theology in the Americas" in August 1975 with fostering "the idea that collaborative theological work on liberation should be the next item on the American theological agenda." Thus "Black Theology today makes room in its formulations for an understanding of liberation that includes the contributions of Native American, Hispanic, Asian, and white brothers and sisters in struggle for the humanity made possible for all by the cross of Christ." Unfortunately, he says, "many white American theologians do not seem to be enthusiastic about the possibility of a renewal of theology along these lines." Nevertheless, Dr. Wilmore believes that ethnic theologies "open the way for American churches to better understand indigenous theologies in the Third World and make an important contribution to the internationalization of the mission of American Christianity." Gayraud S. Wilmore, Director of Black Church Studies at Colgate Rochester/ Bexley Hall/ Crozer Theological Seminary in Rochester, New York, is the author of *Black Religion and Black Radicalism* (Doubleday, 1972). He is a minister of the United Presbyterian Church in the U.S.A., and a member of the Faith and Order Commission of the World Council of Churches. This article first appeared in the October 1978 issue of the *Occasional Bulletin of Missionary Research*, published by the Overseas Ministries Study Center in Ventnor, New Jersey.

Most black American scholars in the field of religion and theology contend that Black Theology, as critical reflection about God and religious faith from the perspective of racial oppression and African cultural adaptation in America, began with the first black American "Independent Churches" in the eighteenth century.[1] The 1960s, however, brought the first attempts since Garveyism to produce a more or less systematic Black Christian Theology.[2] In the immediate post-civil rights period, the focus was reparations and black power considered in the light of the gospel. The flood of books and articles has diminished during the last three years, but interest in Black Theology continues, with the international scene and the renewal of the black church providing a new basis for contextualization.[3]

When the Society for the Study of Black Religion (SSBR) was organized in 1970, a second phase of black theological formation in the United States became evident.[4] The earlier work of the Theological Commission of the National Conference of Black Churchmen (NCBC) was largely in response to current political developments and had an ad hoc quality. Under the SSBR, Black Theology took on greater credibility as an academic discipline. But it was the participation of black scholars in the Detroit conference on Theology in the Americas, in August 1975, which sensitized certain key leaders to issues that Black Theology could address only by broadening its context in an engagement with other ethnic minority and Third World theologians.

Two hundred Latin American and North American Christians met in the ghetto of Detroit during the week of August 17-24, 1975. The purpose was an extended analysis of the theology of liberation in Latin America, but the conference also dealt

with the new theological winds blowing through the black, native American, Chicano, Puerto Rican, Asian American, and
white working-class churches in the United States. The issues
of feminist theology and traditional Protestant and Catholic liberal theology were faced in subsequent meetings. Keyed to the
vitality of Latin American liberation theology, much of the Detroit conference focused on the socio-economic exploitation of
minorities, the repression of human rights, and the class struggle within both the internal and the external colonies of North
and South America. Theologians, church leaders, and grass-
roots Christians wrestled together over the meaning of God's
action in history, the need for radical transformation, the tensions between Marxism and Christianity, and the task of the
churches in the praxis of liberation.

Out of this meeting came the decision to organize several
projects to continue study and move toward greater collaboration in an attack upon the structures of injustice and domination
at a second hemispheric conference to be convened in 1980. The
Black Theology Project, chaired by Dr. Charles Spivey, former
president of Payne Theological Seminary (A.M.E.) and pastor
of Quinn Memorial Chapel in Chicago, rapidly arose as the most
successful of the several continuation projects sponsored by
Theology in the Americas.[5]

The Detroit conference made a decisive impact on black
theologians. Since 1975, a network of small groups of pastors,
professors, church people, and social activists has been developed and nurtured by the staff of the Black Theology Project. In
the summer of 1977, the Project sponsored in Atlanta what is
probably the most significant conference ever held on the subject of Black Theology and its relation to the black church and
community.[6]

What have been some of the consequences of the transcul-
tural and interracial encounters with black theologians orches-
trated by Theology in the Americas? Recent statements and
activities seem to point in the direction of a less exclusive introspective obsession with the American race problem than was
characteristic of the earliest development of Black Theology.
The black-white dichotomy shows signs of breaking up,
yielding to a widening perspective on human oppression which

recognizes the importance of the class and cultural analyses of other theologians—especially the Latin Americans. But there should be no misunderstanding here. Black theologians are still concerned with racist oppression. Despite the insistence of the Latinos that they exaggerate race and color and give too little attention to the class factor, blacks continue to argue that as far as the North American experience is involved, the contradictions within American Christianity are closely related to and aggravated by their historic connection with color prejudice.

The basic problem addressed by Black Theology is the ideological role that racism plays in the culture of the North Atlantic Christian community. A culture which equated the authority and omnipotence of Euroamerican white men with the authority and omnipotence of God himself. A culture which for almost two thousand years created deity in the image of the white man and gave to God the attributes of Caucasian idealization. That is essentially the religious basis of the ideology of the Christian West and the cause of much of the oppression that blacks and other non-white minorities have experienced. Black Theology, therefore, is about the disestablishment of this ideology, the dismantling of the old order based upon it, the liberation from ideology to reality by disengaging the black religious experience and its theological interpretation from the appropriation of an imposed unreality. Its purpose is the development of an inner-directed, self-determined theological reflection grounded in the praxis of liberation from white domination in all areas of faith and life.

What Black Theology affirms is the opposite of the ideology that distorts the Christian faith to make God identical with the culture of white domination. It is, rather, that God has identified himself with the oppressed of every race and nation, and is present in their suffering, humiliation, and death. The violence perpetrated upon the oppressed is violence against God. Their death is God's assassination. But God raised Jesus from death and because we see in him the faces of the poor, oppressed peoples of the world—and particularly black people denigrated by both Jewish and Christian biblical interpretation—black theologians speak unabashedly of the Black Messiah, this oppressed and assassinated God who is risen to give life and hope to all who are oppressed. This Black Messiah who is the Oppressed Man of God, who is seen in the faces of the poor, oppressed black people, and whose death and resurrection is their rising to new life and power, is the meaning of the gospel of liberation that stands opposite to the ideology of domination by which the God of the Christian culture of Europe and America was fabricated before and after the Enlightenment.[7]

The failure of Enlightenment optimism to purge the West of the idea of white supremacy means that the seminal Black Theology of Afro-American Christians in the nineteenth and twentieth centuries was the first self-conscious and consistent attempt to break with the ideological foundation of Euroamerican culture. It is possible to identify, as a consequence of this critical discontinuity between black and white theology, three specific contributions that black theologians have made to the theological enterprise in Europe and North America since the mid-1960s.

First, Black Theology discovered on indisputable biblical grounds that the liberation of the poor and oppressed, of which blacks are a prominent example in Western civilization, is at the heart of the Christian faith. It is not that this truth had not been known before, but it had been either suppressed or ignored whenever it surfaced over the millennia of Judeo-Christian history. Black Theology has helped us to rediscover that this is what our faith is about—the liberation of human beings from every form of oppression.

Second, Black Theology demonstrates that Jesus Christ can be de-Americanized without losing his essential meaning as the incarnate Son of God who takes away the sin of the world by his cross and resurrection. Black Theology authenticated an apprehension of Jesus of Nazareth in cultural symbols and contexts other than those of white American society. In so doing, it provides an example or model for the indigenization of theology in other societies and cultures. Subsequent developments in the United States within Hispanic, native American, and Asian American theologies show that this de-Americanization, de-Westernization of Christ opened the way for other ethnic groups to identify with him in the depths of their own historical experience. We now see the oppressed and assassinated Messiah rising in cultural symbols other than those of the white people of the West.

Third, Black Theology has legitimated a return to the religious genius of the ancestors who came from places other than Europe. It discovered traces of God's visitation in the primal non-Christian traditions of the past. Because of the work black historians and theologians have done on the African inheritance in black religion in the New World, the beliefs, insights, and religious imagination of "primitive" blacks can be appropriated as correctives to the deficiencies of the Western version of the Christian faith.

All of this is not to suggest that Black Theology does not have excesses and deficiencies of its own. Black theologians regarded American reality almost exclusively in terms of black and white. The attempt to understand Scripture and God's action in history in a way that made sense to oppressed blacks makes it too easy to invest skin color with ontological significance. Certainly the black-white dualism dramatically symbolizes a basic aspect of Western experience without which much of it cannot be decoded. But the black-white dichotomy leaves out other important areas of church and societal experience—particularly those reflecting the experience of red, brown, and yellow people. Moreover, the oppression of women, Appalachian whites, homosexuals, and other groups in American life must qualify dualistic analysis.

All theology, Black Theology included, is contextual and situational. We do not know of any school of Christian theology that is universal. The claim of some white theologians that what they call theology is the universal understanding of the faith for modern people is not only ridiculous, but an arrogant falsification of the nature of all theological reflection. Since 1975, black theologians are less tempted to fall into this way of thinking about their work than formerly. Of course, they continue to make the interpretation of the gospel to the poor and oppressed blacks of North America their primary vocation. But Black Theology today makes room in its formulations for an understanding of liberation that includes the contributions of native American, Hispanic, Asian, and white brothers and sisters in their struggle for the humanity made possible for all by the cross of Christ. Most black theologians are now prepared to enter into the "pentangular" discussion of American theology proposed by Benjamin A. Reist.[8]

One problem is that blacks have too often had the experience of seeing other non-white ethnic groups break ranks with them to trade on a preferred status with whites. Bitter memories counsel caution in the opinion of those who continue to contend that a broadly inclusive program on liberation theology is still premature.

There are also other problems. A pluralistic theology, like ecumenism, ought not mean a democratization of thought in the sense that the lowest common denominator becomes the norm of truth. The desire for consensus should not be permitted to adulterate the distinctive gifts which each group has to bring from its own history and cultural inheritance. Moreover, the issue is complicated by the fact that if theological pluralism leads to a more faithful praxis of liberation, it must not only present the implications of the gospel for American minorities, but also the texture of the faith when it is filtered through the cultures and experiences of the people of Africa, Asia, Latin America, and the Pacific.

This means that the task of theology leading to authentic pluralism in a world context is fraught with enormous dangers and difficulties. It can, nevertheless, begin in the United States with its unique racial and cultural composition. The work of black theologians over the last ten years provides American churches with foundational resources. Theology in the Americas, the first research group to promote the idea that collaborative theological work on liberation should be the next item on the American theological agenda, deserves much greater support from the churches than it has received thus far.

Judging by their silence, many white American theologians do not seem to be enthusiastic about the possibility of a renewal of theology along these lines. Baffled by the demise of neo-orthodoxy since the black revolution of the 1960s, they tend to see only confusion, fragmentation, and an exaggerated religious pluralism that produces theological fads unlikely to stand the test of time and the enormous new challenges of the twenty-first century. Those who find in process philosophy the only acceptable basis for a new systemization speak of an emerging Gestalt that will reject all dualism and view the reality of God, people, and nature as an organic whole, interdependent congeries connected in ways that verify the bio-spiritual analysis of modern psychology and the expanding, open-ended process conceptions of the physicists. These theologians have much to contribute in the areas of science and technology, particularly as they apply to bioethics and ecology, and their suggestions of an evolving, androgynous God makes contact with a central emphasis in some feminist theology.

But for all its interest in futurism and relevance to the difficult and pressing problems of the age of robots and computers—the science of the First World—many white theologians seem, to the theologians of liberation among the non-white minorities, to be one step removed from the immediate and monotonously routine problems of economic exploitation, political oppression, and cultural domination. These problems call for the conscientization and mobilization of the submerged masses of the United States and the Third World. The revival of conservative evangelicalism, the pop religion and mystification inundating the middle class white churches, which are in retreat from social action, renders them not only unresponsive to process theology but oblivious to its existence. Black Theology and the other ethnic theologies of liberation may frighten the white churchgoing public, but the truth they speak about the meaning of the gospel and the judgment and grace of God cannot be evaded. Process theology does not attack the soft underbelly of American religion—its hedonism, its racism, and its worship of a privatistic, domesticated God.

There is no guarantee that the new context of Black Theology will provide an acceptable basis for wider collaboration or even that the God of the black, Hispanic, and native American theologians will turn out to be the God of the Bible who is no respecter of persons and races. The folk religious base of the ethnic theologies spells certain dangers as well as an opportunity for a revolution of the oppressed masses. It is nevertheless true that these theologies open the way for American churches better to understand indigenous theologies in the Third World and make an important contribution to the internationalization of the mission of American Christianity. The convergence of non-white ethnicity and theology in the United States, to the extent that it avoids trivialization and the suburban captivity of the mainline churches, can recall neglected themes in biblical religion and can tap into subterranean streams which flow together at the deepest levels of our common humanity and need. Robert N. Bellah, a perceptive critic of the current American religious pluralism, is correct in his observation that

> The survival of ethnic identities seems to me only meaningful in the context of the survival of religious identities. Religion provides an essential mediation between the ethnic group and the larger culture of the modern world. Not only does religion often preserve the deepest symbols of ethnic identity, it also exerts a pull away from ethnic particularity to that which is morally and religiously universal.[9]

NOTES

1. This is one of the basic discoveries of ethnohistorical research since 1964 and is elaborated in my *Black Religion and Black Radicalism* (New York: Doubleday, 1972). Further work is needed to show how the study of the present-day African Independent Churches, if important differences are respected, throws light on the theological development of black religious institutions in the United States and the Caribbean, which began to break away from the white churches in the 1700s.

2. Randall K. Burkett has done valuable work on Garveyism as a black religious movement of the 1920s. See his *Black Redemption: Churchmen Speak for the Garvey Movement* (Philadelphia: Temple Univ. Press, 1978).

3. For a survey of most of the literature, see J. Deotis Roberts, Sr., "Black Theological Ethics: A Bibliographical Essay," *Journal of Religious Ethics* (Jan. 3, 1975), 69-109. The most important recent book is James H. Cone, *God of the Oppressed* (New York: Seabury Press, 1975), although several Ph.D. dissertations by younger black scholars should be published. One that has been published is Allan A. Boesak, *Farewell To Innocence: A Socio-Ethnical Study on Black Theology and Power* (Maryknoll, N.Y.: Orbis Books, 1977). Two recent paperbacks on Black Theology published abroad are Bruno Chenu, *Dieu Est Noir: Histoire, Religion et Theologie des Noirs Americains* (Paris: Le Centurion, 1977), and Rosino Gibellini, ed., *Theologia Nera* (Brescia, Italy: Queriniana, 1978).

4. The SSBR's chief architect was C. Shelby Rooks, president of Chicago Theological Seminary. Its founding was related to the increased attention given to the academic study of black religion since 1968 by the Association of Theological Schools (ATS). See the issue of *Theological Education* on the theme "The Black Religious Experience and Theological Education" (Spring 1970). The SSBR includes most of the 158 black scholars teaching (full- and part-time in 1976) in ATS-related seminaries. It has a working group of theologians, many of whom are also members of the Theological Commission of the National Conference of Black Churchmen. Within the last few years, the SSBR sponsored two consultations on Black Theology in dialogue with African and Caribbean theologians: Accra, Ghana, 1974, and Kingston, Jamaica, 1976. The papers of the Accra meeting were published in the *Journal of Religious Thought*, 22/2 (1975).

5. Theology in the Americas has its office at the Interchurch Center, 475 Riverside Drive, New York, N.Y., and is headed by Sergio Torres, an exiled priest-theologian who also staffs the new Ecumenical Association of Third World Theologians.

6. The "Message to the Black Church and Community" with commentary by Shawn Copeland, adopted by the Atlanta conference, and the keynote address by James H. Cone, appeared in *Cross Currents* (Feb. 27, 1977), 140-156, and are reprinted in this volume.

7. Although the Enlightenment intellectuals opposed slavery, their argument that blacks were a separate species did considerable damage. In the end, the polygenist theorists "frequently denied that the nonwhite races were people at all and maintained that the missionary efforts among them were wholly wasted." Thomas F. Gossett, *Race: The History of an Idea in America* (Dallas: S.M.U. Press, 1963), p. 54.

8. Benjamin A. Reist, *Theology in Red, White and Black* (Philadelphia: Westminster Press, 1975).

9. Robert N. Bellah, *The Broken Covenant* (New York: Seabury Press, 1975), pp. 108-109.

Message to
the Black Church
and Community

*Drafted and Adopted by the National
Conference of the Black Theology Project,
Atlanta, August 1977*

This statement comes from what has been described (by
Gayraud S. Wilmore in the previous essay) as "probably the
most significant conference ever held on the subject of Black
Theology and its relation to the black church and community."
Sponsored by the Black Theology Project of "Theology in the
Americas" (a nationwide coalition growing out of the conference of North and South Americans held in Detroit in August
1975), the Atlanta conference brought together two hundred
Catholic and Protestant clergy and laity, men and women. The
theme of the message from the conference is *liberation:* "Black
theology understands 'good news' as freedom and Jesus Christ
as the Liberator." The church, it says, has a responsibility to
help oppressed people "overcome their powerlessness, rise up
and take charge of their lives." Furthermore, the black
church—"the only institution over which black people have
total control"—must reassert its power, and "gospel power
must be translated into community power." Most notably, the
Atlanta message goes beyond previous black thinking which
focused on racism as the root of social evils, and clearly acknowledges that racism, sexism, and monopolistic capitalism
are all "roots of the crisis." The document furthermore opens
the way for a new level of cooperation between blacks and
non-blacks—"We embrace *all* of God's children who hunger
and thirst for justice and human dignity." As one observer has

noted: "A necessary period of 'separatism,' as blacks recovered a sense of their own dignity and worth, may be drawing to a close with the implementation of this message." The September 1977 issue (vol. 2, no. 3) of *Theology in the Americas Newsletter* (475 Riverside Drive, Rm. 1268, New York, N.Y. 10027) published the message together with an introduction and commentary.

Grace, liberation and peace in struggle unto all who are in Jesus Christ and to all the world's suffering people.

Gathered here in the City of Atlanta from all parts of God's world to examine the meaning and implications of Black Theology for our day, we greet you in the name of that same Jesus Christ, the Black Messiah and Liberator.

Why we have come to Atlanta

We have come in quest of authentic liberation for ourselves and all people. We have come seeking God's will for our people in a time of crisis. We believe that the black church and community stand at a point of profound transition.

Together, we can go forward to a deeper understanding of present reality and a fuller measure of freedom. Or, forsaking the distinctive heritage of our faith and history, we can fall back into even greater oppression and exploitation. In North America and throughout the black world, our present situation demands that we master those processes of thought and action which can refine and enhance our theological understanding for practical application to every aspect of our common life.

We give thanks to God for the black church's witness to His creation, providence and redemption. Without our church, we would have ceased to be as a people. Thus, this assembly in Atlanta makes bold to speak the hard truth, in love, to both the black church and the black community, confessing our own part in whatever sins may be laid against both as we pray for God's gracious pardon and renewal.

By the power of the Holy Spirit, in this place, we have decided to embolden our stand with Jesus Christ for the preaching of good news to the poor, the healing of broken hearts, the releasing of captives, the recovering of sight to the blind, the setting at liberty of the oppressed—for proclamation of the acceptable year of our Lord.

The message of Black Theology

We speak from the perspective we call Black Theology: *Black*—because our enslaved foreparents appropriated the Christian Gospel and articulated its relevance to our freedom struggle with incisive accents that black women and men have sounded ever since. *Theology*—because our people's perception of human life and history begins with God, who works in the person of Jesus Christ for liberation from every bondage.

Therefore, Black Theology is "God-talk" that reflects the black Christian experience of God's action and our grateful response. Black Theology understands the "good news" as freedom and Jesus Christ as the Liberator.

Black Theology is formulated from our reading the Bible as we experience our suffering as a people. Black Theology moves between our church and our community: the church proclaims the message and the message reverberates back upon the church, enhanced by the religious consciousness of black people, including those who stand outside of the institutional church but are not beyond God's grace and His revelation.

The God of Moses and Joshua, of sister Ruth and brother Amos, of our African ancestors and our slave forebearers, has revealed Himself in Jesus Christ, the Black Messiah. He has heard the cry of our people, captive to the racist structures of this land, and is come to deliver us as He came to Israel of old in Egypt-land. In our day, the blackness of Jesus is a religious symbol of oppression and deliverance from oppression; of His struggle and victory over principalities, powers and wickedness in the high places of this age.

The failure of traditional Christianity

We cannot affirm the present religious situation in the USA. One of the greatest tragedies of American Christianity has been its failure to comprehend the physical as well as spiritual nature of human beings. With few exceptions, the church has attempted to address the spiritual needs of people while negating their physical and material requirements. Traditional theology has failed to see that ultimate salvation and historical liberation are inseparable aspects of the indivisible gospel of Jesus.

We disassociate ourselves from such piecemeal Christianity. Any gospel that speaks the Truth of God in the black community must deal with the issues of life here and now as well as with the transcendent dimension of the proclamation. The gospel cannot surrender to blind tradition or emotional effusion that render people insensible to the pain and conflict of earthly experience.

The church must come out from behind its stained-glass walls and dwell where mothers are crying, children are hungry, and fathers are jobless. The issue is survival in a society that has defined blackness as corruption and degradation. Jesus did not die in a sanctuary, nor did Martin Luther King, Jr. In those places where pain was the deepest and suffering the most severe, there Jesus lived and suffered, died and was resurrected.

As long as innocent children continue to die in tenement fires, as long as families have to live in winter without heat, hot water and food, as long as people are forced to live with rats and roaches, the gospel must be heard in judgment against the disorder of society, and the church has a responsibility—not to point people to the future life when all troubles will cease, but to help them overcome their powerlessness, rise up and take charge of their lives.

The power of the black church

We reject the notion that the black church has no power. Each and every week, black ministers interact with more people than do any other community leaders. Indeed, many black ministers have limited their roles to visiting the sick, burying the dead, marrying the lovers, and presiding over institutional trivia, while leaving responsibility for real social change to politicians and social agencies whom they feel to be more qualified than themselves. But the black preacher is still the natural leader and the black church continues to be the richest source of ethically motivated leadership, lay and clergy, in our community.

The black church must re-assert its power to transform our neighborhoods into communities. Our church possesses gospel power which must be translated into community power, for there can be no authentic community in a condition of powerlessness.

The desperation of the black middle class

We are concerned also about people whose desperation is not abject material poverty but poverty of soul and spirit. We do not believe that better jobs and bigger houses, color televisions and latest model cars prove that people have attained the abundant life of which Jesus spoke. That abundant life cannot be experienced by a people captive to the idolatry of a sensate and materialistic culture.

We abhor the capitulation of some of our people to values based on the assumption that things make for security and that distance from the distressed masses makes for a trustworthy barricade against the racism that holds us all in contempt. Commitment to physical gratification as the purpose of life and voidance of the gospel's moral, ethical standards provide false foundations for hard choices. Such false values divide and separate a people who would be free.

The identification of black liberation with the material success of a few, physically and mentally severed from the black masses, makes mockery of the unity essential for the salvation of us all. Even the material good fortune of that few is poisoned by emptiness and isolation from the people's struggle without which the mission of Jesus Christ can be neither understood nor undertaken.

The roots of the crisis

The issue for all of us is survival. The root problem is human sinfulness which nurtures monopolistic capitalism, aided by racism and abetted by sexism.

Our crisis is spiritual, material and moral. Black people

seem unable to effectively counter disruptive forces that undermine our quality of life. We seem unable to collectively define our situation, discover the nature of our problems, and develop sustained coalitions that can resolve our dilemmas.

Exploitative profit-oriented capitalism is a way of ordering life fundamentally alien to human value in general and to black humanity in particular. Racism and capitalism have set the stage for despoilation of natural and human resources all around the world. Yet those who seriously challenge these systems are often effectively silenced. We view racism as criminality and yet we are called the criminals.We view racism as a human aberration, yet we are called the freaks. The roots of our crisis are in social, economic, media and political power systems that prevent us from managing the reality of our everyday lives.

It is this intolerable, alien order that has driven us to Atlanta seeking a word from the Lord out of the wellsprings of black theological tradition.

The inseparability of the black church and black community

The black church tradition of service to its people is documented in our history books, our poetry, our drama and our worship. This tradition will not permit us to separate ourselves from our African heritage which is characterized by the sharing of resources and talents by all. Therefore, the black church and the community which it serves are one in the Spirit of God, Who does not differentiate between the secular and the sacred and Who binds us inseparably to one another.

Our victimization by the rich, the powerful, and the greedy makes it necessary for us to continually renew the tradition of our forebearers who stood in the foreground of the struggle for freedom. The black church is the only institution over which black people have total control. That church must remain in service among black people wherever they may reside.

That church must be one with and inseparable from our brothers and sisters around the world who fight for liberation in a variety of ways, including armed struggle. We affirm whatever methods they decide best in their particular situations and make no pious and hypocritical judgments which condemn those efforts to bring an end to their oppression, recognizing that we in this country have ourselves been compelled to make similar choices and may be so compelled again.

Because of racism and imperialism, domestic and foreign, we black people are an international community of outlaws and aliens in our respective homelands and in those communities where we have chosen or been forced to reside. The loving servanthood of the black church has been and is, today, an inescapable necessity. Therefore, we do not reject the disinherited, for they are us. We do not reject the disenfranchised, for they are us.

Rather we embrace all of God's children who hunger and thirst for justice and human dignity. We rededicate and recommit ourselves, and the black churches in whose leadership we participate, to the struggle for freedom from injustice, racism and oppression. This we declare to be the essential meaning of Black Theology as defined by those who conceive it, nurture it and affirm it as a source of inspiration and reflective action for all black people and for all the exploited and oppressed peoples of the world who are grasped by its truth for their situations.

The witness of the past, hope of the future

Here in Atlanta, as we have struggled over ideas and realities, as we have worshiped in the black tradition, we have felt ourselves surrounded by a great cloud of witnesses. Richard Allen, David Walker, Nat Turner, Henry MacNeil Turner, Sojourner Truth, Harriet Tubman, Henry H. Garnet, Frederick Douglas, W.E.B. DuBois, Marcus Garvey, Malcolm X, Martin Luther King, Ralph Featherstone, Paul Robeson, Fannie Lou Hamer—the innumerable hosts of our ancestors, heroes unknown and unsung. Their blood cries out from the ground. They endured trials and tribulation; braved hate-crazed mobs; were attacked, beaten and lynched; watched loved ones killed before their eyes without surrendering their integrity or dignity as they took up the cross of struggle. Of them this world is not worthy.

In their company and in the company of generations yet unborn, whose life and liberty will be shaped by our deeds, we call upon our church and our community to join us in the warfare that shall know no end, until we shall be perfected together in that kingdom of justice, love and peace which moves relentlessly toward us by the dominion of Jesus the Christ, our Lord and Liberator. AMEN

The Reverend Benjamin Chavis
(McCane, N.C. Correctional Center)
Honorary chairman

The Reverend Dr. Charles S. Spivey
Chairman

The Reverend Muhammad Kenyatta
Executive director

Sister M. Shawn Copeland, O.P.
Program director

The Reverend Dr. Gayraud S. Wilmore
Editor

Black Theology and the Black Church

Where Do We Go From Here?

James H. Cone

Further evidence of significant new global dimensions in Black Theology comes from James H. Cone, who is Charles A. Briggs Professor of Systematic Theology at Union Theological Seminary in New York City, and author of *Black Theology and Black Power*, *A Black Theology of Liberation*, and *The God of the Oppressed*. In this essay Cone discusses the need "to open up the reality of black church experience and its revolutionary potential to a world context." Being "sensitive to the complexity of the world situation," he says, means for the process of liberation that "our starting point in terms of racism is not negated but enhanced when connected with imperialism and sexism." Cone sums up: "We must create a global vision of human liberation and include in it the distinctive contribution of the black experience. We have been struggling for nearly 400 years! What has that experience taught us that would be useful in the creation of a new historical future for all oppressed peoples? And what can others teach us from their historical experience in the struggle for justice? This is the issue that black theology needs to address." Reprinted from the summer 1977 issue (vol. XXVII, no. 2) of *Cross Currents* (Mercy College, Dobbs Ferry, N.Y. 10522), this paper was first presented as an address to the Black Theology Project conference of Theology in the Americas at Atlanta, Georgia in August 1977.

Since the appearance of black theology in the late 1960's, much has been written and said about the political involvement of the black church in black people's historical struggle for justice in North America. Black theologians and preachers have rejected the white church's attempt to separate love from justice and religion from politics because we are proud descendents of a black religious tradition that has always interpreted its confession of faith according to the people's commitment to the struggle for earthly freedom. Instead of turning to Reinhold Niebuhr and John Bennett for ethical guidance in those troubled times, we searched our past for insight, strength and the courage to speak and do the truth in an extreme situation of oppression. Richard Allen, James Varick, Harriet Tubman, Sojourner Truth, Henry McNeal Turner and Martin Luther King, Jr. became household names as we attempted to create new theological categories that would express our historical fight for justice.

It was in this context that the "Black Power" statement was written in July 1966 by an ad hoc National Committee of Negro Churchmen.[1] The cry of Black Power by Willie Ricks and its political and intellectual development by Stokely Carmichael and others challenged the black church to move beyond the models of love defined in the context of white religion and theology. The black church was thus faced with a theological dilemma: either reject Black Power as a contradiction of Christian love (and thereby join the white church in its condemnation of Black Power advocates as un-American and unchristian), or accept Black Power as a sociopolitical expression of the truth of the gospel. These two possibilities were the only genuine alternatives before us, and we had to decide on whose side we would take our stand.

We knew that to define Black Power as the opposite of the Christian faith was to reject the central role that the black church has played in black people's historical struggle for freedom. Rejecting Black Power also meant that the black church would ignore its political responsibility to empower black people in their present struggle to make our children's future more humane than intended by the rulers in this society. Faced with these unavoidable consequences, it was not possible for any self-respecting church-person to desecrate the memories of our mothers and fathers in the faith by siding with white people who murdered and imprisoned black people simply because of our persistent audacity to assert our freedom. To side with white theologians and preachers who questioned the theological legitimacy of Black Power would have been similar to siding with St. George Methodist Church against Richard Allen and the Bethelites in their struggle for independence during the late 18th and early 19th centuries. We knew that we could not do that, and no amount of white theological reasoning would be allowed to blur our vision of the truth.

But to accept the second alternative and thereby locate Black Power in the Christian context was not easy. First, the acceptance of Black Power would appear to separate us from Martin Luther King, Jr., and we did not want to do that. King was our model, having creatively combined religion and politics, and black preachers and theologians respected his courage to concretize the political consequences of his confession of faith. Thus we hesitated to endorse the "Black Power" movement, since it was created in the context of the James Meredith March by Carmichael and others in order to express their dissatisfaction with King's continued emphasis on non-violence and Christian love.[2] As a result of this sharp confrontation between Carmichael and King, black theologians and preachers felt themselves caught in a terrible predicament of wanting to express their continued respect for and solidarity with King, but disagreeing with this rejection of Black Power.

Secondly, the concept of Black Power presented a problem for black theologians and preachers not only because of our loyalty to Martin Luther King, but also because many of us had been trained in white seminaries and had internalized much of white people's definition of Christianity. While the rise and growth of independent black churches suggested that black people had a different perception of the gospel than whites, yet there was no formal theological tradition to which we could turn in order to justify our definition of Black Power as an expression of the Christian gospel. Our intellectual ideas of God, Jesus, and the Church were derived from white European theologians and their textbooks. When we speak of Christianity in theological categories, using such terms as revelation, incarnation and reconciliation, we naturally turn to people like Barth, Tillich and Bultmann for guidance and direction. But these Europeans did not shape their ideas in the social context of white racism and thus could not help us out of our dilemma. But if we intended to fight on a theological and intellectual level as a way of empowering our historical and political struggle for justice, we had to create a new theological movement, one that was derived from and thus accountable to our people's fight for justice. To accept Black Power as Christian required that we thrust ourselves into our history in order to search for new ways to think and be black in this world. We felt the need to explain ourselves and to be understood from our own vantage point and not from the perspective and experiences of whites. When white liberals questioned this approach to theology, our response was very similar to the bluesman in Mississippi when told he was not singing his song correctly: "Look-a-heah, man, dis yere *mah song,* en I'll sing it howsoevah I pleases."[3]

Thus we sang our Black Power songs, knowing that the white church establishment would not smile upon our endeavors to define Christianity independently of their own definitions of the gospel. For the power of definition is a prerogative that oppressors never want to give up. Furthermore, to *say* that love is compatible with Black Power is one thing, but to demonstrate this compatibility in theology and the praxis of life is another. If the reality of a thing was no more than its verbalization in a written document, the black church since 1966 would be a model of the creative integration of theology and life, faith and the struggle for justice. But we know that the meaning of reality is found *only* in its historical embodiment in people as structured in societal arrangements. Love's meaning is not found in sermons or theological textbooks but rather in the creation of social structures that are not dehumanizing and oppressive. This insight impressed itself on our religious consciousness, and we were deeply troubled by the inadequacy of our historical obedience when measured by our faith claims. From 1966 to the present, black theologians and preachers, both in the church and on the streets, have been searching for new ways to confess and to live our faith in God so that the black church would not make religion the opiate of our people.

The term "Black Theology" was created in this social and religious context. It was initially understood as the theological arm of Black Power, and it enabled us to express our theological imagination in the struggle of freedom independently of white theologians. It was the one term that white ministers and theologians did not like, because, like Black Power in politics, black theology located the theological starting point in the black experience and not the particularity of the western theological tradition. We did not feel ourselves accountable to Aquinas, Luther or Calvin but to David Walker, Daniel Payne and W.E.B. DuBois. The depth and passion in which we express our solidarity with the black experience over against the Western tradition led some black scholars in religion to reject theology itself as alien to the black culture.[4] Others, while not rejecting theology entirely, contended that black theologians should turn primarily to African religions and philosophy in order to develop a black theology consistent with and accountable to our historical roots.[5] But all of us agreed that we were living at the beginning of a new historical moment, and this required the development of a *black* frame of reference that many called "black theology."

The consequence of our affirmation of a black theology led to the creation of black caucuses in white churches, a permanent ecumenical church body under the title of the National Conference of Black Churchmen, and the endorsement of James Forman's "Black Manifesto." In June 1969 at the Interdenominational Theological Center in Atlanta and under the aegis of NCBC's Theological Commission, a group of black theologians met to write a policy statement on black theology. This statement, influenced by my book, *Black Theology and Black Power*, which had appeared two months earlier, defined black theology as a "theology of black liberation."[6]

Black theology, then, was not created in a vacuum and neither was it simply the intellectual enterprise of black professional theologians. Like our sermons and songs, black theology was born in the context of the black community as black people were attempting to make sense out of their struggle for freedom. In one sense, black theology is as old as when the first African refused to accept slavery as consistent with religion and as recent as when a black person intuitively recognizes that the confession of the Christian faith receives its meaning only in relation to political justice. Although black theology may be considered to have formally appeared only when the first book was published on it in 1969, informally, the reality that made the book possible was already present in the black experience and was found in our songs, prayers, and sermons. In these outpourings are expressed the black visions of truth, pre-eminently the certainty that we were created not for slavery but for freedom. Without this dream of freedom, so vividly expressed in the life, teachings, and death of Jesus, Malcolm, and Martin, there would be no black theology, and we would have no reason to be assembled in this place. We have come here today to plan our future and to map out our strategy because we have a dream that has not been realized.

To be sure, we have talked and written about this dream. Indeed, every Sunday morning black people gather in our churches, to find out where we are in relation to the actualization of our dream. The black church community really believes that where there is no vision the people perish. If people have no dreams they will accept the world as it is and will not seek to change it. To dream is to know what is ain't supposed to be. No one in our time expressed this eschatological note more clearly than Martin Luther King, Jr. In his "March on Washington" address in 1963 he said: "I have a dream that one day my four children will live in a nation where they will not be judged by the color of their skin but by the content of their character." And the night before his death in 1968, he reiterated his eschatological vision: "I may not get there with you, but I want you to know tonight that we as a people will get to the promised land."

What visions do we have for the people in 1977? Do we still believe with Martin King that "we as a people will get to the promised land"? If so, how will we get there? Will we get there simply by preaching sermons and singing songs about it? What is the black church doing in order to actualize the dreams that it talks about? These are hard questions, and they are not intended as a put-down of the black church. I was born in the black church in Bearden, Arkansas, and began my ministry in that church at the early age of sixteen. Everything I am as well as what I know that I ought to be was shaped in the context of the black church. Indeed, it is because I love the church that I am required, as one of its theologians and preachers, to ask: When does the black church's actions deny its faith? What are the activities in our churches that should not only be rejected as unchristian but also exposed as demonic? What are the evils in our church and community that we should commit ourselves to destroy? Bishops, pastors, and church executives do not like to disclose the wrong-doings of their respective denominations. They are like doctors, lawyers, and other professionals who seem bound to keep silent, because to speak the truth is to guarantee one's exclusion from the inner dynamics of power in the profession. But I contend that the *faith* of the black church lays a claim upon all church people that transcends the social mores of a given profession. Therefore, to cover-up and to minimize the sins of the church is to guarantee its destruction as a community of faith, committed to the liberation of the oppressed. If we want the black church to live beyond our brief histories and thus to serve as the "Old Ship of Zion" that will carry the people home to freedom, then we had better examine the direction in which the ship is going. Who is the Captain of the Ship, and what are his economic and political interests? This question should not only be applied to bishops, but to pastors and theologians, deacons and stewards. Unless we are willing to apply the most severe scientific analysis to our church communities in terms of economics and politics and are willing to confess and repent of our sins in the struggle for liberation, then the black church, as we talk about it, will remain a relic of history and nothing more. God will have to raise up new instruments of freedom so that his faithfulness to liberate the poor and weak can be realized in history. We must not forget that God's Spirit will use us as her instrument only insofar as we remain agents of liberation by using our resources for the empowerment of the poor and weak. But if we, like Israel in the Old Testament, forget about our Exodus experience and the political responsibility it lays upon us to be the historical embodiment of freedom, then, again like Israel, we will become objects of God's judgment. It is very easy for us to expose the demonic and oppressive character of the white church, and I have done my share of that. But such exposures of the sins of the white church, without applying the same criticism to ourselves, is hypocritical and serves as a camouflage of our own shortcomings and sins. Either we mean what we say about liberation or we do not. If we mean it, the time has come for an inventory in terms of the authenticity of our faith as defined by the historical commitment of the black denominational churches toward liberation.

I have lectured and preached about the black church's involvement in our liberation struggle all over North America. I have told the stories of Richard Allen and James Varick, Adam Clayton Powell and Martin Luther King. I have talked about the double-meaning in the Spirituals, the passion of the sermon and prayer, the ecstasy of the shout and conversion experience in terms of an eschatological happening in the lives of people, empowering them to fight for earthly freedom. Black theology, I have contended, is a theology of liberation, because it has emerged out of and is accountable to a black church that has always been involved in our historical fight for justice. When black preachers and laypeople hear this message, they respond enthusiastically and with a sense of pride that they belong to a radical and creative tradition. But when I speak to young blacks in colleges and universities, most are surprised that such a radical black church tradition really exists. After hearing about David Walker's "Appeal" in 1829, Henry H. Garnet's "Address to the Slaves" in 1843, and Henry M. Turner's affirmation that "God is a Negro" in 1898, these young blacks are shocked. Invariably they ask, "Whatever happened to the black churches of today?" "Why don't we have the same radical spirit in our preachers and churches?" Young blacks contend that the black churches of today, with very few exceptions, are not involved in liberation but primarily concerned about how much money they raise for a new church building or the preacher's anniversary.

This critique of the black church is not limited to the young college students. Many black people view the church as a hindrance to black liberation, because black preachers and church members appear to be more concerned about their own institutional survival than the freedom of poor people in their communities. "Historically," many radical blacks say, "the black church was involved in the struggle but today it is not." They often turn the question back upon me, saying: "All right, granted what you say about the historical black church, but *where* is an institutional black church denomination that still embodies the vision that brought it into existence? Are you saying that the present day AME Church or AME Zion Church has the same historical commitment for justice that it had under the leadership of Allen and Payne or Rush and Varick?" Sensing that they have a point difficult to refute, these radicals then say that it is not only impossible to find a black church denomination committed to black liberation but also difficult to find a local congregation that defines its ministry in terms of the needs of the oppressed and their liberation.

Whatever we might think about the unfairness of this severe indictment, we would be foolish to ignore it. For connected with this black critique is our international image. In the African context, not to mention Asia and Latin America, the black church experiences a similar credibility problem. There is little in our theological expressions and church practice that rejects American capitalism or recognizes its oppressive character in Third World countries. The time has come for us to move beyond institutional survival in a capitalistic and racist society and begin to take more seriously our dreams about a new heaven and a new earth. Does this dream include capitalism or is it a radically new way of life more consistent with African socialism as expressed in the *Arusha Declaration* in Tanzania?[7]

Black theologians and church people must now move beyond a mere reaction to white racism in America and begin to extend our vision of a new socially constructed humanity for the whole inhabited world. We must be concerned with the quality of human life not only in the ghettoes of American cities but also in Africa, Asia and Latin America. Since humanity is one, and cannot be isolated into racial and national groups, there will be no freedom for anyone until there is freedom for all. This means that we must enlarge our vision by connecting it with that of other oppressed peoples so that together all the victims of the world might take charge of their history for the creation of a new humanity. As Frantz Fanon taught us: if we wish to live up to our people's expectations, we must look beyond European and American capitalism. Indeed, "we must invent and we must make discoveries. . . . For Europe, for ourselves and for humanity, we must turn over a new leaf, we must work out new concepts, and try to set afoot a new [humanity]."[8]

New times require new concepts and methods. To dream is

not enough. We must come down from the mountain top and experience the hurts and pain of the people in the valley. Our dreams need to be socially analyzed, for without scientific analysis they will vanish into the night. Furthermore, social analysis will test the nature of our commitment to the dreams we preach and sing about. This is one of the important principles we learned from Martin King and many black preachers who worked with him. Real substantial change in societal structures requires scientific analysis. King's commitment to social analysis not only characterized his involvement in the civil rights movement but also led him to take a radical stand against the war in Viet Nam. Through scientific analysis, King saw the connection between the oppression of blacks in the U.S.A. and America's involvement in Viet Nam. It is to his credit that he never allowed a pietistic faith in the other world to become a substitute for good judgment in this. He not only preached sermons about the promised land but concretized his vision with a political attempt to actualize his hope.

I realize, with Merleau-Ponty, that "one does not become a revolutionary through science but through indignation."[9] Every revolution needs its Rosa Parks. This point has often been overlooked by Marxists and other sociologists who seem to think that all answers are found in scientific analysis. Mao Tse-tung responded to such an attitude with this comment: "There are people who think that Marxism is a kind of magic truth with which one can cure any disease. We should tell them that dogmas are more useless than cow dung. Dung can be used as fertilizer."[10]

But these comments do not disprove the truth of the Marxists' social analysis which focuses on economics and class and is intended as empowerment for the oppressed to radically change human social arrangements. Such an analysis will help us to understand the relation between economics and oppression not only in North America but throughout the world. Liberation is not a process limited to black-white relations in the United States; it is also something to be applied to the relations between rich and poor nations. If we are an African people, as some of the names of our churches suggest, in what way are we to understand the political meaning of that identity? In what way does the economic investment of our church resources reflect our commitment to Africa and other oppressed people in the world? For if an economic analysis of our material resources does not reveal our commitment to the process of liberation, how can we claim that the black church and its theology are concerned about the freedom of oppressed peoples? As an Argentine peasant poet said:

> They say that God cares for the poor
> Well this may be true or not,
> But I know for a fact
> That he dines with the mine-owner.[11]

Because the Christian church has supported the capitalists, many Marxists contend that "all revolutions have clashed with Christianity because *historically* Christianity has been structurally counter-revolutionary."[12] We may rightly question this assertion and appeal to the revolutionary expressions of Christianity in the black religious tradition, from Nat Turner to Martin Luther King. My concern, however, is not to debate the fine points of what constitutes revolution, but to open up the reality of the black church experience and its revolutionary potential to a world context. This means that we can learn from people in Africa, Asia and Latin America, and they can learn from us. Learning from others involves listening to creative criticism; to exclude such criticism is to isolate ourselves from world politics, and this exclusion makes our faith nothing but a reflection of our economic interests. If Jesus Christ is more than a religious expression of our economic and sexist interests, then there is no reason to resist the truth of the Marxist and feminist analyses.

I contend that black theology is not afraid of truth from any quarter. We simply reject the attempt of others to tell us what truth is without our participation in its definition. That is why dogmatic Marxists seldom succeed in the black community, especially when the dogma is filtered through a brand of white racism not unlike that of the capitalists. If our long history of struggle has taught us anything, it is that if we are to be free, we black people will have to do it. Freedom is not a gift but is a risk that must be taken. No one can tell us what liberation is and how we ought to struggle for it, as if liberation can be found in words. Liberation is a process to be located and understood only in an oppressed community struggling for freedom. If there are people in and outside our community who want to talk to us about this liberation process in global terms and from Marxist and other perspectives, we should be ready to talk. But *only* if they are prepared to listen to us and we to them will genuine dialog take place. For I will not listen to anybody who refuses to take racism seriously, especially when they themselves have not been victims of it. And they should listen to us *only* if we are prepared to listen to them in terms of the particularity of oppression in their historical context.

Therefore, I reject dogmatic Marxism that reduces every contradiction to class analysis and thus ignores racism as a legitimate point of departure in the process of liberation. There are racist Marxists as there are racist capitalists, and we must struggle against both. But we must be careful not to reject the Marxist's social analysis simply because we do not like the vessels that the message comes in. If we do that, then it is hard to explain how we can remain Christians in view of the white vessels in which the gospel was first introduced to black people.

The world is small. Both politically and economically, our freedom is connected with the struggles of oppressed peoples throughout the world. This is the truth of Pan-Africanism as represented in the life and thought of W.E.B. DuBois, George Padmore, and C.L.R. James. Liberation knows no color bar; the very nature of the gospel is universalism, i.e., a liberation that embraces the whole of humanity.

The need for a global perspective, which takes seriously the struggles of oppressed peoples in other parts of the world, has already been recognized in black theology, and small beginnings have been made with conferences on African and black theologies in Tanzania, New York, and Ghana. Another example of the recognition of this need is reflected in the dialogue between black theology in South Africa and North America. From the very beginning black theology has been influenced by a world perspective as defined by Henry M. Turner, Marcus Garvey, and the Pan-Africanism inaugurated in the life and work of W.E.B. DuBois. The importance of this Pan-African perspective in black religion and theology has been cogently defended in Gayraud Wilmore's *Black Religion and Black Radicalism*. Our active involvement in the "Theology in the Americas," under whose aegis this conference is held, is an attempt to enlarge our perspective in relation to Africa, Asia, and Latin America as well as to express our solidarity with other oppressed minorities in the U.S.

This global perspective in black theology enlarges our vision regarding the process of liberation. What does black theology have to say about the fact that two-thirds of humanity is poor and that this poverty arises from the exploitation of the poor nations by rich nations? The people of the U.S.A. compose 6% of the world's population, but we consume 40% of the world resources. What, then, is the implication of the black demand for justice in the U.S. when related to justice for all the world's victims? Of the dependent status we experience in relation to white people, and the experience of Third World countries in relation to the U.S.? Thus, in our attempt to liberate ourselves from white America in the U.S., it is important to be sensitive to the complexity of the world situation and the oppressive role of the U.S. in it. African, Latin American, and Asian theologians, sociologists and political scientists can aid us in the analysis of this complexity. In this analysis, our starting point in terms of racism is not negated but enhanced when connected with imperialism and sexism.

We must create a global vision of human liberation and include in it the distinctive contribution of the black experience. We have been struggling for nearly 400 years! What has that experience taught us that would be useful in the creation of a new historical future for all oppressed peoples? And what can others teach us from their historical experience in the struggle for justice? This is the issue that black theology needs to address. "Theology in the Americas" provides a framework in which to address it. I hope that we will not back off from this important task but face it with courage, knowing that the future of humanity is in the hands of oppressed peoples, because God has said: "Those that hope in me shall not be put to shame" (Is. 49:23).

NOTES

1. This statement first appeared in the *New York Times*, July 31, 1966, and is reprinted in Warner Traynham's *Christian Faith in Black and White* (Wakefield, Mass.: Parameter, 1973).

2. For an account of the rise of the concept of Black Power in the Civil Rights Movement, see Stokely Carmichael and Charles Hamilton, *Black Power: The Politics of Black Liberation* (New York: Random House). For Martin Luther King's viewpoint, see his *Where Do We Go From Here: Chaos or Community?*

3. Cited in Lawrence W. Levine, *Black Culture and Black Consciousness* (New York: Oxford University Press, 1977), p. 207.

4. This is especially true of Charles Long who has been a provocative discussant about black theology. Unfortunately, he has not written much about this viewpoint. The only article I know on this subject is his "Perspectives for a Study of Afro-American Religion in the United States," *History of Religions*, Vol. 11, #1, August 1971.

5. The representatives of this perspective include Gayraud S. Wilmore, *Black Religion and Black Radicalism* (New York: Doubleday, 1972), and my brother, Cecil W. Cone, *Identity Crisis in Black Theology* (Nashville: AMEC, 1976).

6. This statement was issued on June 13, 1969 and is also reprinted in Warner Traynham, *op. cit.*

7. See Julius Nyerere, *Ujamaa: Essays on Socialism* (Dar es salaam: Oxford University Press, 1968).

8. Frantz Fanon, *The Wretched of the Earth* (New York: Grove Press, 1966), p. 255.

9. Cited in Jose Miguez Bonino, *Christians and Marxists* (Grand Rapids, Michigan: Eerdmans, 1976), p. 76.

10. Cited in George Padmore, *Pan-Africanism or Communism* (New York: Anchor Books, 1972), p. 323.

11. Cited in Bonino, *Christians and Marxists* (Grand Rapids, Michigan: Eerdmans, 1976), p. 71.

12. A quotation from Giulio Girardi, cited in Bonino, *Christians and Marxists* (Grand Rapids, Michigan: Eerdmans, 1976), p. 71.

We Shall Overcome

Andrew Young

Speaking to a convocation at Howard University, a predominantly black institution in Washington, D.C. from which he graduated, Ambassador Andrew Young urges black men and women in America to continue their demands for freedom and justice, but not just for themselves. "The extent to which we are committed to justice and freedom," he says, "will be determinded by how much we cry out for others who cannot help themselves." Invoking the vision of Martin Luther King, Jr., Young affirms that "all people are bound together in a single garment of destiny inextricably woven into a network of mutuality." Specifically, he calls for "an integration of the foreign and domestic policies of this nation; . . . to realize that there is an interdependence in this world that must be adhered to; that we cannot just turn our backs on the problems of the rest of the world without somehow suffering from them ourselves; and that we have been given too much." Black Americans, he says, rightly are this nation's "best critics," but they "also have the responsibility to be its advocates." Despite the problems of the world, Mr. Young argues, "we who are the descendants of black men and women in slavery should face the future with the same faith, hope and promise with which they faced it." Andrew Young, an ordained minister of the United Church of Christ, became United States Ambassador to the United Nations on January 10, 1977. A former Congressman and leader of the Civil Rights movement with Martin Luther King, Jr., Ambassador Young gave the convocation address at the 110th anniversary of the founding of Howard University on March 2, 1977, from which this previously unpublished excerpt is included in *Mission Trends* by permission of Howard University and the Ambassador.

In a sense, we are still living under the prophecy of W. E. B. DuBois who in 1906 said that the problem of the twentieth century will be the problem of the color line. We have been dogged by that problem throughout the days of our lives, and we will be throughout all the days of our future unless we can somehow in this century wipe racism from the face of this earth.

Politically, God put us in a strange and powerful position before we even knew where we were and why we were here. We somehow were congregated in the South and made cotton king, and then escaped to the North and centered in the major urban areas. That somehow produced the difference in winning and losing. We produced the difference between this nation moving forward and this nation slipping back.

In 1960, black men and women responded to the leadership of Martin Luther King, Jr., and they saw in John F. Kennedy someone who would be concerned about their well-being and they went to the polls in greater numbers than before and elected John F. Kennedy president of the United States by less than one vote per precinct. Dick Gregory said they did it in Chicago where folks from Mississippi voted four and five times for all the years they would not let them vote down there.

But the fact remains that when there was a massive understanding of the political situation and when black voters got involved in determining the destiny of this nation, this nation moved forward under the leadership of John F. Kennedy. Even after his assassination, we continued to fulfill the promises of the New Frontier in a Great Society under the leadership of Lyndon Johnson. Yet, the politics of assassination set us back. We suffered as we lost the leadership of Martin Luther King and Robert Kennedy back-to-back. We floundered in our ghettos when the leadership of Malcolm X was taken from us. As a result of a few assassinations, we found this, the strongest nation in the history of mankind, literally morally retarded under the leadership of Richard Nixon and Gerald Ford. In a sense, they are not solely to blame, for people in 1968 said, ''The vote does not make any difference. All white folks are the same. You cannot trust any of them.'' We know better now, but for eight years we paid for that misinformation.

In the 1976 election, however, we came back and redeemed

ourselves once again. For the first time in the history of the United States of America, the black community determined who would be president of the United States. I do not know about you, but from where I sit on the inside, I have not been disappointed. Hardly a Cabinet meeting passes that the President does not ask members of the Cabinet how they are doing in hiring members of minority groups and women. Hardly an opportunity comes up for him to remind them of his commitment to the poor and the oppressed in this nation that he does not take that opportunity to urge upon them the kinds of appointments and policies that will involve all Americans in the mainstream of this wonderful experiment in democracy. Yes, we have come a long way, but we still have a long way to go. Perhaps the South Georgia President who knows how difficult that road might be, and who has trod it himself throughout all of his life, might well be the one who can lead this nation—with our help—to move beyond the stigma of race and class between the shores of these two mighty oceans.

Any administration, no matter how noble and decent, gets caught up in its own immediate priorities. It gets paralyzed by bureaucratic necessities, and if there is to be any breakthrough of any significance, it is going to be produced by people who require it and who need it, demanding that their problems be met; that their needs be responded to; and that, literally, their hunger be fed. Just because we elected a President does not assure us that the kingdom has come. It only assures us that there is an Administration in power that will respond to those questions which we raise and those issues which we urgently put forward.

The burden is still on us to cry out in our demand for freedom and justice. I hope that in our cries for freedom and justice, we will not only cry for ourselves—because when you cry only for yourself, the tendency is for people not to pay much attention to you—but I think the extent to which we are committed to justice and to freedom will be determined by how much we cry out for others who cannot help themselves. Black men and women in the United States of America can never be free so long as black men and women in South Africa are not free.

There is a sense here of the continued prophecy of Martin Luther King: that all people are bound together in a single garment of destiny inextricably woven into a network of mutuality; that the problems of Southern Africa will inevitably be reflected in the Middle East; when they are reflected in the Middle East, inevitably it has something to do with the price of oil; and when the price of oil is affected, the number of jobs in the ghetto are affected. We are still, no matter how much we have progressed, the last hired and the first to be fired. When there are economic fluctuations in this nation's economy, more often than not, they are brought on by economic fluctuations in the world.

In the area of foreign policy, we found Martin Luther King telling us—though we could not understand—that the bombs you drop on Vietnam will explode at home. They will explode at home in unemployment; they will explode at home in violence and despair; they will explode at home in drug addiction; and they will explode at home in racism and right-wing reactions. They will polarize your society, and when you are immoral in your practices abroad, inevitably down the road at home you will end up in a Watergate and pay the price for your immorality at home.

There comes a point in the affairs of man when moral preachments are not just philosophy and theology. In today's world, morality becomes economic and political reality. If one is insensitive and if a nation such as ours loses its claim to moral credibility, then our ability to lead in almost any issues in the world is affected. I think we have taken a step in the right direction and I would hope that as a fulfillment of the promise we made to this Administration by our support, and that this Administration made to us, we will have an integration of the foreign and domestic policies of this nation; that we will help this nation to realize that there is an interdependence in this world that must be adhered to; that we cannot just turn our backs on the problems of the rest of the world without somehow suffering from them ourselves; and that we have been given too much.

There is a sense in which with all of its faults, this political system and this economic order has produced more in the way of revolutionary changes for more people than any other on the face of the earth. While we are on the short-end of the stick sometimes as far as this order is concerned, and perhaps rightly so are its best critics, I think we also have the responsibility to be its advocates.

This is for me perhaps the best of all times. It is a time of tremendous pressure, but it is also a time of tremendous opportunity. It is a time when we see clearly all the problems of the world, but it is also a time when we have more resources at our command to deal with all those problems than mankind has ever had in history. So, I would say that we who are the descendants of black men and women in slavery should face the future with the same faith, hope and promise with which they faced it. Then we—and all we stand for—shall overcome.

Evangelism and
the Struggle for Power

William Pannell

Looking back at the Civil Rights struggle in America, William Pannell laments that "evangelicals for the most part . . . were conspicuously absent from that historical struggle." The reason, he explains, is that "most people committed to evangelism in the evangelical sense of the word are also committed to a conservatism that identifies the *status quo* with the will of God; hence most evangelicals could only deplore the 'excesses' of the movement and wish that the preachers who led marches would get back to preaching the Gospel." Pannell—formerly an evangelist with Tom Skinner Associates of Brooklyn, New York, and now on the faculty of Fuller Theological Seminary in Pasadena, California—maintains that "Christians devoted to an evangelism which counts converts in order to achieve personal significance, or organizations which need converts to satisfy supporting constituencies found the highway to Selma uncongenial." It is Pannell's contention that "this false conservatism which characterizes most of the evangelical movement reveals a theological perspective that . . . is virtually blind to corporate iniquity," and accounts for "the failure of evangelicals to understand the nature of institutional power and its relationship to the personal sin of racial bigotry." In discussing the relationship of evangelism to the struggle for power, Dr. Pannell reflects upon the black experience and concludes that, as with Jesus on the cross, there can be power in powerlessness. His essay first appeared in the April 1974 issue of the *International Review of Mission*, which is published in Geneva, Switzerland by the Commission on World Mission and Evangelism of the World Council of Churches.

Like most evangelicals who are black, I came to the issue of power rather late. Raised amid the comforts of the evangelical ghetto, we sallied forth to evangelize the pagan masses of our generation. The question of power *v.* powerlessness was never raised, since we felt we were in touch with the only real power—the Gospel of Jesus Christ.

This stance, and practice, was sincere. It was also to be expected since we all graduated from evangelical colleges and Bible institutes. From a cultural and theological perspective we were white men. The question of power and its effect upon the powerless masses would never be brought up in these circles. For one thing, white people in North America play power games continuously without realizing it. Power, to white people, is assumed. Furthermore, our mentors wouldn't raise the issue even if aware of it, because they knew we non-white brothers were powerless. They didn't want us to get any ideas. It was a form of paternalism borrowed from the early plantation era in American history, and paternalism dies hard.

We were innocent, believing in the honor and integrity of the leaders to whom we were exposed. From them we heard about the "regions beyond" and received the challenge to dedicate ourselves to the task of world-wide missions. We assumed that we would be allowed to participate fully once the commitment was made. Many young blacks made that commitment, yet today nearly all of us relate to the missions enterprise from outside established mission structures. No one can be charged for this. As with segregation, nobody is responsible. Yet there have been no cries of anguish that we are not involved. The result of this exclusion is that the combat that rages between the conciliar and non-conciliar forces over the question of mission and missions is little understood by black evangelicals. Most do not know such a squabble exists. A few of us, now older and less naive, understand the nature of the conflict and manage to duck our heads as the verbal shells scream across the DMZ. To read the literature of both sides, one would almost conclude that the battle is an ancient one—Westerners still haggling over the rights to keep non-Westerners from their proper place of responsibility in the body of Christ.

My own awakening to the relationship between evangelism and power came in the early sixties with the dawning of the

Civil Rights struggle. Initially critical of the leadership of the movement, I came to see that there were large questions impinging upon black survival to which we evangelists were not speaking. I came to see that there were conditions of powerlessness to which evangelists ought not to speak; the greater need was for action. There were tables to be overturned and money changers to be cast out. In short, I came to see that black people, the embodiment of "powerless conscience" understood the radical nature of the cross at deeper levels than most of us who were called evangelicals. Good news to black people, and others of good will, became the possibility that with God "we shall overcome."

The spectacle of black people living out their discipleship in the form of confrontation is worth noting. It is perfectly consistent with the history of black people in American life, and striking in the history of black religious leadership. The existence of the black church in America testifies to the black person's acceptance of the relationship between embracing the cross and in its name confronting evil powers. The black church is protest by its very existence; it is a form of judgment upon society and the larger religious community. The black preacher has consistently related his understanding of the Gospel to the need for social justice. He has preached release to the captives.

Commenting upon the distinctly religious nature of the Civil Rights movement in the early sixties, Harry Golden observed that the black man has chosen two weapons in the fight for dignity: "One is the writ, the brief, the court argument. In short, he uses the law, the oldest complex in our Anglo-American complex. The second weapon is even more remarkable. It is Christianity, the oldest complex in our Western civilization." Golden, celebrated journalist, concluded his remarks by stating that "if Christianity is saving the Negro, so is he saving Christianity."[1]

Interesting. And yet evangelicals for the most part, black as well as white, were conspicuously absent from that historical struggle. Why? How is it that while most black Christians over the past 300 years could see a connection between the preaching of the Gospel and social justice, most evangelical Christians, black and white, have not been so perceptive?

I refer to the Civil Rights struggle in America because it

serves, as does the entire history of black people in America, as a focus for an inquiry into the relationship of evangelism and powerlessness. By extension, this domestic struggle illuminates much of the current flap in mission circles regarding the nature of salvation and the means to its achievement. If we agree that the means by which salvation is announced is the practice of evangelism, then we still need to understand how it is related to the gut concerns of the powerless masses of the world.

I use the word "powerless" to mean the inability of persons to effect change in the crucial areas impinging upon their survival. And survival is understood as encompassing spiritual as well as material well-being. Man does not indeed live by bread alone, but he does need bread. His inability to provide bread for his physical, psychological, social and political needs is the expression of his powerlessness.

It is ironical that those persons most concerned about evangelism did not see in the black men's struggle for justice an opportunity to demonstrate their faith, for if evangelism is anything, it is personal. Hence one would think that a commitment to people in the name of the Gospel would be a commitment to their total human needs. The failure lay in an antipathy to black people as persons and revealed an inadequate anthropology. This silence also revealed a failure to recognize a radical aspect of religion itself. The late Abraham Joshua Heschel observed that "the central commandment is in relation to the person. But religion today has lost sight of the person . . . religion has become an impersonal affair, an institutional loyalty . . . it has fallen victim to the belief that the real is only that which can be registered by fact-finding surveys."[2] Christians devoted to an evangelism which counts converts in order to achieve personal significance, or organizations which need converts to satisfy supporting constituencies found the highway to Selma uncongenial.

Furthermore, most people committed to evangelism in the evangelical sense of the word are also committed to a conservatism that identifies the *status quo* with the will of God, hence most evangelicals could only deplore the "excesses" of the movement and wish that the preachers who led marches would get back to preaching the Gospel. This position reflects what

Helmut Thielicke calls "false conservatism." According to Thielicke, false conservatism "expresses itself in the inclination to accept conditions as they are. . . . A corrupt social order, which keeps part of humanity living at substandard economic levels while allowing another class to exploit and profiteer, is regarded as a matter of divine providence . . . calling for simple acceptance and submission."[3] Thielicke sees the political problem this creates: "Between a rationalization of the *diaconia* such as is pursued by the modern welfare state, and a purely individualized love of neighbor which cannot cope with the collective misery, there is a middle zone of Christian social obligation which the church has fatally ignored."[4]

This false conservatism which characterizes most of the evangelical movement reveals a theological perspective that sees the benefits of our Lord's passion as aimed at solving personal rather than systemic ills. It is virtually blind to corporate iniquity. Admittedly, there needs to be this emphasis, for it is a biblical one. As the late L. Nelson Bell stated it, "corporate sins are but the elongated shadow of personal sins" and in arguing for revival and moral rectitude in America, he is correct. However, the failure of evangelicals to understand the nature of institutional power and its relationship to the personal sin of racial bigotry, precluded their involvement in the struggle for social justice. Committed to a "privatistic" understanding of sin, the conservative churches were rendered inadequate in dealing with sin's more corporate manifestations.

Rosemary Ruether, speaking of this view of sin, observes that "it is clear that for St. Paul, the state of sin, alienation and brokenness between man and God, does not result simply in individual 'bad acts' but stands within the corporate structure of alienation and oppression which has raised up a social and cosmic 'anti-creation.' . . . This individualistic concept of sin ignores this social-cosmic dimension of evil. A concentration on individualistic repentance has led in Christianity, to a petty and privatistic concept of sin which involved the person in obsessive compunction about individual (mostly sexual) immorality while having no ethical handle at all on the great structures of evil which we raise up corporately to blot out the face of God's good creation."[5]

John Howard Yoder has put the issue in even sharper focus. Commenting on the tendency of modern evangelism to relate the Gospel to man's sense of loneliness and alienation, Yoder asserts that "for Jesus in his time, and for increasing numbers of us in our time, the basic human problem is seen in less individualistic terms. The priority agenda for Jesus, and for many of us, is not mortality or anxiety, but unrighteousness, injustice. The need is not for consolation or acceptance, but for a new order in which people may live together in love."[6]

Black people have understood this, though not always in theological perspective. They have not concerned themselves only with matters of personal salvation or love and acceptance. They have known that the issue of survival was not only a matter of love, but also of justice, that in order to ensure justice, indeed in order to express love, it was necessary to assume a position of power in relation to the "enemy." The clash became a confrontation between "powerless conscience and conscienceless power." This is a crucial aspect of the cross. At Calvary is worked out the ultimate confrontation between the weakness of God and the power of men, between the sagacity of men and the foolishness of God. That cross was the judgment of this world-system, the casting out of the prince of this world. It is the ultimate expression of the justice of God and the guarantee that in consequence of Christ's travail there will be a new order established in the earth. The cross of Christ is the definitive act of a holy God by which he declares the end of the old order. Hence, if any one is in Christ the old is finished and done, the new has come. Christ becomes the head of a whole new order in which justice is an essential characteristic.

Yet this new order is intensely personal; a new order requires new people. It is the purpose of the Holy Spirit to confront persons with the central demand of that cross which is repentance. It is repentance that contains the core experience necessary for change and the reordering of one's priorities in favor of God. The good news is that God offers forgiveness to all those who repent. Those who are broken at the cross are restored in pardon and baptized into a new family. For them, the kingdom of God has come.

The irony of the cross is that the one hanged there chose

weakness as the way to become the power of God unto salvation. It was this choice which was Christ's supreme act of faith, and which made it possible for God through him to destroy principalities and powers. Though his death expresses weakness, it is clearly a calculated weakness; it is a voluntary weakness. In what seems a curious contradiction, Jesus claimed the authority to lay down his life—the power to be weak. Powerless people need a message of good news that promises a duplication of this splendid irony. They need to know that this is the principle by which all life is realized. It is in this sense that Rollo May writes of the relationship between powerlessness and innocence: "There is a way, however, of confronting one's powerlessness by making it a seeming virtue. This is the conscious divesting on the part of the individual of his power; it is then a virtue not to have it. I call this innocence . . . to be free from guilt or sin, guiltless, pure; and in actions it means "without evil influence or effect, or not arising from evil intention.' " May differentiates this condition of innocence from a pseudoinnocence which denies the reality of sin and the forces of evil in society. Capitalizing on naïveté, "it [pseudoinnocence] consists of childhood that is never outgrown, a kind of fixation on the past. It is childishness rather than childlikeness. When we face questions too big and horrendous to contemplate, such as the dropping of the atomic bomb, we tend to shrink into this kind of innocence and make a virtue of powerlessness, weakness and helplessness. This kind of pseudoinnocence leads to utopianism. . . . This kind of innocence does not make things bright and clear as does the first kind; it only makes them seem simple and easy."[7]

This "innocence" is the key to Jesus' strength. He was clear-eyed in his view of sin and the demonic. He knew what it was as a Jew to feel the yoke of political oppression. Yet he was curiously free from self-pity or rancour; in him was no guile, nor did he resort to clever manipulation to achieve his ends. The good news he personified was that in the midst of the stark realities of corporate evil, it was possible, indeed crucial, not only to be wise as serpents, but also harmless as doves.

The powerless also need a message that informs them of the relationship between physical and psychological impotence. This is especially important in an era when people are emerging to new possibilities of political freedom and responsibility. The Gospel informs those whose lives have been circumscribed by power that it is possible through Christ to be psychologically liberated. Christ died for everyone, therefore all persons are of inestimable worth to God. They count with God; they are profoundly significant. In the power of the resurrected Christ, they perform great exploits. The Gospel strikes at the heart of self-hatred by affirming the worth of all persons.

May is perceptive when he observes that "the central crime of the white man was that he placed the blacks, during several centuries of slavery and one century of physical freedom but psychological oppression, in situations where self-affirmation was impossible."[8] The evangelistic task concerns itself with the psychological dimensions of liberation, for it is here that so much potential for good and evil resides. As May again puts it, "social problems and psychological problems can no longer be isolated from each other."[9] Informed believers readily recognize this as but a dim echo of Christ's own understanding of his role in his time. He had come to "preach the gospel to the poor . . . to heal the brokenhearted . . . to preach deliverance to the captives . . . recovering of sight to the blind, to set at liberty them that are bruised" (Luke 4:18). Yoder sees here more than a neophyte's ordination sermon. "We must conclude," he affirms, "that in the ordinary sense of his words, Jesus, like Mary and John, was announcing the imminent *entrée en vigueur* of a new regime whose marks would be that rich would give to the poor, the captives would be freed, and people would have a new mentality (*metanoia*) if they believed this news."[10] This new attitude would certainly affect one's view of oneself. After all, if the King sends a messenger to the poor and the psychologically oppressed, surely this is cause for a radical re-appraisal of one's selfhood. It is for this reason that the messenger must be careful what he says about sin in calling people to repentance. It is not good news to black people to be told that "black" is synonymous with evil in Scripture. It is not, of course, but many believers do not know the difference between Western culture and Scripture. That all persons are sinners is scripturally sound, but that they are *ipso facto* of no value is blatantly unscriptural.

It is the peculiar burden of the oppressed that they are

called upon to be better than their oppressors. They must be loving, honest and humble, especially humble and loving. The other virtues of honor, strength, courage, and power are reserved for their benefactors. It is a peculiar phenomenon that in spite of the damage this dichotomy has inflicted upon the minority psyche, many minority members have come to accept this view of themselves. Thus it is common to hear spokesmen for the oppressed extol the virtues of their people as if suffering conferred an automatic saintliness upon the multitudes. Such a narrow view of human nature must not go unchallenged. It may be possible to demonstrate that persons who have suffered most seem to have developed a greater capacity for certain qualities usually associated with saintliness, but the connection is tenuous. Israel is one example of a people raised under great oppression who, when liberated, became an oppressor community. Ruether is again helpful: "They [the oppressed] have also been distorted in their inward being in a way that does not immediately make them realized models of redeemed humanity; i.e. the victims are not saints. They have a very considerable task of inward liberation to do."[11] A major facet of this liberation must be experienced in relation to the enemy. It cannot be accomplished in isolation. "Yet they must also keep somewhere in the back of their minds the idea that the dehumanization of the oppressor is really their primary problem to which their own dehumanization is related primarily in a relationship of effect to cause."[12]

This necessary perspective on one's own culpability in the face of evil is another facet of the cross and evangelism. At the cross all persons are guilty before God; here there are no righteous ones, no haves and have nots. Here no stones are thrown, for all have sinned. This is the necessary and radical confrontation between one's personal alienation from God and a God who assumes in himself the causes of that alienation. "For he who knew no sin, became sin for us, that we might become the righteousness of God in him" (II Cor. 5:21).

Jesus, in commanding his followers to love their enemies, was stating his understanding that the real enemy was within, and that a failure to subdue that "oppressor" rendered people incapable of successfully resolving a confrontation with the enemy "out there." Any evangelism that fails to bring the power of the cross to bear on the sin of the oppressed can have nothing to say to the oppressor either, for the cross of Christ is the judgment of God upon the whole system of humanity. The relationship of the preaching of the cross to the condition of powerlessness is that it exposes the pretensions of the oppressed that they are inherently, or by virtue of their sufferings, better than the powerful. The cross is the death of such arrogance, the birth of humility and wholesome self-criticism.

At a recent conference on evangelism, a black student from a major seminary in America rose to address the small group of delegates. "While I am in sympathy with much that is being said here," he said, "my own feeling is that evangelism itself is the problem." I can only speculate on what he meant, but I am sure he at least had in mind the probability that evangelism has become part of a middle class function removed from and unmoved by the sufferings of humankind. To him evangelism has become institutionalized, reflecting the myopia of secular establishments.

The cure for this myopia is the cross. The institution of evangelism must die if the evangelist is to be free as a person to relate to other persons; success must be sacrificed to the passion to preach the good news to those about whom our Lord is most concerned; popularity must be offered up in favor of a declaration against the sins of a society which offend the honor of God in whose image man is created. What is needed is the evangelist-prophet, men who practice Heschel's understanding of the historic role:

> . . . the prophet is a man who feels fiercely. God has thrust a burden upon his soul, and he is bowed and stunned at man's fierce greed. Frightful is the agony of man; no human voice can convey its full terror. Prophecy is the voice that God has lent to the silent agony, a voice to the plundered poor, to the profaned riches of the world. It is a form of living, a crossing point of God and man. God is raging in the prophet's words.
> The prophets had disdain for those to whom God was comfort and security; to them God was a challenge, an in-

cessant demand. . . . While others are callous, and even
callous to their callousness and unaware of their insensitiv-
ity, the prophets remain examples of supreme impatience
with evil, distracted by neither might nor applause, by
neither success nor beauty.[13]

NOTES

1. Harry Golden: *Mr. Kennedy and the Negroes* (New York:
Crest Books, 1964), pp. 16, 17.

2. Abraham Joshua Heschel: "The Abiding Challenge of Religion," in *The Center Magazine* (Santa Barbara, Calif.), March/April
1973, p. 47.

3. Helmut Thielicke: *Theological Ethics,* Vol. II (Philadelphia:
Fortress Press, 1969), p. 627.

4. *Ibid.*

5. Rosemary Ruether: *Liberation Theology* (New York: Paulist
Press, 1972), p. 8.

6. John Howard Yoder: *The Original Revolution* (Scottdale, Pa.:
Herald Press, 1971), p. 18.

7. Rollo May: *Power and Innocence, The Search for the Sources
of Violence* (New York: W. W. Norton, 1972), p. 39.

8. *Ibid.*, p. 43.

9. *Ibid.*, p. 44.

10. John Howard Yoder: *The Politics of Jesus* (Grand Rapids,
Mich.: Wm. B. Eerdmans Publishing Co., 1972), p. 39.

11. Ruether, *op. cit.* p. 12.

12. *Ibid.*, p. 13.

13. Heschel, *op. cit.*, p. 47.

A Black Nun
Looks at Black Power

Mary Roger Thibodeaux, S.B.S.

To be both black and a Catholic Sister is to belong to two "emerging" groups. To help others understand the thoughts and feelings of one in this position, Sister Mary Roger Thibodeaux, S.B.S., has written a series of reflections that are vivid with compassion, indignation and hope concerning the oppression of black people in American society and the church. These excerpts are from her book *A Black Nun Looks at Black Power* (Sheed & Ward, 1972), and are reprinted by permission of Sheed Andrews & McMeel, Inc. Thibodeaux, a Sister of the Blessed Sacrament, teaches at St. Anselm's School and is Directress of St. Anselm's Convent in Chicago. She also serves as Associate Professor of Urban Ministry in the summer graduate program at LaSalle College in Philadelphia.

I believe
    that the message
      is loud and clear:
      Only insofar as
Blacks have access to America
    will America
      have access to God.

*   *   *

I tremble
    for so many
      Americans
        when
I reflect that God is just!

* * *

Will someone kindly tell me,
        will someone let me know,
            when the FBI starts
its all-out war
        on the Ku Klux Klan?

        When we read of the Grand Wizard
seeking refuge
        in Algiers or Cuba,
            then we'll know that America
is waking up to equality.

* * *

The Book of Exodus
        does not spare our feelings.
            It paints a fairly complete picture
                of the life
        of an oppressed people.
The first thing that comes to mind is
        hard work.
            Work done for extra-long hours
and with little or no pay
        was the lot of the Hebrews
and is the lot of many others today.
        Yet, God saved the Hebrews.
Yahweh has never failed His own.
        America would do well
            to keep this in mind.

* * *

No matter how often
        we are scorned in this land—
            because it is our land
(in more ways than some care to admit)—
        we will continue to enrich it
            with our unique presence.

* * *

American society
     can learn much from Black women.
Black women have borne the burdens
     of so many other living things.

* * *

Are there any others in America
     who can be as true
          to themselves
as Black women are?

Life has never been
     a little womanly game to us—
we are a serious lot—
     called upon
          to bind
the wounds of all.

     Has it been written
at the head of the Book
     that Black people
will forever
     be exploited?

* * *

The Bible is very clear in stating
     that Jesus Christ came
          to save sinners—
Perhaps, our Church leaders
     ignore us
          for the earth's greats
because they know
     we are not the sinners.

* * *

I am a Black nun
       Seeking, wondering, doubting,
          hoping and praying.
I am a Black nun
       Singing, talking, laughing,
          crying and dying.
I am a Black nun—
       No more begging,
       No more cringing,
       No more shaming.
Shaming no more,
       no more, no more!
I am a Black nun . . .

Black Perspectives
on Evangelization
of the Modern World

The National Office for Black Catholics

Black Catholics in America sense much of the same "paternalism and arrogance" experienced by blacks in other mainline, predominantly white Christian churches. When the Roman Catholic Synod of Bishops was preparing to meet in 1974 to discuss "Evangelization in Today's World," black Catholics saw this as "a unique opportunity to redefine evangelization from a black perspective," and issued a statement which urged that their own "thoughtful reflection on our collective experience and history in the Catholic Church must be incorporated into any contemporary blueprint for guiding Catholic ministry among black people." After charging that "the institutional church in America . . . is entrapped in the same systematic racism which regulates all other institutions of this country," the statement declares that " 'evolution-through-revolution' may be our only option." If, however, the church is to have credibility in the black community, urgent consideration must be given to the need for indigenous black leadership in the Catholic Church, and for "authentic liturgical expressions based on [black] culture and heritage." This "historic document, prepared entirely under black Catholic auspices," was published in 1974 by the National Office for Black Catholics, 1234 Massachusetts Avenue, N.W., Washington, D.C. 20005.

Introduction

As a result of growing black consciousness and the strides

toward self-determination which took place in the 1960's, black people in the United States have openly and honestly assessed the implications and significance of their presence in predominantly white Christian churches, including the Roman Catholic Church. This assessment has been from a theological, philosophical, psychological and sociological perspective. The policies and practices of mainline churches, although cloaked in gospel garments, were found to be characterized by paternalism and cultural arrogance. Black people have demanded that Christian churches take new directions. This demand undoubtedly has been influenced to some extent by ''secular'' development, but in actuality was sparked by a sincere concern to bring about a greater consistency between the church's stated mission and its practice, particularly as it relates to a whole racial group—namely black Americans. It is, therefore, nothing less than a call for a total revamping of the traditional notion and practice of evangelization in the black community.

Evangelization in the modern world is a topic of special importance to black Catholics in America. For us, the 1974 World Synod of Bishops presents a unique opportunity to redefine evangelization from a black perspective. We are at a point when our own thoughtful reflection on our collective experience and history in the Catholic Church must be incorporated into any contemporary blueprint for guiding Catholic ministry among black people.

For black Catholics, considerations regarding the updating of evangelization in the black community start where revelation begins—in the culture and ethos of the people. The basis of our analysis is an awareness that *Faith* has been the sustaining force of black life in America. The traditional black church, with its emphasis on the saving presence of God throughout history, and on Christ as Liberator, has been the backbone of our constant struggle for freedom. That a people survive, grow and indeed become strong despite their being the most frequent victims of unemployment, imprisonment, miserable housing, and the debilitating effects of drugs and disease, can only be a sign of the Spirit working among us. The black man's unique perspective emphasizes the ability of the human soul, seemingly abandoned in its trials and torments, to survive and to be loyal to God through his goodness and by living the gospels. Our survival in spite of the bitter experiences and atrocities encountered in the effort to realize our full human dignity in America, gives particular cause for us to resonate the redeeming and supporting grace of God. We feel that these experiences, far surpassing in magnitude the suffering that other men undergo, can and do give hope and guidance to all desiring the great fruits of evangelization.

That black people have remained in predominately white churches is more an affirmation of their convictions about the consonance between the Gospel and the struggle for liberation, than an endorsement of the policies and practices of the institutional church. The institutional church in America, for whatever reason, is entrapped in the same systematic racism which regulates all other institutions of this country. Surely this indictment should move those in authority over the church to a serious examination of conscience.

Black presence in the predominantly white Christian church is also an affirmation that Christian faith, rooted firmly in an uncompromised Gospel, speaks with clarity and directness to the heart of the black experience—namely the individual as well as collective quest for recognition of human dignity and personal worth. It is further a challenge. A challenge to the Christian community to take up, unhesitatingly, its obligation to participate in a major way in the fight against injustice and oppression.

Such an affirmation has numerous implications for the evangelization process. It speaks forcefully to the awareness and attitudes which must prevail among those who would exercise this mission on behalf of the Catholic Church. It establishes unquestionably that the task in the black community is not a matter of proclaiming the Good News to a people who have never heard of Jesus Christ. And while this affirmation does necessitate a deep reflection by the Catholic Church upon the propriety of the *techniques* and *methods* utilized in its so-called "black apostolate," techniques and methods cannot be the primary focus.

In America a far more profound question emerges—the fusion of Gospel truth and cultural experience. The black community must be encountered where it actually is as opposed to where interpreters of the "phenomenology" of black evolution may think it is. Despite similarities with the past, the circumstances of the black condition today are not what they were fifty, twenty or even ten years ago. If the Church's reflection on "Evangelization in the Modern World" is to be productive for the black community, then it must consider as real that community's awareness of itself, its assessment of its needs, and its statement of aspirations. It is this comprehension of the existential condition of black people for what it is that will reveal to all of us what God calls his Church today.

As black Catholics we have searched the experience of our people in America, our history in the Catholic Church, and our relationship to the Church today. Our conviction is the need to see all of these elements in their proper relationship if we are to make a proper assessment of the evangelizing process today. This is the occasion for an indepth analysis of priestly ministry, the recruitment of vocations, parochial education, the role of the permanent diaconate and the character of parish life as they relate to the black community. From this analysis should emerge ethical guidelines rooted in the gospel reality which will create the new directions required for modern society.

In constructing this document on evangelization, we have formulated a definition consistent with our understanding of Mission and of Church. Our consideration is then focused on the persons—namely priests, religious and laity—whose responsibility it is to proclaim the Gospel. Interwoven through our discussion is an understanding of the social and cultural context in which their work will be carried out. Finally we will consider the various structures and practices through which our faith is communicated.

Definition of Evangelization

Our understanding of the mission of the People of God is derived from the Scriptures. Reading the Scriptures carefully, we find that Christ Himself frequently quoted the Old Testament as a reliable guide for discerning God's methods of instructing us. We also find that He cited the ancient prophecies to verify the fact that He is the "Sent One," the One Who is to be listened to. Christ commands the apostles to evangelize the whole world, witnessing to what He has already taught, to value as He valued. "And so the apostolic preaching, which is expressed in a special way in the inspired books, was to be preserved by a continuous succession of preachers until the end of time." With this in mind, we are able to formulate a functional definition of evangelization.

Evangelization is that process whereby a person is led to make a commitment to Christ, dedicate himself to a Christian mode of activity in society, and thereby become a vital member of the local church or the local community. Evangelization also involves the continuing formation of the Christian community to a conformity with Christ and the principles of the Gospel, in an attempt to bring people into a new relationship with one another through their common commitment. This community constantly extends itself, witnessing to the establishment of a new covenant—a reconstructed order, in which every person is free to live out the fullness of his God-given dignity.

The Challenge Today

It is our commitment to Christ and inner convictions about the reality of the Gospel message which produces the imperative to respond to the fact of evangelization. It demands a radical kind of commitment. On the one hand, we are encouraged by and give acknowledgement to those blacks who, witnessing to the values of Christ, have uncompromisingly condemned the hypocrisy of preaching the Gospel through words only. Their inspiration has been the vision of a Christianity truly lived. On the other hand, we are keenly aware of the experiences of many black men and women who, acting from these same convictions, and exercising their own role in the process of evangelization, have been cautioned to prudence and patience. They have been told that in the evolution of time the Gospel will be implemented. However, the constrictions of the times in which we live tell us that "evolution—through—revolution" may be our only option.

The example of the ancient prophets, of Christ Himself, the

apostles and the early fathers of the Church give us a simple lesson: false prudence and/or false patience should not be allowed to deter the total and complete witnessing of the Gospel.

We should not be comfortable in assuming that because of the centrality of the Christian faith in the past history of black Americans the process of evangelization will be easy today. On the contrary, there are serious challenges arising from (1) the philosophical and psychological transitions which black people have undergone in recent years, as well as (2) the degrading and dehumanizing social conditions in which society continues to force us to live. The single result of both these challenges is that many black people, especially the young, question the *credibility* of the institution certainly, and at times Christianity itself.

*   *   *

Liturgy is the primary expression of our communion with God and the most vital element of our union within the ecclesial community. *Through liturgy black people express, in a communal manner, our praise and gratitude for God's continuing presence in the midst of our liberation struggle.*

In liturgy we celebrate all that makes us a people, including the fact that we have survived in the face of adversity, and that we are committed to struggle on towards the achievement of a society in which our personhood and dignity will be recognized by all people. In liturgy we also celebrate our conviction that it is God who has obviously preserved us, that it is in the Word spoken in Jesus Christ His Son which liberates us, and that His Spirit makes possible in us the adherence to the promise He has given.

In liturgy we celebrate all that makes us a people. This faith and hope cannot be witnessed in a ritual that has its derivation totally outside our cultural context. Every aspect of the elements which make the liturgy reflective and make it the worship experience of a particular people in a particular place must be rooted in the cultural experiences and expressions from which the people draw strength, inspiration and hope. Liturgy can be the most enriching experience that black people have in the Church, and as such the most practical of its methods of evangelization.

It is in the interest of the Church itself not only to permit but to *actively encourage black Catholics to develop authentic liturgical expressions based on their culture and heritage*. It should periodically evaluate these efforts, and officially endorse them when satisfied that they are authentic in all respects.

This can be accomplished by being supportive of the efforts which black Catholics have already begun in this direction, and by promoting the programs which they offer.

Those responsible for pastoral ministry should be encouraged to seek out opportunities for re-educating themselves in the liturgical aspect of their ministry. They should especially seek to understand the nature and practice of *worship* from a black perspective, the importance and technique of preaching the Word in the black community, and the centrality of music to the spiritual experience. Besides understanding these things themselves, they should endeavor to extend this awareness throughout the parish community. In each parish there should be a committee which is responsible for its liturgical practice, working closely with the pastoral team.

The priority of this concern should be reflected in the budget of the parish.

As regards evangelization, there is no other consideration that is more important. Nor is there any other place where a modernization of evangelization should begin than with liturgical practice in black parishes throughout the country.

As a final word, we wish to reaffirm that *the objective of evangelization in any sector or on any level is the establishment of the Church*. There are perceptible ways of evaluating whether or not, in fact, this is what is being achieved as a result of the personnel, resources and effort designated for this purpose. The Church itself has stated the most obvious of these in a variety of ways on numerous occasion. The guideline is clear and precise: *The Church is established in a given locality or among a particular people when it is capable of continuing the life and mission of the Church from its own resources*. It is for this reason that the most prevalent emphasis in this paper is given to the need for *indigenous leadership* in the black Catholic community.

If this paper, and indeed the World Synod itself, is to represent anything more than a timely exercise, then the focus of its call is clear enough. We certainly realize that there are other considerations to be given to the discussion of evangelization in the United States, and we believe they should be given. Conversely, our reflections on this topic from a black perspective are a call for implementation of the pluralistic view which Pope Paul has so frequently spoken of, and which is an essential characteristic of the country in which we live. These reflections are a call for our representatives at the synod to reflect this pluralism at the World Synod.

The document is, in itself, historic. It undoubtedly represents the first American black Catholic response to a World Synod of Bishops, prepared entirely under black Catholic auspices.

Naturally an overview of this nature can be given in only the most general terms. There are many elements here that must be further specified for practical purposes and use. Even so, it genuinely reflects the earnest concerns of black Catholics about the future of the Church in their community. It is our hope and trust that the document will not cease to have purpose and meaning with the synod, but will continue to be a functional guideline for evangelization in the black community for all persons entrusted with that task.

III: Feminist Experience

Crisis in Sex and Race:

Black Theology vs. Feminist Theology

Rosemary Ruether

There is "an undeclared war," according to Rosemary Ruether, "brewing between" black theology and feminist theology. Actually, there are three groups against each other: white women, black women, and black men—common victims of white male domination—and "each group tends to suppress the experience of its racial and/or sexual counterpart." After describing "the inability of the black (male) movement in America to deal with sexism," Ruether charges that black theology is middle class and "primarily addresses *white* people." But feminist theology, she says, is also showing signs of elitism and "a kind of 'separatist' ideology." She contends that "an independent black feminism . . . is the essential element that is needed to cut through the mystifications of white male power that set the three subordinate groups against each other." Formerly on the faculty of Howard University's School of Religion, Rosemary Ruether is now Georgia Harkness Professor of Applied Theology at Garrett-Evangelical Theological Seminary in Evanston, Illinois. Her article is reprinted from the April 15, 1974 issue of *Christianity and Crisis*.

The two most important expressions of liberation theology to emerge from the American experience in the late sixties are black theology and feminist theology. Unfortunately, an undeclared war is brewing between them. First white male-dominated seminaries across the country adjusted their self-absolutizing perspective slightly to find a few crumbs for Black Studies. More recently they divided these crumbs even further to create a parallel corner for Women's Studies. Thereby these two expressions of criticism of the dominant social context of theological education have been set up to compete with each other.

The ruling class typically puts minority groups at each other's throats, and this could well be another example, unless blacks and women themselves figure out how to avoid the trap. The black caucuses, appearing a year or two earlier than the women's groups, have generally denied reciprocal solidarity with the women's movement. (Some black seminary professors here and there are notable exceptions.) The second women's movement, like the first, arose as women working for black liberation began to address the issues of their own liberation. Initially women analyzed their own oppression by comparing it to racism. Then, finding their own concern scorned by blacks, they withdrew in hurt alienation.

Are these two causes quite unrelated? Are blacks correct in denying solidarity with the women's movement, and are feminists specious in comparing sexism to racism? I would argue that historically racism and sexism have been interrelated but not exactly "parallel." Rather, they have been interstructural elements of oppression within the overarching system of domination by white males.

Moreover, this interstructuring has the effect of alienating white women, black women and black men from each other. Each group tends to suppress the experience of its racial and/or sexual counterpart. The black movement constantly talks as though "blacks" means black males. Hence it conceals an opposition between black males and black females. The women's movement fails to integrate the experience of poor and nonwhite women. Much of what it means by the "female experience" is in fact class-bound, restricted to the experience of a fairly atypical group of white, usually childless, women who are blocked in their efforts to break into the bastions of white, male, upper-class privilege.

We must understand these oppositions—between black *males* and black *females*, and between *white* females and *black* females—in order to understand the complexity of the interpenetration of racism and sexism in a class society. Simplistic references to sexism in general and racism in general will not suffice.

Black Theology: Sexist?

James Cone is the most notable of the younger, militant black theologians. He appears to reject any coordination between black theology and women. He has cited only part of the key scriptural passage Galatians 3:28: "In Christ there is neither slave nor free, black nor white." Class oppression is reduced to racism, and women are omitted from St. Paul's vision of human liberation. Cone has declared that women are not a "people" and do not have a "church," implying that they cannot be a liberation movement. Recently he has indicated to this author that these statements have been misunderstood, that he does not negate the women's movement as a legitimate liberation struggle. Nevertheless, he has come to symbolize for the women's movement the pervasive rebuff by black caucuses, toward which most women react with sadness and hopes of better relations and some with anger and counterrejection. Why this tension?

The tension arises not because sexism is irrelevant to black "manhood" but because it is all too uncomfortably relevant. However, this does not make black men male chauvinists in the same way as white men. Rather, the hostility springs from the humiliation of the black male at the hands of white males. The black (male) movement has been unable to sort out the way in which this humiliation has been not just racist but an interstructuring of racism and sexism.

A white Southern churchwoman recently sketched for me a model of the racist-sexist system of classical Southern society. It looked something like this:

White (elite) male
— — —over— — —
White (elite) female

$\qquad\qquad$ ———over———
$\qquad\qquad$ Black female
$\qquad\qquad$ ———over———
$\qquad\qquad\qquad$ X

In this system the white, upper-class male ruled supreme. He dominated a society divided by sex, class and race. Within the interface of sex and race, white females and black females were made the opposite sides of each other. The white woman was the dependent ornament in the parlor; the black woman was exploited for sex and work in the kitchen.

The black male was at the bottom, reduced to an asexual beast of burden, denied any self-affirmation through sexual identity. Marginalized as a human being, he was dependent not only on the white "massa" and "missus" but on his own woman as well. It is this unnameable humiliation that rankles behind the inability of the black (male) movement in America to deal with sexism—with either white *or black* women.

This situation has meant that the black church generally has played a different role in the sexual identity of the black minister than in that of the white minister. The white minister is often thrown into a confused posture toward his maleness. This is because white society considers religion and morality "feminine." It is a nice thing for women and children; it belongs in the private domestic sector; it has no place in the world of "real men" and should not get mixed up in business or politics. The virtues of Christianity are those of the "feminine": sweetness, passivity, private "feelings." The white minister is thrown into a threatened posture toward the women's movement because in white culture his own "manliness" is in doubt.

The black church has functioned in the opposite way. It was the one institution run and owned by the black community. It was their one place of public, corporate self-affirmation, the seedbed of whatever training was available for black politics and organizational development. In a society where black maleness was marginalized and placed under constant threat of "castration" (literally as well as figuratively) by the dominant sexist-racist society, the black minister became the one true "man" of the black community, the surrogate patriarch for a scorned manliness.

Even if everywhere else the black family was disjointed, in the church father was clearly on top and mother was in the kitchen cooking the chicken. Functioning as a compensatory patriarchal figure for the whole community, the minister often became superpatriarchal, a symbol of pride for his people to whom they could transfer the privileges denied to them.

Black women have recently tried to challenge the tendency to make them the victims of this development of black manliness. They have tried to suggest that the strength of the black woman under oppression should be regarded with pride, not humiliation, as a part of the black experience. They have suggested that this strength makes possible an alternate paradigm for black male-female relations: They need not be patterned after white male dominance but can be truly reciprocal and mutually enhancing. They declare their full solidarity with the development of black manhood, but they protest a covert insistence that they walk ten paces behind in order to give the illusion that the black man is walking ten paces ahead. This is a delusionary form of manliness that fails to appreciate and build upon the true possibilities of the experience of the black family that remained strong under the experience of oppression.

In the writings of black women one glimpses their fundamental experience of functioning as the "reality principle" for the entire race. They not only upheld the economic viability of the family unit, giving strength to the new generation, but also bore the ego frustration of the black man. This experience grows the more bitter when the black woman finds herself rejected precisely at the moment when she feels compelled to reject the "feminine" role in order to assert her truthful character as the "reality principle."

The black man, in turn, is constantly pulled after the white woman, who represents the illusionary "feminine" and the forbidden fruits of sexual dominance. No wonder these groups are constantly tempted to turn on each other—the black man blaming the black woman, the black woman blaming the white woman, the white woman retreating in a hurt alienation that could change into a racist reaction—instead of recognizing that despite their outwardly different conditions they share a common victimization under the superstructure of white patriarchy.

Black Theology: Middle Class?

In addition to representing the aspiration of the black community for "manliness," the black church has also been the traditional path toward the *embourgeoisement* of the black community. Consequently, it also has had the tendency to lose contact with the actual condition of the masses and become an enclave of "respectability," alienated and threatened by the chaotic conditions of the impoverished blacks, especially in the Northern city. The black masses, therefore, have often turned toward cultic and even anti-Christian movements to express their own experience of oppression. They have villified the black minister—respected as the "proper" spokesman for the black community by whites—as a "crook" and an Uncle Tom.

The lower class has developed its own ways of affirming its different experience of sexuality. It is more comfortable with the nonbourgeois family patterns so deplored by Patrick Moynihan. This pattern is incorrectly described as "matriarchy," since the woman is hardly "dominant" in the usual sense of that word. But there is an autonomy and reciprocity quite different from the standard bourgeois model. Ultimately it is the woman who stands firm. She is the "ground of being" of the people in a way that finds its ambivalent celebration. Even as she is decried for her "lip," it is this toughness and realism that is the foundation of black survival.

On the portico of the main auditorium at Howard University there is a gigantic mural of black history that consists of four male and two female figures. The males are Martin Luther King, Malcolm X, Frederick Douglass and an anonymous rebel slave. The first three are posed in rhetorical stances, talking, while the fourth pulls the chain from his back. The females, Harriet Tubman and Sojourner Truth, are shown in fighting stances, pulling the chains off their people and carrying guns. They are depicted as participating militantly in the liberation of their people. I know of no other group in America that could— and would be willing to—show the women of its history in this fashion.

The tension between black churchmen and the women's movement, then, seems to represent the defensive perspective of the black, middle-class, patriarchal church. It concentrates on confronting the racism of its counterparts in the white church. But it has not yet opened itself up to the disturbing countertrends in the lower-class black community that not only conflict with bourgeois male and female stereotypes but also are alienated from middle-class values and the Christian identity as well.

The Limits of "Black Caucus Theology"

These remarks do not discredit the validity of the theology being done by Cone in a particular context. His theology is an effective and appropriate instrument for its primary task. I would call this "black caucus theology." By this I mean that it is shaped to function in a confrontational fashion within a white power base. It places demands of conscience on white power and seeks to appropriate its advantages for the training of black leadership. But contrary to what Cone himself often declares, I think his kind of theology primarily addresses *white* people. Its content originally was little penetrated by the spirit of the black experience as an alternate source of theological themes. Its substance was taken from German dialectical theology, something Cone has continually defended as appropriate. He has essentially turned white theology upside down in order to reveal its hidden racist ideology. This is a valid and authentically prophetic use of theology within these social limits.

Cone's prophetic reversal of white theology remains too vaguely "universalist" for the concrete tasks of a radical black church. He spends much time justifying the idea that a white person may become "black" in a moral sense. He accepts an empty and negative definition of "blackness." Defining it essentially as "the oppressed," he gives little suggestion of what blackness might mean as an alternative culture in its own right. His recent book, *The Spirituals and the Blues*, has begun to correct this.

I believe that Cone's theology is appropriate for the task of confronting white power in the black caucus situation. However, it may be inadequate for the integral self-development of the black community itself, i.e. as black theology for black people. As a white middle-class female I presume no superior knowledge of blackness. But as a former teacher at the Howard School of Religion, I simply suggest something rather evident from the different sitz-im-leben of the black seminary in the black church and community, which has a much fuller reality than what appears to whites in the special psychology of the black caucus in the white institution.

The black community needs the transfer of power and skills from white institutions. Black caucuses have an important role here. What is still not evident is whether this power and these skills will really be transferred. One wonders whether black caucuses are not being led in the centrifugal path of the black middle class in militant disguise. The new willingness of white society to promote the skilled black person to full citizenship creates the possibility of disenfranchising this leadership group from the poor black community. We are beguiled into thinking that racism is overcome because a small elite gains new visibility and honor. We are prevented from seeing that the black masses in the ghettos are experiencing a worsening condition that they can no longer tolerate.

A relevant black church must perhaps become far more integrally black if it is to address itself to this situation. It must transform itself to overcome the split between the bourgeois black church and the unchurched black masses. It must become more like the Black Muslims or the Garveyite movements in the sense of focusing on building communal structures of social cooperation by and for blacks within the black community itself. It must take the initiative, in a vast movement of new morale, in transferring resources from white society and building resources from within the black community to transform the "ghetto" from a place of deprivation to a place of positive black communal expression and development.

The symbols that the black church inherited from evangelical Christianity may be too limited for this task. It may have to reach much more toward "soul," toward symbols developed by blacks alienated from the church, and also towards the Caribbean and Africa to find a "blackness" that is not simply anti-white but can rejoice in itself. Perhaps only Mother Africa can provide some symbols that the uprooted, stolen people cannot derive from the land of slavery: symbols for the soul-self, for the goodness of the body-self, for the integration of humankind in nature, the rootedness of peoplehood in the land.

The development of women's caucuses in seminaries and feminist theology, parallel to that of the black movement, is a phenomenon of the last few years. However, already there is evidence that women's caucuses may be creating a social encapsulation similar to that of black caucuses. This encapsulation, moreover, has social roots in the history of white feminism in America.

Feminist Theology: Elitist?

The women's movement in America arose in the 1830's among Southern elite and New England Brahmin women turned abolitionists. Its concept of the oppression of women was fueled by its sympathy with the antislavery cause. When the 14th Amendment enfranchised the black male and excluded women—using the word "male" as a description of citizenship for the first time in American constitutional tradition (previously the "generic" term "man" was used)—the more militant thought the amendment should be rejected until it included both race and sex. Thereafter they acquiesced in the increasing drift of the women's movement away from equalitarian views toward a racist and class bias.

As the women's movement became a mass movement in the 1880's, it was influenced by the general abandonment of romantic heroic reformism for a racist social Darwinism. Even the Social Gospel movement, strong in preaching against the exploitation of labor, acquiesced to the leading scientific dogma of Negro inferiority and never overcame its bourgeois paternalistic concept of the reformer as an expression of *noblesse oblige*. Increasingly the movement drifted toward a view that women should be enfranchised in order to double the vote of the white, Protestant, middle class and thereby assure the supremacy of this ruling class over the rising tide of blacks and immigrant Catholics and Jews. It thereby also took for granted the de facto reversal of the 14th Amendment in the Jim Crow laws.

At the same time the women's movement backed away from its earlier radical confrontation with the stereotypes of masculinity and femininity and the place of the woman in the home. Instead it accepted the stereotype of the feminine "lady," whose beneficent role in the home should now shine forth into the public arena.

The new women's movement of the 1960's also arose out of

an alliance with and, then, a traumatic experience of rejection by the black civil rights and white male radical movements. It has typically sought to go beyond the limits of the old women's movement and to challenge the stereotypes of the feminine and the sexual relations of male and female in home and society. It seems little disposed, therefore, to fall for a new version of the "white lady" myth. Yet its alienation from other radical movements, especially black liberation, and its recourse to a kind of "separatist" ideology—that talks about the oppression of women as more basic than any other form of oppression in a way that makes women a separate cause unrelated to other kinds of oppression—may be working its own kind of subtle social encapsulation.

This separatist concept helps to obscure the way in which the oppression of women is structurally integrated with that of class and race. Sociologically, women are a sexual caste within every class and race. They share a common condition of women: dependency, secondary existence, domestic labor, sexual exploitation and the projection of their role in procreation into a total definition of their existence.

But this common condition takes profoundly different forms as women are divided against each other by class and race. No woman of an oppressed class and race, therefore, can separate her female struggle from its context in the liberation of her own community. It is impossible for a black woman to join a women's movement that ignores racial oppression, however much she may want to lead the black movement beyond patriarchalism.

Women of the elite class and race easily fall into an abstract analysis of women's oppressed status that they believe will unite *all* women. They ignore their own context of class and race privilege. Their movement fails to connect with women of oppressed groups, and it becomes defined by a demand for "rights" commensurate with the males of their group, oblivious to the unjust racist and class context of these privileges. It may not be wrong to seek such "equality," but it is dangerous to allow the ideology of the women's movement to remain confined to this perspective.

Feminist Theology: Anti-female?

Theology done in the context of women's caucuses in elite universities tends also to be alienated from the *experience* of most women. Motherhood is a negative trip, and the chief ethical word one has to say about it is "abortion." Abortion is a necessary evil at this time, which I wish all women to have available to them if they need it. The elite woman, who competes with the career pattern of the elite male, is subverted at the point of her capacity to have children. She is usually forced to choose between the two. Absolutized, however, this perspective on motherhood really accepts the "phallic morality" (to use Mary Daly's phrase) that women have decried. It accepts a feminist antifemaleness that loathes women at the point of the specificity of female difference.

Maternity has been the root of female oppression because it represents the one power that men do not have and upon which all men depend for their existence. Not to be able to rescue maternity as a positive symbol for women in a way that can be liberating is really a capitulation to the male false consciousness that tries to convert female potency into the female weakness through which women are subjugated. Sexism cannot be understood, historically or psychologically, unless it is recognized that it rests not on female weakness but on the suppression of female power. Sexism is an elaborate system of handicaps that males erect around women to make female potency appear to be the point of their weakness and dependency, thereby suppressing from cultural consciousness the truth of male dependency. Women who strive for an equality by accepting this male negation of the female remain encapsulated in male false consciousness.

As all early mythology shows, our fundamental images of ontology draw on maternity as a biological fact of all our existence. Fathering is essentially external, while the origin of each of us in the mother's womb is the fundamental anthropological-existential basis of language about ground and substance. Hence, the first power on earth was "Mother Power"—ontologically, if not politically. In suppressing

Mother Power women must recognize themselves as cooperators from the first. The fact is that women almost never take advantage of their own power for political domination. Even neurotic "momism" is really a creation of male chauvinism, which squeezes women's power into a confined space. But the fundamental mothering function is one that seeks to build up the autonomous existence of men and children—even at her own expense. Sexism arises at the point where men take advantage of this nurturing function to refuse reciprocity and erect a political structure of dependency that vaunts the male as a priori and transcendent, thereby denying his real foundations in Mother Power.

If women must unmask these false superstructures today, it cannot be in a way that betrays the lifebuilding aspect of female life for an adoption of misogynism. Rather, women's liberation will only gain general support from women when it can be revealed as a necessity that also expresses the mandate of the woman as the foundation of the survival of the race. Male false consciousness has created an antagonistic concept of self and social and ecological relations that is rapidly destroying mankind and the earth. Not only have the personhood and cultural gifts of women been suppressed by this, but males themselves have been allowed to remain in an adolescent form of vainglorious psychology that is no longer compatible with human survival.

Women must reject male chauvinism at the point of the oppression of their own personhood and autonomy. But they must also reject it at the point of motherhood for the sake of the survival of their children. It is at this point that the dialogue between white feminism and black feminism is vital. White feminism easily capitulates to a female version of male misogynist psychology. Only the experience of black women can unmask what is suppressed beneath this pretense of the "natural superiority of the male" and show its real roots. Black women inevitably ground a militant feminism not only in their liberation as persons but also in the validation of woman as mother, fighting for the survival of her children. Their experience reveals what patriarchal mythology conceals: The first power is Mother Power, and patriarchy arises by suppressing and concealing this grounding of the male in the female.

The history of white male chauvinism, with its interstructuring of sexism and racism, is bent on alienating black women and white women and making their contrary experiences incommunicable to each other. When black and white women can penetrate each other's experience and recognize each other as common victims of a total structure of white male domination, this will be the moral victory that will cut the Gordian knot of white male dominance. An independent black feminism that can articulate the distinctive character of the black female experience in a way that can reveal this total structure of oppression, then, is the essential element that is needed to cut through the mystifications of white male power that set the three subordinate groups against each other.

Perhaps only black feminism can give us a strong image of womanhood before patriarchy reduced it to shattered fragments. The white patriarchal God has alienated us from our bodies, each other and the earth. The black patriarchal God is prophetic on the side of the oppressed. He represents the transcendent Almighty who assures the weak that there is a power in heaven stronger than the mighty on earth. But absolutized, he promises more apocalyptic warfare in reverse. The white lady of Mariology always lands woman on her knees before her "divine Son" as the sublimated, and the sexually alienated, servant of the male ego.

One needs to glimpse again the primordial power of the mother-symbol as Ground of Being to restore an ontological foundation to the "wholly other" God of patriarchy. The Christian effort to overcome gnosticism and apocalypticism and to integrate the God of the messianic future with the divine Ground of Being failed because it continued to be based on the patriarchal denigration of the female. Only a regrounding of the power of the future within the power of the primordial matrix can refound the lost covenant of man with nature and give us a theology for the redemption of the earth.

Feminist Theology
as a Critical Theology
of Liberation

Elisabeth Schüssler Fiorenza

Elisabeth Schüssler Fiorenza argues that the Christian tradition
is recorded very largely by theologians who consciously or unconsciously have understood it "from a patriarchal perspective
of male dominance." Such a tradition of doing theology functions to justify the church's discriminatory practice toward
women. What could feminists contribute, she asks, to a new
understanding and doing of theology which, in turn, would influence basic Christian attitudes and institutional church practices? Dr. Schüssler Fiorenza proposes the rewriting of "the
Christian tradition in such a way that it becomes not only his-
story but as well her-story recorded and analyzed from a
feminist point of view." Convinced that Christian faith and theology are "capable of transcending their own ideological sexist
forms," she suggests that theologians will contribute to "the
development of a humanized theology" by insisting that the
"so-called feminine values" are in fact human and especially
Christian values, and should be used "to define the whole of
Christian existence and the practice of the Christian churches."
She concludes with a critique of the Mary and Mary Magdalene
images and myths as an example of the feminist search for a
new liberating focus and interpretation. The author has her
Th.D. from Münster, Germany, and teaches theology at the
University of Notre Dame. Her essay first appeared in the De-
cember 1975 *Theological Studies* (vol. 36. no. 4), published in
Baltimore.

Feminism and Theology

The analyses of the women's liberation movement have uncovered the sexist structures and myth of our culture and society.[1] As racism defines and oppresses black people because of their color, so sexism stereotypes and limits people because of their gender. That women are culturally oppressed people becomes evident when we apply Paulo Freire's definition of oppression to the situation of women:

> Any situation in which 'A' objectively exploits 'B' or hinders his [*sic*] pursuit of self-affirmation as a responsible person is one of oppression. Such a situation in itself constitutes violence, even when sweetened by false generosity, because it interferes with man's [*sic*] ontological and historical vocation to be more fully human.[2]

In a sexist society woman's predominant role in life is to be man's helpmate, to cook and work for him without being paid, to bear and rear his children, and to guarantee him psychological and sexual satisfaction. Woman's place is in the home, whereas man's place is in the world earning money, running the state, schools, and churches. If woman ventures into the man's world, then her task is subsidiary, as in the home; she holds the lowest-paid jobs, because she supposedly works for pocket money; she remains confined to women's professions and is kept out of high-ranking positions. G. K. Chesterton's ironical quip sums up the struggles and results of the suffrage movement: "Millions of women arose and shouted: No one will ever dictate to us again—and they became typists." In spite of a century of struggle for equality, women have not yet succeeded in getting leading positions and equal opportunity in the public and societal realm. On the contrary, they were incorporated into the economic system and moral values of our sexist culture, which merely organized women's capabilities for its own purposes.[3]

Feminist Critique of Culture and Religion

Whereas the suffrage movement did not so much attempt to change society as mainly to integrate women into it, in the conviction that women would humanize politics and work by virtue of their feminine qualities,[4] the new feminist movement radically criticizes the myth and structures of a society and culture which keep women down. The women's liberation movement demands a restructuring of societal institutions and a redefinition of cultural images and roles of women *and* men, if women are to become autonomous human persons and achieve economic and political equality.

The feminist critique of culture has pointed out that nature and biology are not the "destiny" of women, but rather sexist culture and its socialization. Women are denied the full range of human potentiality; we are socialized to view ourselves as dependent, less intelligent, and derivative from men. From earliest childhood we learn our roles as subservient beings and value ourselves through the eyes of a male culture.[5] We are the "other," socialized into helpmates of men or sex objects for their desire. Journals, advertisements, television, and movies represent us either as dependent little girls (e.g., to address "baby"), as sexy and seductive women, or as self-sacrificing wives and mothers. Teachers, psychologists, philosophers, writers, and preachers define us as derivative, inferior, and subordinate beings who lack the intelligence, courage, and genius of men.

Women in our culture are either denigrated and infantilized or idealized and put on a pedestal, but they are not allowed to be independent and free human persons. They do not live their own lives, but are taught to live vicariously through those of husband and children. They do not exercise their own power, but manipulate men's power. They usually are not supposed to express their own opinion, but to be silent or to voice only that of their fathers, husbands, bosses, or sons. Not only men but women themselves have interiorized this image and understanding of woman as inferior and derivative. Often they themselves most strongly believe and defend the "feminine mystique."[6] Since women have learned to feel inferior and to despise themselves, they do not respect, in fact they even hate, other women. Thus women evidence the typical personality traits of oppressed people who have internalized the images and notions of the oppressor.

In the face of this cultural image and self-understanding of women, feminism first maintains that women are human persons, and it therefore demands free development of full personhood for all, women and men. Secondly, feminism maintains that human rights and talents or weaknesses are not divided by sex. Feminism has pointed out that it is necessary for women to become independent economically and socially in order to be able to understand and value themselves as free, autonomous, and responsible subjects of their lives. If women's role in society is to change, then women's and men's perceptions and attitudes toward women have to change at the same time.

Feminism has therefore vigorously criticized all institutions which exploit women, stereotype them, and keep them in inferior positions. In this context, feminist analysis points out that Christianity had not only a major influence in the making of Western culture and sexist theology,[7] but also that the Christian churches and theologies still perpetuate the "feminine mystique" and women's inferiority through their institutional inequalities and theological justifications of women's innate difference from men. Christian ethics has intensified the internalization of the feminine, passive attitudes, e.g., meekness, humility, submission, self-sacrifice, self-denying love, which impede the development of self-assertion and autonomy by women. "The alleged 'voluntarism' of the imposed submission in Christian patriarchy has turned women against themselves more deeply than ever, disguising and reinforcing the internalization process."[8]

Responses to Feminist Critique

As society and culture often respond to the feminist analysis and critique with denial, co-optation, or rejection, so do the Christian churches and theologians in order to neutralize the feminist critics so that the social and ecclesial order remains unchanged.

1) They deny the accuracy and validity of the feminist analysis and critique. They point out that women are in no way inferior and oppressed but superior and privileged; e.g., Pope Paul's various statements on the superior qualities of women thus serve to support the "feminine mystique." Since women

have most thoroughly internalized the ideals and values of this mystique, this repudiation is most effectully carried out by women themselves. Middle-class and middle-aged women who have learned to suppress their own interests, abilities, and wishes in order to support their husbands' egos and careers feel that they become obsolete because of the feminist critique. They sense that the abolition of gender stereotypes and traditional roles threatens the value and security of their lives. As in the nineteenth century the Beecher sisters glorified domesticity and sang the praises of motherhood,[9] so today some women's groups behind the anti-ERA campaign idolize women's security in marriage and their protection by law. They support their claim by theological references to the divinely ordained order of creation.[10] Theological arguments justify the privileged status of middle-class women. These women do not realize that they are only one man away from public welfare and that even middle-class women's economic status and self-identity is very precarious indeed.

2) Another way of dealing with the feminist critique is to co-opt it by acknowledging some minor points of its analysis. The establishment can adopt those elements of the feminist critique which do not radically question present structures and ideologies. For instance, Paul VI maintains that the Church has already recognized "the contemporary effort to promote 'the advancement of women' " as "a sign of the times" and he demands legislation to protect women's equal rights "to participate in cultural, economic, social, and political life."[11] Yet he maintains that women have to be excluded from hierarchical orders on the grounds of an antiquated and simply false historical exegesis.[12] Similarly, "liberal" Protestant theologians and churches pay lip service to the equal rights of women; for, even though they ordain women, they erect "qualifying standards" and "academic quotas" which effectively keep women out of influential parish or seminary positions.[13] Some theologians participate in this process of co-optation after the feminist movement has become "acceptable" in intellectual circles and in the publishing industry. In writing articles and books on women in the New Testament or in the Christian tradition, in filling Church commissions on "the role of women in the

Church," they not only demonstrate they are still in charge but also enhance their professional status. Another way of co-opting the feminist critique is to turn women against women—"religious" women against "lay" women, moderate theologians against radical ones—or to endow certain women with "token status" in order to turn them against their not so "well-educated" or so "well-balanced" sisters.

3) Where co-optation of the feminist critique is not possible, outright rejection and condemnation often takes its place. The reaction is often very violent, because the feminist demand for institutional and theological change is always a demand for far-reaching personal change and giving up of centuries-old privileges. Whereas the "liberal" Christian press and "liberal" Christian theologians in general pay lip service to the goals of the women's movement, they often label it "anti-Christian," because the feminist critique holds, to a great part, Christianity responsible for the "rationalization" of women's inferior status in our culture. In other words, male theologians are accountable for the ideologization of women's image and role in Christian theology. Being male and being male theologians, they no longer can uphold their "liberal" attitude toward the feminist cause, since they are already personally involved. They declare Christian feminism as "anti-male" and "anti-Christian" in order to avoid radical conversion and radical change.

> Those of us who are men can not escape the crisis of conscience embodied in that moment [the ordination of Episcopal women] because whatever our politics on the issue, we are as men associates in the systematic violence done to women by the structures of male supremacy. . . .

> As men we must support the movement for equality by women, even as it becomes more radical. And, as men, we must examine and repent of our own parts in the sexist mindset that dehumanizes us. . . .[14]

The unwillingness for radical repentance and fundamental

change is the Achilles' heel of the liberal male theologian and churchman.

Christian feminists respond to the systematic violence done to women by ecclesial institutions and male representants basically in two different ways. They do not differ so much in their analysis and critique of the cultural and ecclesial establishment and its ideologies, but more in their politics and strategies. Those who advocate an exodus and separation from all institutional religion for the sake of the gospel and the experience of transcendence point, as justification, to the history of Christianity and their own personal histories, proving that the submission of women is absolutely essential to the Church's functioning. In the present Christian structures and theologies women can never be more than marginal beings.[15] Those Christian feminists who hope for the repentance and radical change of the Christian churches affirm their own prophetical roles and critical mission within organized Christianity. They attempt to bring to bear their feminist analysis and critique in order to set free the traditions of emancipation, equality, and genuine human personhood which they have experienced in Christian institutions and traditions, but brand them in order to change them. Aware that not only Christian institutions but also Christian theology operates in a sexist framework and language, they attempt to reconceptualize and to transform Christian theology from a feminist perspective.

Feminist Theology as a Critical Theology

Historical studies and hermeneutical discussions have amply demonstrated that theology is a culturally and historically conditioned endeavor. Moreover, historical-critical studies and hermeneutical-theological reflection have shown that not only theology but also the revelation of God in Scripture is expressed in human language and shares culturally conditioned concepts and problems. Revelation and theology are so intertwined that they no longer can be adequately distinguished. This hermeneutical insight is far-reaching when we consider that Scripture as well as theology is rooted in a patriarchal-sexist culture and shares its biases and prejudices. Scripture and theology express truth in sexist language and images and participate in the myth of their patriarchal-sexist society and culture.

The feminist critique of theology and tradition is best summarized by the statement of Simone Weil: "History, therefore, is nothing but a compilation of the depositions made by assassins with respect to their victims and themselves."[16] The hermeneutical discussion has underlined that a value-free, objectivistic historiography is a scholarly fiction. All interpretations of texts depend upon the presuppositions, intellectual concepts, politics, or prejudices of the interpreter and historian. Feminist scholars, therefore, rightly point out that for all too long the Christian tradition was recorded and studied by theologians who consciously or unconsciously understood it from a patriarchal perspective of male dominance. Since this androcentric cultural perspective has determined all writing of theology and of history, their endeavor is correctly called his-story. If women, therefore, want to get in touch with their own roots and tradition, they have to rewrite the Christian tradition and theology in such a way that it becomes not only his-story but as well her-story recorded and analyzed from a feminist point of view.

Yet a hermeneutical revision of Christian theology and tradition is only a partial solution to the problem. Radical Christian feminists, therefore, point out that the Christian past and present, and not only its records, victimized women. A hermeneutics which merely attempts to *understand* the Christian tradition and texts in their historical settings, or a Christian theology which defines itself as "the actualizing continuation of the Christian history of interpretation," does not suffice,[17] since it does not sufficiently take into account that tradition is a source not only of truth but also of untruth, repression, and domination. Critical theory as developed in the Frankfurt school[18] provides a key for a hermeneutic understanding which is not just directed toward an actualizing continuation and a perceptive understanding of history but toward a criticism of history and tradition to the extent that it participates in the repression and domination which are experienced as alienation. Analogously (in order to liberate Christian theologies, symbols, and institutions), critical theology uncovers and criticizes Christian traditions and theologies which stimulated and perpetuated violence, alienation, and oppression. Critical theology thus has as its methodological presupposition the Christian community's constant need for renewal. Christian faith and life are caught in the middle of history and are therefore in constant need of prophetic criticism in order not to lose sight of their eschatological vision. The Christian community finds itself on the way to a greater and more perfect freedom which was initiated in Jesus Christ. Christian theology as a scholarly discipline has to serve and support the Christian community on its way to such eschatological freedom and love.

Toward a Liberated and Liberating Theology

Feminist theology presupposes as well as has for its goal an emancipatory ecclesial and theological praxis. Hence feminists today no longer demand only admission and marginal integration into the traditionally male-dominated hierarchical institutions of the churches and theology; they demand a radical change of these institutions and structures. They do this not only for the sake of "equal rights" within the churches, but because they are convinced that theology and Church have to be liberated and humanized if they are to serve people and not to oppress them.

Although we find numerous critical analyses of hierarchical church structures,[19] we do not find critical evaluations of the theological profession as such. Most recently, however, liberation theologians have pointed out that theology in an American and European context is "white" theology and, as such, shares in the cultural imperialism of Europe and America.[20] Theology as a discipline is the domain of white clerics and academicians and thus excludes, because of its constituency, many different theological problems and styles within the Christian communities. Whereas in the Middle Ages theology had its home in cloisters and was thus combined with an ascetic life style, today its place is in seminaries, colleges, and universities. This *Sitz im Leben* decisively determines the style and content of theology. Since theology is mainly done in an academic context, its questions and investigations reflect that of the white, middle-class academic community. Competition, prestige, promotion, quantity of publications, and acceptance in professional societies are often primary motivations for the members of the theological guild.

Feminist theology maintains that this analysis of the life-setting of theology does not probe far enough. Christian theology is not only white-middle-class but white-middle-class-male, and shares as such in cultural sexism and patriarchalism. The "maleness" and "sexism" of theology is much more pervasive than the race and class issue. The writers of the Old Testament lived in Palestine, and Augustine in North Africa, but their theology is no less male than Barth's or Rahner's. Today established theologians often feel free to tackle the social, class, and race issue, precisely because they belong as males to the "old boys club," and they themselves are neither poor nor oppressed. They generally do not, however, discuss the challenges of feminist theology, precisely because they refuse to begin "at home" and to analyze their own praxis as men in a sexist profession and culture. Therefore the much-invoked unity between theory and praxis has to remain an ideology.

Since the New Testament beginnings and the subsequent history of Christianity were immersed in cultural and ecclesial patriarchy, women—whether white or black or brown, whether rich or poor—never could play a significant rather than marginal role in Christian theology. When women today enter the theological profession, they function mostly as "tokens" who do not disturb the male consciousness and structures, or they are often relegated to "junior colleagues" dependent on the authority of their teachers, to research assistants and secretaries, to mother figures and erotic or sex partners; but they are very rarely taken as theological authorities in their own right. If they demand to be treated as equals, they are often labeled "aggressive," "crazy," or "unscholarly."

How women feel in a sexist profession is vividly illustrated in an experiment which Professor Nelle Morton devised. In a lecture "On Preaching the Word,"[21] she asked her audience to imagine how they would feel and understand themselves and theology if the male-female roles were reversed. Imagine Harvard Divinity School, she proposed, as a school with a long female theological tradition. All the professors except one are women, most of the students are women, and all of the secretaries are men. All language in such an institution has a distinctly feminine character. "Womankind" means all humanity; "women" as generic word includes men (Jesus came to save all women). If a professor announces a course on "the doctrine of women" or speaks about the "motherhood of God," she of course does not want to exclude men. In her course on Christian anthropology, Professor Ann maintains that the Creator herself made the male organs external and exposed, so that man would demand sheltering and protection in the home, whereas she made the female reproductive organs compact and internal so that woman is biologically capable of taking her leadership position in the public domain of womankind.

> Once in a while a man gets nerve enough to protest the use of Mother God, saying that it does something to his sense of dignity and integrity. Professor Martha hastens to explain that no one really believes that God is female in a sexual sense. She makes it quite clear that in a matriarchal society the wording of Scripture, of liturgy and theology, could only come out in matriarchal imagery.[22]

This experiment in imagination can be extended to all theological schools or professional societies. Imagine that you are one of the few men at a theological convention, where the female bishop praises the scholarly accomplishments of all the women theologians without noticing that there are some men on the boards of this theological society. Or imagine that one of the

Roman Catholic seminarians tells you, who cannot be ordained because you are a man, that (after her ordination) she will be essentially different from you. If your consciousness is raised and you complain that you are not considered a full human being in your church, then a liberal colleague might answer you that you yourself should protest, since after all it is not her problem but yours. And all this is done to you in the name of Christian sisterhood!

Such an experiment in imagination can demonstrate better than any abstract analysis how damaging the masculine language and patterns of theology are to women. Therefore feminist theology correctly maintains that it is not enough to include some token women in the male-dominated theological and ecclesial structures. What is necessary is the humanization of these structures themselves. In order to move towards a "whole theology," women and men, black and white, privileged and exploited persons, as well as people from all nations and countries, have to be actively involved in the formulation of this new theology, as well as in the institutions devoted to such a "catholic" theologizing.

What, then, could feminists contribute to such a new understanding and doing of theology? Naturally, no definite answer can be given, since feminist theology is an ongoing process which has just begun.[23] I do not think that women will contribute specifically feminine modes to the process of theology.[24] However, I do think that feminist theologians can contribute to the development of a humanized theology, insofar as they can insist that the so-called feminine values,[25] e.g., concreteness, compassion, sensitivity, love, relating to others, and nurturing or community are human and especially central Christian values, which have to define the whole of Christian existence and the practice of the Christian churches. Feminist theology thus can integrate the traditionally separated so-called male-female areas, the intellectual-public, and the personal-emotional. Insofar as it understands the personal plight of women in a sexist society and church through an analysis of cultural, societal, and ecclesial stereotypes and structures, its scope is personal and political at the same time.

Against the so-called objectivity and neutrality of academic theology, feminist theology maintains that theology always serves certain interests and therefore has to reflect and critically evaluate its primary motives and allegiance. Consequently, theology has to abandon its so-called objectivity and has to become partisan. Only when theology is on the side of the outcast and oppressed, as was Jesus, can it become incarnational and Christian. Christian theology, therefore, has to be rooted in emancipatory praxis and solidarity. The means by which feminist theology grounds its theologizing in emancipatory praxis is consciousness-raising and sisterhood. Consciousness-raising makes theologians aware of their own oppression and the oppression of others. Sisterhood provides a community of emancipatory solidarity of those who are oppressed and on the way to liberation. Consciousness-raising not only makes women and men aware of their own situation in a sexist society and church, but also leads them to a new praxis insofar as it reveals to us our possibilities and resources. Expressed in traditional theological language: feminist theology is rooted in conversion and a new vision; it names the realities of sin and grace and it leads to a new mission and community.[26]

As theology rooted in community, feminist theology finds its expression in celebration and liturgy.[27] Feminist theologians maintain that theology has to become again communal and wholistic. Feminist theology expresses itself not only in abstract analysis and intellectual discussion, but it employs the whole range of human expression, e.g., ritual, symbol, drama, music, movement, or pictures. Thus feminist celebrations do not separate the sacral and the profane, the religious and the daily life. On the contrary, the stuff of feminist liturgies is women's experience and women's life. In such liturgies women express their anger, their frustrations, and their experience of oppression, but also their new vision, their hopes for the coming of a "new heaven and earth," and their possibilities for the creation of new persons and new structures.

In conclusion: Since feminist theology deals with theological, ecclesial, and cultural criticism and concerns itself with theological analysis of the myths, mechanisms, systems, and institutions which keep women down, it shares in the concerns of and expands critical theology. Insofar as it positively brings to word the new freedom of women and men, insofar as it promotes new symbols, myths and life styles, insofar as it raises new questions and opens up different horizons, feminist theology shares in the concerns and goals of liberation theology.[28] But because Christian symbols and thought are deeply embedded in patriarchal traditions and sexist structures, and because women belong to all races, classes, and cultures, its scope is more radical and universal than that of critical and liberation theology. Feminist theology derives its legitimization from the eschatological vision of freedom and salvation, and its radicalism from the realization that the Christian Church is not identical with the kingdom of God.

Tension between Christian Vision and Praxis

Christian feminism is fascinated by the vision of equality, wholeness, and freedom expressed in Gal 3:27 ff.: in Christ Jesus "there is neither Jew nor Greek, neither slave nor free, neither male nor female." This magna carta of Christian feminism was officially affirmed by Vatican II in the Constitution on the Church (no. 32): "Hence there is in Christ and in the Church no inequality on the basis of race and nationality, social condition or sex, because there is neither Jew nor Greek . . . (Gal 3:28)." Yet this vision was never completely realized by the Christian Church throughout its history. The context of the conciliar statement reflects this discriminatory praxis of the Church, insofar as it maintains the equality for all Christians only with respect to salvation, hope, and charity, but not with respect to church structures and ecclesial office. The failure of the Church to realize the vision of Gal 3:28-29 in its own institutions and praxis had as consequence a long sexist theology of the Church which attempted to justify the ecclesial praxis of inequality and to suppress the Christian vision and call of freedom and equality within the Church.

A feminist history of the first centuries could demonstrate

how difficult it was for the ecclesial establishment to suppress the call and spirit of freedom among Christian women.[29] Against a widespread theological apologetics which argues that the Church could not liberate women because of the culturally inferior position of women in antiquity, it has to be pointed out that the cultural and societal emancipation of women had gained considerable ground in the Greco-Roman world. Paul, the post-Paul tradition, and the Church Fathers, therefore, not only attempted to limit or to eliminate the consequences of the actions of Jesus and of the Spirit expressed in Gal 3:28, but also reversed the emancipatory processes of their society.[30] They achieved the elimination of women from ecclesial leadership and theology through women's domestication under male authority in the home or in the monasteries. Those women who did not comply but were active and leading in various Christian movements were eliminated from mainstream Christianity. Hand in hand with the repression and elimination of the emancipatory elements within the Church went a theological justification for such an oppression of women. The androcentric statements of the Fathers and later church theologians are not so much due to a faulty anthropology as they are an ideological justification for the inequality of women in the Christian community. Due to feminist analysis, the androcentric traits of patristic and Scholastic theology are by now well known.[31]

Less known, however, is how strong the women's movement for emancipation was in the various Christian groups. For instance, in Marcionism, Montanism, Gnosticism, Manicheism, Donatism, Priscillianism, Messalianism, and Pelagianism, women had authority and leading positions. They were found among the bishops and priests of the Quintillians (cf. Epiphanius, *Haer.* 49, 2, 3, 5) and were partners in the theological discourses of some church theologians. In the Middle Ages women had considerable powers as abbesses, and they ruled monasteries and church districts that included both men and women.[32] Women flocked to the medieval reform movements and were leaders among the Waldenses, the Anabaptists, the Brethren of the Free Spirit, and especially the Beguines. The threat of these movements to the church establishment is mirrored in a statement of an East German bishop, who "complained that these women [the Beguines] were idle, gossiping vagabonds who refused obedience to men under the pretext that God was best served in freedom."[33] Such an emancipatory her-story is surfacing in the story of the mystics of the twelfth-to-fourteenth centuries[34] or in that of the witches; in figures like Catherine of Siena, Elizabeth I of England, Teresa of Avila; in groups like the Sisters of the Visitation or the "English Ladies" of Mary Ward, in Quakerism or Christian Science.

Feminist theology as critical theology is driven by the impetus to make the vision of Gal 3:28 real within the Christian community. It is based on the conviction that Christian theology and Christian faith are capable of transcending their own ideological sexist forms. Christian feminists still hope against hope that the Church will become an all-inclusive, truly catholic community. A critical analysis of the Christian tradition and history, however, indicates that this hope can only be realized if women are granted not only spiritual but also ecclesial equality. Twelve years ago, in my book on the ministries of women in the Church, I maintained that women have to demand ordination as bishops,[35] and only after they have attained it can they afford to be ordained deacons and priests. Today I would add that the very character of the hierarchical-patriarchal church structure has to be changed if women are to attain their place and full authority within the Church and theology. The Christian churches will only overcome their patriarchal and oppressive past traditions and present theologies if the very base and functions of these traditions and theologies are changed.[36] If there is no longer a need to suppress the Spirit who moves Christian women to fully participate in theology and the Church, then Christian theology and community can become fully liberated and liberating. Church Fathers and theologians who do not respect this Spirit of liberty and freedom deny the Christian community its full catholicity and wholeness. Feminist theologians and Christian feminists will obey this call of the Spirit, be it within or outside established church structures. They do it because of their vision of a Christian and human community where all oppression and sin is overcome by the grace and love of God.

Christian feminists are well aware that this vision cannot be embodied in the "old wineskins" but has to be realized in new theological and ecclesial structures. If change should occur, a circular move is necessary.[37] Efforts concentrated on bringing women's experience and presence into the Church and theology, into theological language and imagery, will not succeed unless the ecclesial and theological institutions are changed to support and reinforce the new feminist theological understanding and imagery. On the other hand, efforts to change the ecclesial and theological institutions cannot be far-reaching enough if theological language, imagery, and myth serve to maintain women's status as a derivative being in church and theology. Structural change and the evolution of a feminist theology, and nonsexist language, imagery, and myth, have to go hand in hand.

Toward New Symbols, Images, and Myths

Whereas theology appeals to our rational faculties and intellectual understanding, images and myths provide a world view and give meaning to our lives. They do not uphold abstract ideals and doctrines but rather provide a vision of the basic structure of reality and present a model or prototype to be imitated. They encourage particular forms of behavior and implicitly embody goals and value judgments. Insofar as a myth is a story which provides a common vision, feminists have to find new myths and stories in order to embody their goals and value judgments. In this search for new feminist myths integrating the personal and political, the societal and religious, women are rediscovering the myth of the mother goddess,[38] which was partially absorbed by the Christian myth of Mary, the mother of God.

Yet feminist theologians are aware that myths have also a stabilizing, retarding function insofar as they sanction the existing social order and justify its power structure by providing communal identity and a rationale for societal and ecclesial institutions. Therefore, exactly because feminist theologians value myths and images, they have first to analyze and to "demythologize" the myths of the sexist society and patriarchal religion in order to liberate them.

Feminist Critique of the Mary-Myth

Since the "myth of Mary" is still today a living myth and functions as such in the personal and communal life of many Christian women and men,[39] it is possible to critically analyze its psychological and ecclesial functions. From the outset it can be questioned whether the myth can give to women a new vision of equality and wholeness, since the myth almost never functioned as symbol or justification of women's equality and leadership in church and society, even though the myth contains elements which could have done so. As the "queen of heaven" and the "mother of God," Mary clearly resembles and integrates aspects of the ancient goddess mythologies, e.g., of Isis or the Magna Mater.[40] Therefore the myth has the tendency to portray Mary as divine and to place her on an equal level with God and Christ. For instance, Epiphanius, Bishop of Salamis, demonstrates this tendency in the sect of the Collyridians, which consisted mostly of women and flourished in Thracia and upper Scythia: "Certain women adorn a chair or a square throne, spread a linen cloth over it, and on a certain day of the year place bread on it and offer it in the name of Mary, and all partake of this bread."[41] Epiphanius refutes this practice on the ground that no women can exercise priestly functions and makes a very clear distinction between the worship of God and Christ and the veneration of Mary. Through the centuries church teachers maintained this distinction, but popular piety did not quite understand it. The countless legends and devotions to Mary prove that people preferred to go to her instead of going to a majestic-authoritarian God.

Yet, although this powerful aspect of the Mary-myth affected the souls and lives of the people, it never had any influence upon the structures and power relationships in the Church. That the Mary-myth could be used to support the leadership function of women in the Church is shown by the example of Bridget of Sweden,[42] who was the foundress of the Order of the Most Holy Savior, a monastery which consisted of nuns and monks. She justifies the leadership and ruling power of the abbess over women and men with reference to Acts 2, where Mary is portrayed in the midst of the apostles. This instance of a woman shaping the Mary-myth for the sake of the leadership and authority of women is, however, the exception in the history of Mariology.

On the whole, the Mary-myth has its roots and development in a male, clerical, and ascetic culture and theology. It has very little to do with the historical woman Mary of Nazareth. Even though the New Testament writings say very little about Mary and even appear to be critical of her praise as the natural mother of Jesus (Mk 3:31-35),[43] the story of Mary was developed and mythologized very early in the Christian tradition. Even though some aspects of this myth, e.g., the doctrine of her immaculate conception or her bodily assumption into heaven, were only slowly accepted by parts of the Christian Church, we find one tenor in the image of Mary throughout the centuries: Mary is the *virginal* mother. She is seen as the humble "handmaiden" of God who, because of her submissive obedience and her unquestioning acceptance of the will of God, became the "mother of God."[44] In contrast to Eve, she was, and remained, the "pure virgin" who was conceived free from original sin and remained all her life free from sin. She remained virgin before, during, and after the birth of Jesus. This myth of Mary sanctions a double dichotomy in the self-understanding of Catholic women.

First, the myth of the virginal mother justifies the body-soul dualism of the Christian tradition. Whereas man in this tradition is defined by his mind and reason, woman is defined by her "nature," i.e., by her physical capacity to bear children. Motherhood, therefore, is the vocation of every woman regardless of whether or not she is a natural mother.[45] However, since in the ascetic Christian tradition nature and body have to be subordinated to the mind and the spirit, woman because of her nature has to be subordinated to man.[46] This subordination is, in addition, sanctioned with reference to Scripture. The body-spirit dualism of the Christian tradition is thus projected on women and men and contributes to the man-woman dualism of polarity which in modern times was supported not only by theology but also by philosophy and psychology.[47] Moreover, the official stance of the Roman Catholic Church on birth control and abortion demonstrates that woman in distinction from man has to remain dependent on her nature and is not allowed to be in control of her biological processes.[48] According to the present church "fathers," as long as woman enjoys the sexual pleasures of Eve, she has to bear the consequences. Finally, all the psychological qualities which are associated with mothering, e.g., love, nurture, intuition, compassion, patience, sensitivity, emotionality, etc., are now regarded as "feminine" qualities and, as such, privatized. This stereotyping of these *human* qualities led not only to their elimination from public life but also to a privatization of Christian values,[49] which are, according to the New Testament, concentrated and climaxed in the command to love.

Second, the myth of the virginal mother functions to separate the women within the Roman Catholic community from one another. Since historically woman cannot be both virgin and mother, she has either to fulfil her nature in motherhood or to transcend her nature in virginity. Consequently, Roman Catholic traditional theology has a place for women only as mother or nun. The Mary-myth thus sanctions a deep psychological and institutional split between Catholic women. Since the genuine Christian and human vocation is to transcend one's nature and biology, the true Christian ideal is represented by the actual biological virgin who lives in concrete ecclesial obedience. Only among those who represent the humble handmaiden and ever-virgin Mary is true Christian sisterhood possible. Distinct from women who are still bound to earthly desires and earthly dependencies, the biological virgins in the Church, bound to ecclesial authority, are the true "religious women." As the reform discussions and conflicts of women congregations with Rome indicate, dependency on ecclesial authority is as important as biological virginity.

The most pressing issue within the Catholic Church is, therefore, to create a "new sisterhood" which is not based on sexual stratification. Such a new sisterhood is the *sine qua non* of the movement for ordination within the Roman Catholic community.[50] Otherwise the ordination of some women, who are biological virgins and evidence a great dependency on church authority, not only will lead to a further clericalization and hierarchization of the Church, but also to an unbridgeable metaphysical split between woman and woman.[51]

Traditional Mariology thus demonstrates that the myth of a woman preached to women by men can serve to deter women from becoming fully independent and whole human persons. This observation has consequences for our present attempts to emphasize feminine imagery and myth in feminist theology. As long as we do not know the relationship between the myth and its societal functions, we cannot expect, for example, that the myth of the mother goddess in itself will be liberating for women. The myth of the "Mother God"[52] could define, as the myth of the "mother of God" did, woman primarily in her capacity for motherhood and thus reduce woman's possibilities to her biological capacity for motherhood. We have to remain aware that the new evolving myths and images of feminist theology necessarily share the cultural presuppositions and stereotypes of our sexist society and tradition, into which women as much as men are socialized. The absolute precondition of new liberating Christian myths and images is not only the change of individual consciousness but that of societal, ecclesial, and theological structures as well.

Yet, at the same time, feminist theologians have to search for new images[53] and myths which could incarnate the new vision of Christian women and function as prototypes to be imitated. Such a search ought not to single out and absolutize one image and myth but rather put forward a variety of images and stories,[54] which should be critical and liberating at the same time. If I propose in the following to contemplate the image of Mary Magdalene, I do not want to exclude that of Mary of Nazareth, but I intend to open up new traditions and images for Christian women. At the same time, the following meditation on Mary Magdalene might elucidate the task of feminist theology as a critical theology of liberation.

Image of Mary Magdalene, Apostle to the Apostles

Mary of Magdala was indeed a liberated women. Her encounter with Jesus freed her from a sevenfold bondage to destructive powers (Lk 8:3). It transformed her life radically. She followed Jesus.

According to all four Gospels, Mary Magdalene is the primary witness for the fundamental data of the early Christian faith: she witnessed the life and death of Jesus, his burial and his resurrection. She was sent to the disciples to proclaim the Easter kerygma. Therefore Bernard of Clairvaux correctly calls her "apostle to the apostles."[55] Christian faith is based upon the witness and proclamation of women. As Mary Magdalene was sent to the disciples to proclaim the basic events of Christian faith, so women today may rediscover by contemplating her image the important function and role which they have for the Christian faith and community.

Yet, when we think of Mary Magdalene, we do not think of her first as a Christian apostle and evangelist; rather we have before our eyes the image of Mary as the sinner and the penitent woman. Modern novelists and theological interpreters picture her as having abandoned sexual pleasure and whoring for the pure and romantic love of Jesus the man. This distortion of her image signals deep distortion in the self-understanding of Christian women. If as women we should not have to reject the Christian faith and tradition, we have to reclaim women's contribution and role in it. We must free the image of Mary Magdalene from all distortions and recover her role as apostle.

In her book *A Different Heaven and Earth,* Sheila Collins likens this exorcising of traditions to the process of psychoanalysis. "Just as the neurotic who has internalized the oppressive parent within himself (herself) must go back to the origin of the trouble in his (her) childhood, so the oppressed group, if it is to move from a condition of oppression to one of liberation, or from self-contempt to self-actualization, must go back to its origins in order to free itself from its psychic chain."[56] Just as black people[57] search history for models of identification that indicate the contributions of blacks to culture and history, just as they strive to eliminate racist interpretations of history and culture, so too women and men in the Church must attempt to rewrite Christian history and theology in order to recover aspects that have been neglected or distorted by patriarchal historians and theologians.

A close examination of the Gospel traditions discloses already in the beginning of the tradition a tendency to play down the role of Mary Magdalene and the other women as witnesses and proclaimers of the Easter faith. This tendency is apparent in the Markan tradition, which stresses that the women "said nothing to anyone, for they were afraid" (16:8). It is also evident in the comment of Luke that the words of the women seemed to the Eleven and those with them "an idle tale and they did not believe them" but instead checked them out (24:11). It is, moreover, reflected in the Lukan confessional statement "The Lord has risen indeed and appeared to Simon" (24:34). This Lukan confession corresponds to the pre-Pauline credal tradition quoted in 1 Cor 15:3 ff., which mentions Cephas and the Eleven as the principal Resurrection witnesses, but does not refer to any of the women. This tendency to play down the witness of Mary Magdalene is also apparent in the redaction of the fourth Gospel that takes pains to ensure that the Beloved Disciple, but not Mary Magdalene, is the first believer in the Resurrection (20:1-18).

The apocryphal traditions acknowledge the spiritual authority of Mary Magdalene, but can express her superiority only in analogy to men. They have Jesus saying: "I will make her male that she too may become a living spirit resembling you males. For every women who makes herself male will enter the kingdom of heaven.''[58]

The liturgy and the legend of the Western Church have identified Mary Magdalene with both the sinner in the house of Simon and the woman who anointed Jesus' feet before his death. Modern piety stresses the intimacy and love of the woman Mary for the man Jesus.

In looking at these various interpretations of Mary Magdalene, we find our own situation in the Church mirrored in her distorted image. Women still do not speak up "because they are afraid''; women still are not accepted in theology and the Church in positions of authority but only in junior ranks and special ministries because they are women. The measure of humanity and Christianity is still man even when we stress that the term is generic, for only those women can "make it'' who play the male game. Love and service is still mainly the task of women.

Looking at this distorted image of Mary Magdalene and of ourselves, we are discouraged and in danger of trying to avoid suffering. Thus we tend to fall back into the bondage of the "seven evil spirits'' of our culture. Let us therefore recall the statement of Bernard: Mary and the other women were chosen to be the "apostles to the apostles.'' The first witness of women to the Resurrection—to the new life—is, according to all exegetical criteria of authenticity, a historical fact, for it could not have been derived from Judaism nor invented by the primitive Church. Christian faith and community has its foundation in the message of the "new life'' proclaimed first by women.

NOTES

1. The literature on the women's liberation movement is so extensive that it is impossible here to mention all works from which I have learned. Especially helpful were V. Gornick & B. K. Moran, *Woman in Sexist Society: Studies in Power and Powerlessness* (New York, 1971); J. Hole and E. Levine, *Rebirth of Feminism* (New York, 1971); E. Janeway, *Man's World, Woman's Place: Studies in Social Mythology* (New York, 1971); *Kursbuch 17: Frau, Familie,*

Gesellschaft (Frankfurt, 1969); A. Vesel Mander & A. Kent Rush, *Feminism as Therapy* (New York, 1974); B. Roszak and T. Roszak, *Masculine/Feminine: Readings in Sexual Mythology and the Liberation of Women* (New York, 1969); S. Rowbotham, *Woman's Consciousness, Man's World* (London, 1973).

2. P. Freire, *Pedagogy of the Oppressed* (New York, 1970) pp. 40 f.

3. Cf. the various analyses in *Liberation Now! Writings from the Women's Liberation Movement* (New York, 1971); C. Bird, *Born Female: The High Cost of Keeping Women Down* (New York, 1968); J. Huber, *Changing Woman in a Changing Society* (Chicago, 1974).

4. B. Wildung Harrison, "Sexism in the Contemporary Church: When Evasion Becomes Complicity," in A. L. Hageman, ed., *Sexist Religion and Women in the Church* (New York, 1974) pp. 195-216, makes the very helpful distinction between "radical" or "hard" feminism and "soft" feminism. See also her article "The Early Feminists and the Clergy: A Case Study in the Dynamics of Secularization," *Review and Expositor* 72 (1975) 41-52. For the documentation and analysis of the first women's movement, cf. E. Flexner, *Century of Struggle: The Woman's Rights Movement in the United States* (Cambridge, 1966); A. S. Kraditor, ed., *Up from the Pedestal: Selected Writings in the History of American Feminism* (Chicago, 1968).

5. This is elucidated from a linguistic point of view by R. Lakoff, *Language and Woman's Place* (New York, 1975).

6. Cf. the now classic analysis of B. Friedan, *The Feminine Mystique* (Baltimore, 1965).

7. S. de Beauvoir's analysis is still paradigmatic: *The Second Sex* (New York, 1961); see also the discussion of her position by M. Daly, *The Church and the Second Sex* (London, 1968) pp. 11-31.

8. M. Daly, *Beyond God the Father: Toward a Philosophy of Women's Liberation* (Boston, 1973) pp. 140 and 98-106. Cf. also D. G. Kennedy Neville, "Religious Socialization of Women within U.S. Subcultures," in Hageman, *Sexist Religion,* pp. 77-91; N. van Vuuren, *The Subversion of Women as Practiced by Churches, Witch-Hunters and Other Sexists* (Philadelphia, 1973), deals with the "traits due to victimization" from a historical perspective.

9. See G. Kimball, "A Counter Ideology," in J. Plaskow and J. Arnold Romero, *Women and Religion* (Missoula, 1974) pp. 177-87; D. Bass Fraser, "The Feminine Mystique: 1890-1910," *Union Seminary Quarterly Review* 27 (1972) 225-39.

10. M. H. Micks, "Exodus or Eden? A Battle of Images," *Anglican Theological Review* 55 (1973) 126-39.

11. Cf. E. Carroll, "Testimony at the Bicentennial Hearings of the Catholic Church, Feb. 4, 1975, on Woman."

12. See *National Catholic Reporter,* May 2, 1975, p. 17. [In Oc-

tober 1976 the Vatican Congregation for the Doctrine of the Faith issued a declaration on the ''Admission of Women to the Ministerial Priesthood.'' A point-by-point commentary by several authors to this official statement is *Women Priests: A Catholic Commentary on the Vatican Declaration,* eds. Leonard and Arlene Swidler (Paulist Press, 1977), wherein Dr. Fiorenza has two essays—Editors.]

13. Anonymous, ''How to Quench the Spirit without Really Trying: An Essay in Institutional Sexism,'' *Church and Society,* Sept.-Oct. 1972, pp. 25-37; N. Ramsay Jones, ''Women in the Ministry,'' in S. Bentley Doely, *Women's Liberation and the Church: The New Demand for Freedom in the Life of the Christian Church* (New York, 1970) pp. 60-69.

14. J. Carroll, ''The Philadelphia Ordination,'' *National Catholic Reporter,* Aug. 16, 1974, p. 14.

15. See M. Daly's ''autobiographical preface'' and her ''feminist postchristian introduction'' to the paperback edition of *The Church and the Second Sex* (New York, 1975). Cf. also S. Gearhart, ''The Lesbian and God-the-Father,'' *Radical Religion* 1 (1974) 19-25.

16. S. Weil, *The Need for Roots* (New York, 1971) p. 225.

17. Against E. Schillebeeckx, *The Understanding of Faith* (New York, 1974).

18. J. Habermas, ''Der Universalitätsanspruch der Hermeneutik 1970,'' in *Kultur and Kritik* (Frankfurt, 1973) pp. 264-301; *id.,* ''Stichworte zu einer Theorie der Sozialisation 1968,'' *ibid.,* pp. 118-94. For a discussion of Habermas and the critical theory, see the Spring-Summer 1970 issue of *Continuum,* which was prepared by Francis P. Fiorenza. Cf. also A. Wellmer, *Critical Theory of Society* (New York, 1974) esp. pp. 41-51.

19. See, e.g., E. C. Hewitt and S. R. Hiatt, *Women Priests: Yes or No?* (New York, 1973); C. H. Donnelly, ''Women-Priests: Does Philadelphia Have a Message for Rome?,'' *Commonweal* 102 (1975) 206-10. C. M. Henning, ''Canon Law and the Battle of Sexes,'' in R. Radford Ruether, *Religion and Sexism: Images of Woman in the Jesus and Christian Traditions* (New York, 1974) 267-91; L. M. Russell, ''Women and Ministry,'' in Hageman, *Sexist Religion,* pp. 47-62; cf. the various contributions on ministry in C. Benedicks Fischer, B. Brenneman, and A. McGrew Bennett, *Women in a Strange Land* (Philadelphia, 1975), and the NAWR publication *Women in Ministry* (Chicago, 1972). I find most helpful the collection of articles by R. J. Heyer, *Women and Orders* (New York, 1974).

20. See F. Herzog, ''Liberation Theology Begins at Home,'' *Christianity and Crisis,* May 13, 1974, and ''Liberation Hermeneutics as Ideology Critique?'' *Interpretation* 28 (1974) 387-403.

21. N. Morton, ''Preaching the Word,'' in Hageman, *Sexist Religion,* pp. 29-46, and ''The Rising Women Consciousness in a Male Language Structure,'' in *Women and the Word: Toward a Whole Theology* (Berkeley, 1972) pp. 43-52.

22. Morton, "Preaching the Word," p. 30.

23. See P. A. Way, "An Authority of Possibility for Women in the Church," in Doely, *Women's Liberation*, pp. 77-94; also M. A. Doherty and M. Earley, "Women Theologize: Notes from a June 7-18, 1971 Conference," in *Women in Ministry*, pp. 135-59. For a comprehensive statement of what Christian feminist theology is all about, see the working paper of N. Morton, "Toward a Whole Theology," which she gave at the Consultation of the World Council of Churches on "Sexism," May 15-22, 1974, in Berlin.

24. Here I clearly distance myself from those Christian feminists and authors leaning in the direction of Jungian psychology. The "equal or better but different" slogan is too easily misused to keep women in their traditional place. Nevertheless I appreciate the attempt to arrive at a distinct self-identity and contribution of women based on female experience. For such an attempt, cf. S. D. Collins, *A Different Heaven and Earth* (Valley Forge, 1974).

25. For philosophical analyses of how these "feminine" values contribute to women's oppression, see J. Farr Tormey, "Exploitation, Oppression and Self-Sacrifice," *Philosophical Forum* 5 (1975) 206-21, and L. Blum, M. Homiak, J. Housman, and N. Scheman, "Altruism and Women's Oppression," *ibid.*, pp. 222-47.

26. See *Women Exploring Theology at Grailville*, a packet prepared by Church Women United, 1972, and S. Bentley and C. Randall, "The Spirit Moving: A New Approach to Theologizing," *Christianity and Crisis*, Feb. 4, 1974, pp. 3-7.

27. Cf. the excellent collection of feminist liturgies by A. Swidler, *Sistercelebrations: Nine Worship Experiences* (Philadelphia, 1974), and S. Neufer Emswiler and T. Neufer Emswiler, *Women & Worship: A Guide to Non-Sexist Hymns, Prayers and Liturgies* (New York, 1974).

28. L. M. Russell, *Human Liberation in a Feminist Perspective: A Theology* (Philadelphia, 1974); J. O'Connor, "Liberation Theologies and the Women's Movement: Points of Comparison and Contrast," *Horizons* 2 (1975) 103-13.

29. Cf. my article "The Role of Women in the Early Christian Movement," *Concilium* 7 (January 1976).

30. See the excellent article by K. Thraede, "Frau," in *Reallexikon für Antike und Christentum* 8 (Stuttgart, 1973) 197-269, with extensive bibliographical references. Cf. also C. Schneider, *Kulturgeschichte des Hellenismus* 1 (Munich, 1967) 87-117, and W. A. Meeks, "The Image of the Androgyne: Some Uses of a Symbol in Earliest Christianity," *History of Religion* 13 (1974) 167-80, who also point out that the emancipation of women in Hellenism provoked in some groups misogynist reactions.

31. Representative is the work of R. Radford Ruether; see especially her article "Misogynism and Virginal Feminism in the Fathers of the Church," in *Religion and Sexism*, pp. 150-83.

32. See my book *Der vergessene Partner: Grundlagen, Tatsachen*

und Möglichkeiten der beruflichen Mitarbeit der Frau in der Heilssorge der Kirche (Düsseldorf, 1964) pp. 87-91, and J. Morris, *The Lady Was a Bishop: The Hidden History of Women within Clerical Ordination and the Jurisdiction of Bishops* (New York, 1973).

33. N. Cohn, *The Pursuit of the Millennium* (Essential Books, 1957) p. 167.

34. E. L. McLaughlin, "The Christian Past: Does It Hold a Future for Women?" *Anglican Theological Review* 57 (1975) 36-56.

35. Schüssler, *Partner*, pp. 93-97.

36. This is not sufficiently perceived or adequately stressed by G. H. Tavard, *Women in Christian Tradition* (Notre Dame, 1973). See also his statement in his article "Women in the Church: A Theological Problem?" in G. Baum, ed., *Ecumenical Theology No. 2* (New York, 1967) p. 39: "Once a Christian woman knows—not only in her intellect, but in her heart and in her life—that in her mankind is fulfilled, it makes no more difference to her that, in the present circumstances, she cannot be ordained. . . ."

37. This is also pointed out by S. B. Ortner, "Is Female to Male as Nature Is to Culture?" in M. Zimbalist Rosaldo and L. Lamphere, *Woman, Culture and Society* (Stanford, 1974) pp. 67-87.

38. See, e.g., B. Bruteau, "The Image of the Virgin Mother," in Plaskow and Romero, *Women and Religion*, pp. 93-104; Collins, *A Different Heaven*, pp. 97-136.

39. A. M. Greeley, "Hail Mary," *New York Times Magazine*, Dec. 15, 1974, pp. 14, 98-100, 104, 108.

40. For a wealth of historical material, cf. H. Graef, *Mary: A History of Doctrine and Devotion* (2 vols.; London, 1963), and C. Miegge, *The Virgin Mary* (Philadelphia, 1955).

41. Epiphanius, *Panarion* 79. Cf. F. J. Dölger, "Die eigenartige Marienverehrung," *Antike und Christentum* 1 (1929) 107-42.

42. Schüssler, *Partner*, p. 91.

43. The interpretation which points out that the fourth Gospel conceives of Mary as the prototype of a disciple overlooks the fact that the scene under the cross defines her as "mother" in relationship to the "Beloved Disciple."

44. This image of Mary led in Roman Catholic thought to the ideologization of womanhood and to the myth of the "eternal woman." Cf. G. von le Fort, *The Eternal Woman* (Milwaukee, 1954), and my critique in *Partner*, pp. 79-83; see also Teilhard de Chardin, "L'Eternel féminin," in *Ecrits du temps de la guerre (1916-1919)* (Paris, 1965) pp. 253-62; H. de Lubac, *L'Eternel féminin: Etude sur un texte du Père Teilhard de Chardin* (Paris, 1968).

45. G. H. Tavard, *Woman*, p. 136: "Pope Paul clearly asserts one basic notion about woman: all her tasks, all her achievements, all her virtues, all her dreams are derived from her call to motherhood. Everything that woman can do is affected by this fundamental orientation of her being and can best be expressed in terms of, and in relation to, motherhood."

46. V. L. Bullough, *The Subordinate Sex: A History of Attitudes toward Women* (Baltimore, 1974) pp. 97-120.

47. Numerous analyses of the treatment of women in psychoanalysis and psychotherapy exist; cf., e.g., P. Chesler, *Women and Madness* (New York, 1972).

48. Cf. the analyses of phallic morality by M. Daly, *Beyond God*, pp. 106-31; J. Raymond, "Beyond Male Morality," in Plaskow and Romero, *Women and Religion*, pp. 115-25; J. MacRae, "A Feminist View of Abortion," *ibid.*, pp. 139-49.

49. E. Hambrick-Stove, "Liberation: The Gifts and the Fruits of the Spirit," in *Women Exploring Theology at Grailville*.

50. The issue is correctly perceived by G. Moran, "The Future of Brotherhood in the Catholic Church," *National Catholic Reporter*, July 5, 1974, p. 7, and G. B. Kelly, "Brothers Won't Be Priests Because Priests Won't Be Brothers," *ibid.*, July 18, 1975, p. 9 and 14.

51. For an exegetical and theological discussion of the notion of priesthood in early Christianity, see my book *Priester für Gott* (Münster, 1972) pp. 4-60.

52. This does not mean that we ought not to revise our sexist terminology and imagery in our language about God. It is absolutely necessary, in my opinion, that in a time of transition our vision and understanding of God be expressed in female categories and images, However, I do think we have to be careful not to *equate* God with female imagery, in order that Christian women remain free to transcend the "feminine" images and roles or our culture and church and be able to move to full personhood.

53. On the relationship of the image to the self, cf. E. Janeway, "Images of Women," *Women and the Arts: Arts in Society* 2 (1974) 9-18.

54. A creative and brilliant retelling of the biblical aitiological story of the origin of sin is given by J. Plaskow Goldenberg, "The Coming of Lilith," in Ruether, *Religion and Sexism*, pp. 341-43.

55. *Sermones in Cantica*, Serm. 75, 8 (*PL* 183, 1148).

56. *Op. cit.* p. 93.

57. For the justification of such a comparison, cf. H. Mayer Hacker, "Women as a Minority Group," in Roszak, *Masculine/Feminine*, pp. 130-48, especially the comparative chart on p. 140 f.

58. *The Gospel of Thomas*, Logion 114. See also the apocryphal writings *Pistis Sophia, The Gospel of Mary* [Magdalene], and *The Great Questions of Mary* [Magdalene] in Hennecke-Schneemelcher, *New Testament Apocrypha* 1 (Philadelphia, 1963) 256 ff., 339, and 342 f.

The Woman's Creed

Rachel Conrad Wahlberg

"The Woman's Creed" is an effort by Rachel Conrad Wahlberg to enlarge conventional theological categories and to expand the Christian tradition. It is, comments Constance F. Parvey, "a protest against a language about God that is too small, too limited, too restrictive, not expansive enough for the spirituality and life experience of women." The creed envisions "a God that sees woman not only as a complement to man, but as a full and equal person in the care and stewardship of the earth." Rachel Conrad Wahlberg has four grown children and teaches management courses at the University of Texas at Austin. A member of the Lutheran Church in America, she is the daughter of two ministers, she notes, "one ordained, one not ordained." Her mother, she recalls, "was the faith-center of the home and a strong leader in the congregation." Wahlberg's husband and three brothers are also Lutheran ministers. As a college student in the 1940s, she too felt called to the ministry, but "in those days," she explains, "ordination of women was unheard of among Lutherans, so I have had to work out my calling through other channels." "The Woman's Creed" is taken from her book *Jesus and the Freed Woman* (Paulist Press, 1978), which is a sequel to her *Jesus According to a Woman* (Paulist Press, 1975).

(Upon pondering The Apostles' Creed and wondering what it would have been like had women written it)

I believe in God
who created woman and man in God's own image
who created the world
and gave both sexes
the care of the earth.

I believe in Jesus
child of God
chosen of God
born of the woman Mary
who listened to women and like them
who stayed in their homes
who discussed the Kingdom with them
who was followed and financed
by women disciples.

I believe in Jesus
who discussed theology with a woman at a well
and first confided in her
his messiahship
who motivated her to go and tell
her great news to the city.

I believe in Jesus who received anointing
from a woman at Simon's house
who rebuked the men guests who scorned her
I believe in Jesus
who said this woman will be remembered
for what she did—
minister to Jesus.

I believe in Jesus
who acted boldly
to reject the blood taboo
of ancient societies
by healing the audacious woman
who touched him.

I believe in Jesus who healed a woman
on the sabbath
and made her straight
because she was
a human being.

I believe in Jesus
who spoke of God
as a woman seeking the lost coin
as a woman who swept
seeking the lost.

I believe in Jesus
who thought of pregnancy and birth
with reverence
not as punishment—but
as wrenching event
a metaphor for transformation
born again
anguish-into-joy.

I believe in Jesus
who spoke of himself
as a mother hen
who would gather her chicks
under her wings.

I believe in Jesus who appeared
first to Mary Magdalene
who sent her with the bursting message
GO AND TELL . . .

I believe in the wholeness
of the Savior
in whom there is neither
Jew nor Greek
slave nor free
male nor female
for we are all one
in salvation.

I believe in the Holy Spirit
as she moves over the waters

of creation
and over the earth.

I believe in the Holy Spirit
as she yearns within us
to pray for those things
too deep for words.

I believe in the Holy Spirit
the woman spirit of God*
who like a hen
created us
and gave us birth
and covers us
with her wings.

*The Hebrew word for Spirit is feminine.

Women and the Bible:
A Challenge
to Male Interpretations

Virginia Mollenkott

Taking issue with those who cite the Bible as supporting male supremacy and the subordination of women in marriage and in the church, Virginia Mollenkott argues that "one cannot absolutize the culture in which the Bible was written." Biblical culture included slavery and absolute monarchy which the church has de-absolutized, and Mollenkott contends that biblical notions of male supremacy and the subordination of women were also part of biblical culture that must be de-absolutized. She and other biblical feminists "ask that modern Christianity concern itself with fulfilling the visions of a society regenerated by the power of the gospel, instead of clinging to the sinful social order into which the gospel was first introduced." They believe that "by his own practice Jesus showed us that sacred scripture concerning man's behavior toward woman does not always reflect God's highest intentions for the human race." Taking a holistic view of the Bible, Mollenkott maintains that "we are in error to absolutize anything that denies the thrust of the entire Bible toward individual wholeness and harmonious community, toward oneness in Christ." Dr. Mollenkott, author of *Women, Men, and the Bible* (Abingdon Press, 1977), teaches English at William Paterson College in Wayne, New Jersey. Her article was first presented as an address at the Evangelical Women's conference on biblical feminism in November 1975 at Washington, D.C., and is reprinted from the February 1976 issue of *Sojourners* (Washington, D.C.).

We biblical feminists believe that when properly understood, the Bible supports the central tenets of feminism.

Traditionalists cite New Testament instructions about the submission of first-century wives and church women as proof that it is forever the will of God for women to remain in a subordinate role in marriage and in the church. It is understandable that the Bible should seem to traditionalists and even to many secular feminists to support male supremacy, since most of the Old Testament authors assume that patriarchy is the will of God for the social order, while in the New Testament the same assumption prevails, with several notable exceptions: Christ's personal behavior, the ministry of certain women in the early church, and several prophetic flashes which envision the regenerative effects of the gospel on human society.

Because patriarchy is the cultural background of the Scriptures, it is absolutely basic to any feminist reading of the Bible that *one cannot absolutize the culture in which the Bible was written*. We must make careful distinctions between what is "for an age" and what is "for all time." We cannot assume that because the Bible was written against the backdrop of a patriarchal social structure, patriarchy is the will of God for all people in all times.

To clarify by means of a different example, most biblical authors assumed that kings ruled by divine right and that absolute monarchy was the divinely ordained form of government. Yet although traditionalists insist that New Testament instructions to first-century wives and church women are normative for all times and all places, they do not insist on a return to absolute monarchy. In other words, where political government is concerned, both feminists and traditionalists join in de-absolutizing the culture of biblical times. We all agree that one can be a Christian without believing in absolute monarchy. What we feminists are asking is that in the area of sexual politics as well as in the area of national politics, we de-absolutize the biblical culture.

Similarly, both Old and New Testament authors assume that it is the will of God for some people to be the slaves of other people. There was a time when traditionalists argued for that very reason black people could justly be enslaved by whites.

But largely through the efforts of eighteenth and nineteenth century evangelicals who believed that the gospel was intended to lead to an egalitarian society in which the injustices of racism would be abolished, the pro-slavery view is no longer upheld by traditionalists.

On the subject of slavery, as on the subject of monarchy, we have de-absolutized the biblical culture. We all agree that one can be a biblical Christian without believing in slavery; in fact, most of us, even traditionalists, would go farther and say that enslaving other people is a practice *antithetical* to genuine Christianity. Here again, what biblical feminists are asking is that in the area of male-female relationship we be *consistent* about de-absolutizing the biblical culture. We ask that modern Christianity concern itself with fulfilling the visions of a society regenerated by the power of the gospel, instead of clinging to the sinful social order into which the gospel was first introduced.

The apostle Paul knew that the sinful order could not be changed overnight, but he sometimes glimpsed the truth that eventually the principles of the gospel would bring about a more egalitarian society. That seems to be the point of his message to slaves and their masters in Ephesians when he states that there is no discriminatory respect of persons with God—that all people are equal in his sight. The implication is that those who want to reflect the nature of God here on earth should also desist from being "respecters of persons" and should treat one another more nearly as equals. But since Paul could not abolish slavery single-handedly and overnight, he wrote instructions to both masters and slaves which would at least alleviate the conditions of slavery until the gospel had done its full work.

Paul also wrote instructions to first-century wives and husbands which closely parallel the instructions to masters and slaves: "Wives, submit yourselves unto your own husbands, as unto the Lord. . . . Husbands, love your wives, even as Christ also loved the church and gave himself for it" (Ephesians 5:22 and 25). Just as slave masters were reminded that they had a Master in Heaven, first-century heads of families were also reminded that they had a Head in Heaven (1 Corinthians 11:3), and that they were to manifest Christlike self-sacrifice toward their wives. It would seem that in the case of first-century female subordination, as in the case of first-century slavery, people were being told how best to live in an established social order which could not be changed overnight.

Since the Bible is a divine book which reached us through human channels, it is also true that some of the apostle Paul's arguments reflect his personal struggle and show vestiges of the rabbinical training he had received from Gamaliel, training which strongly favored female subordination. Such vestiges seem to be implied in 1 Corinthians 14:34, where women "are commanded to be under obedience, as also saith the law," a reference not so much to the Old Testament as to the social customs and rules of first-century Judaism. The miracle is that Paul so often triumphed over such culturally-instilled preconceptions, most notably in his Galatians 3:28 vision of a classless, non-racist, non-sexist society, "all one in Christ Jesus."

Many biblical feminists fear that if they admit that some of Paul's arguments undergirding female submission reflect his rabbinical training and human limitations, the admission will undercut the authority of scriptures and the doctrine of divine inspiration. Things have come to a bad pass when we have to avoid seeing certain things in scripture (or avoid *admitting* that we see them) in order to preserve our preconceived notions about inspiration. Rather we ought to have so much faith in the God of the Bible that we fearlessly study what is written there.

The fact is that the same apostle Paul who wrote of "no male and female" in Christ also argued for female submission, and did so on the basis of Genesis 2, Adam's creation before Eve (1 Timothy 2:12-13; 1 Corinthians 11:8-9). Either we must recognize that Paul is contradicting Genesis 1 by saying that the creation of Adam and Eve was *not* simultaneous, or we must say that Genesis 1 is not inspired. It is of course possible to harmonize Genesis 1 and 2 by seeing the second chapter as a symbolic and poetic expansion on the first, while viewing the first account as authoritative concerning the simultaneous creation of Adam and Eve—but if we do that, then Paul's argument falls flat. Traditionalists, by insisting on the inerrancy of Paul's argument, are forced to deny the accuracy of Genesis 1, and contradict their own interpretation of inerrancy.

Despite rabbinical theories that Genesis 2 depicts the order of creation and that female submission is based on that order, Paul treated Phoebe and Aquilla and other women as his equals in the Lord's work; and it is time for the Christian community to follow Paul in his transcendence of his limitations instead of clinging to the letter of his struggles with them.

It seems to me far less detrimental to the authority of scripture to recognize that some of Paul's arguments *do* reflect his human limitations, just as the imprecatory Psalms which express David's vindictive hatred of his enemies are reflections of David's human limitations. By gloating over the fall of his enemies David was violating such Old Testament instructions as "Rejoice not when thine enemy falleth" (Proverbs 24:17); yet even the imprecatory Psalms were written for our instruction and learning. And I believe that Paul's arguments for female subordination, which contradict much of his own behavior and certain other passages he himself wrote, were also written for our instruction: to show us a man of God *in process,* and to force us to use our heads and our hearts in working our way through conflicting evidence.

What C. S. Lewis wrote concerning the imprecatory Psalms (see his *Reflections on the Psalms*), I would say concerning Paul's rationalizations for the female submission which was standard in his culture: the passages are distorted by the human instrument, yet they are instructive in showing us an honest man in conflict with himself. Lewis calls David's imprecatory Psalms "contemptible," yet he insists that we must not try to explain them away, nor must we reject the inspirational and devotional value of the Psalms, nor must we try to call hatred a good and pious thing. Rather, we must seek to profit from this record of David's humanity. Similarly, we cannot deny that Paul rationalized female subordination in a theological fashion that he did not employ concerning slavery. Neither can we deny that Paul contradicts these rationalizations in Galatians 3:28, in his many passages on the new creation in Christ, and in his own behavior toward female church leaders. We must open our eyes to these conflicts, demonstrating faith in the God who allowed them to appear in the New Testament. We must conquer our fear that honest attention to what we see in the Bible will undercut the doctrine of inspiration. We must allow the facts of scripture to teach us in what way it is inspired, rather than forcing scripture to conform to our own theories about it.

The Bible was not in error to record David's hatred and the Bible was not in error to record Paul's thought-processes. But *we* are in error to absolutize anything that denies the thrust of the entire Bible toward individual wholeness and harmonious community, toward oneness in Christ. Even if the biblical evidence were fifty percent in support of female subordination and only fifty percent in favor of the quality of mutual submission, ordinary kindness and decency should lead modern Christians to choose in favor of equality. But the evidence for Christian equality is far stronger than that.

Biblical feminism should not seek to root itself in the citation of first-century practices, which for all the purifying impact of the gospel remain to some degree hierarchical, patriarchal, and sexist. Biblical feminism must instead root itself firmly in the major scriptural *doctrines* of the Trinity, of creation in the image of God, of the incarnation, and of regeneration (including the regenerative influence of the gospel in human society).

Christian feminists must stress that biblical language about the nature of God is *metaphorical* language. Women have long been barred from the ministry through specious reasoning about God's maleness and Christ's incarnation as a male. Women have been kept in submission in the home and in the church through reasoning that the male embodies the sovereignty of God while the female embodies the submission which is the proper response to that sovereignty. Lately, radical feminists have been saying that if God is male, then the male is God—a line of reasoning which meant very little to me until recently, when I studied some twenty-seven evangelical books about the role and status of women and discovered that they are indeed filled with worship of the male.

In this connection, the September 1975 issue of *Cosmopolitan* printed a large excerpt from *The Total Woman*; and the only factor which the sexually permissive *Cosmopolitan* editors found it necessary to repudiate was the male idolatry. In their introduction the editors commented that *The Total Woman* is "too blatantly man-worshipping." What a tragic twist, that the secular world should have to point out to people who claim to be Bible-believers that they are "too blatantly man-worshipping"! Where are the prophets in the Christian community? Why are they failing to thunder against such idolatry?

Traditionalists tend to fall into unconscious idolatry when they operate on the assumption that the male relates to God directly while the female relates to God through the authority of the male. This in turn stems from failure to realize the implications of Genesis 1:27, which tells us that both male and female were created in the image of God. Whatever else this may mean, it certainly *must* mean that there is a feminine aspect as well as a masculine aspect in the nature of God.

It would seem from Genesis 1:26 that any attempt to split off the Trinity into separated masculine and feminine persons would be unbiblical: "And God said, Let us make man in *our* image, after *our* likeness: and let *them* have dominion . . . ." This surely implies that both male and female are created in the image of the entire Trinity, and therefore that the entire Trinity possesses both masculine and feminine elements.

Therefore, we ought to re-think our doctrine of the Trinity, which traditionally has been pictured as totally masculine. And there is biblical precedent for understanding the masculine and feminine elements of the Trinity. The "Father" is referred to in maternal as well as paternal terms in both the Old and New Testaments. At least five times the Old Testament pictures God as maternal rather than paternal (cf. Isaiah 42:14, 46:3, 49:15, 66:13, and Psalm 131:2), and in Luke 15 the Lord Jesus Christ pictures God not only as a shepherd seeking his lost sheep and a father welcoming home his prodigal son, but also as a woman seeking for her lost coin.

The Son is pictured not only in the stereotypically feminine aspects of submission to the will of the First Person, but also in the stereotypically masculine roles of the powerful generator, upholder, and judge of the universe (Colossians 1:16, 2 Thessalonians 1:7-8). His incarnation is pictured in human rather than male terms, since the New Testament authors repeatedly refer to him not as *aner*, male, but as *anthropos*, human. As the

Logos Christ is associated with the Old Testament figure of wisdom, always personified as feminine, through whom one is enabled to know and do the will of God (Proverbs 4:4-7).

The Holy Spirit is pictured as femininely brooding over the face of the waters like a hen on her nest, and as the comforter of the Christian (John 14:26) but is also associated with the masculine symbol of a flame of fire (Acts 2:3,4). Throughout mythology the dove, biblically associated with the Holy Spirit, is an androgynous image, embodying both male and female characteristics in one unit. So it seems clear that we have been remiss in failing to grasp the feminine as well as the masculine elements in each of the three persons of the Trinity, no doubt an important element in the unity of the one God who inhabits the universe.

Perhaps the *theological* lesson to be learned from all this is that we are to free ourselves from the delusion that God is to be limited by sexual dichotomies or by any other human limitations, and certainly that we ought to free ourselves from oppressing one sex and idolizing the other on the assumption that God is male.

Perhaps the *psychological* lesson to be learned is that in every male and in every female, there are masculine and feminine components which must be accepted and harmonized in order for the personality to become whole and healthy. If we regard the masculine component in terms of traditional roles, it would include activity, aggressiveness, clarity, logic, and so forth; and traditionally defined, the feminine component would include passivity, submissiveness, tenderness, intuitiveness, nurturance, and the like. Damage is done to the human spirit when these characteristics are assigned to only one sex exclusively—that is, when men are taught to be exclusively and stereotypically "masculine," and women are taught to be exclusively and stereotypically "feminine." When biblical feminists call for psychological androgyny, we are *not* talking about becoming hermaphrodites or homosexuals, and we are *not* talking about unisex; we are talking about developing all aspects of God-given male and female personalities, so that each person becomes a unique and unstereotyped harmony of male and female components. Biologically we remain male and female and relate to each other in that fashion; but we are basically *persons*, whole beings, made in the image of a God whose being apparently mingles what society has defined as masculine and feminine components.

The *sociological* lesson to be learned is that male and female are intended to work in harmonious partnership in society, in the home, and in the church. When men reject their so-called female component they become contemptuous of the opposite sex as well. Instead of manifesting the best qualities of what society calls feminine, such as tenderness, intuitiveness, and nurturance, they develop the negative qualities, such as narcissism and selfishness. And when women reject their so-called masculine component they also become contemptuous of the opposite sex. Instead of developing the better traits of what society terms masculine, such as strength and assertiveness and clear logic, they tend to develop the negative qualities of that "masculine" component, such as opinionatedness and rigid dogmatism. All of this escalates the war of the sexes.

By contrast, the Bible teaches mutual submission and mutual concern, for "neither is the man without the woman, neither the woman without the man, in the Lord. For as the woman is of the man, even so is the man also by the woman; but all things are of God" (1 Corinthians 11:12). Only when the church teaches and acts on the assumption that marriage is a partnership of equals, that the Christian community is a harmonious relating between men and women, and that women as well as men are fully qualified and fully acceptable in all aspects of the Christian ministry and church governance, will the church be true to the biblical teaching that both male and female are made in the image of a God who is both paternal and maternal, both powerful and submissive, both transcendent and immanent.

When the apostle Paul wrote his dazzling vision of a Christian society which recognizes neither Jew nor Greek, neither bond nor free, neither male nor female, certainly he could not have meant that those born Jews and those born Gentiles would lose their ethnic roots. Rather, he meant, according to the context, that those rules and practices which militated against the Gentile converts, forcing them to conform to Jewish stereotypes, would be abolished in the equality of Christian fellowship (Galatians 2:14). Similarly, he could not have meant that Christian males and females would lose their biological distinctives, but rather that in the freedom and psychological wholeness fostered by Christian fellowship, each male and each female would be free to develop his or her gifts and God-given traits without reference to gender-based stereotypes. They would not be forced to conform to sexual stereotyping any more than Gentile converts would be forced to live according to Jewish religious customs.

When Paul says that in Christ there is oneness, there is neither male nor female, he is envisioning the breakdown of all stereotypical behavior, including the hierarchical pattern of male dominance and female submission. He is supporting the concept that a healthy personality involves a harmony between so-called masculine and feminine components in both men and women, while a healthy society involves a harmonious sense of partnership between those who were created biologically male and those who were created biologically female.

What biblical feminism seeks to promote is wholeness both in the individual personality and in the Christian community, the kind of wholeness described in Ephesians 4:13—"till we all come in the unity of the faith, and of the knowledge of the Son of God, unto a perfect person, unto the measure of the stature of the fullness of Christ." At least one aspect of coming "to a perfect person" is reflecting the psychological androgyny of Christ and relating harmoniously and without any rigid role-playing to the members of the opposite sex.

For too long the church has ignored such implications, and blocked genuine friendship between men and women by insisting on a hierarchical pattern of dominance and submission rather than responding to the liberating message of the good news. For too long the church has denied the fulfilment of Christ's great prayer in John 17, a prayer which takes on a new dimension in the light of a Godhead of three persons who each contain a harmony of so-called masculine and feminine elements. Jesus prayed "that they all may be one; as thou, Father, art in me, and I in thee, that they also may be one in us. . . . And the glory which thou gavest me I have given them; that they may be one, even as we are one: I in them, and thou in me, that they may be made perfect in one. . . ." (John 17:21-23). Neither male nor female, all one in Christ Jesus!

In the May 1975 issue of the *Post-American,* traditionalist Thomas Howard writes that trying to defend feminism by listing Sarah and Deborah, Esther and Jael, Anna and Dorcas and Paul's female assistants in the ministry "is self-defeating, since . . . [the list] is embarrassing in its brevity next to the long list of the . . . *male* prophets, apostles, etc." But the point to be made is not that the female list equals or exceeds the male, but rather that in the Bible's patriarchal context, it is amazing and indicative of God's intentions that *any* women are listed at all. Jesus repeatedly had to correct the sexist and stereotyped responses of his male disciples, who were shocked that he would talk to a Samaritan woman and disturbed that mere children should bother the Master and incensed that the Lord would let himself be touched by a fallen woman. What we see operating in the Bible is the power of God similarly moving on human beings, causing them to overcome their prejudices in order to include occasional details about women in leadership roles. It is not the *paucity* of attention to women which is surprising, but rather that there is as much biblical focus on women as actually exists. And biblical feminists emphasize these passages about women precisely because the church has *not* emphasized them, and because Christian women need to be encouraged to believe that they too can be meaningful in God's service, and because the demon of sexism must be exorcised from the modern Christian community.

Regarding incarnation, it is important to remember that Christ's submission was a personal, internal, purely voluntary matter. According to the New English Bible's rendering of Philippians 2:5-8, "the divine nature was his [Christ's] from the first; yet he did not think to snatch at equality with God, but made himself nothing, assuming the nature of a slave. Bearing the human likeness, revealed in human shape, he humbled himself, and in obedience accepted even death—death on a cross." Christ's obedience was not to something external to himself; rather, it was the fusing of his own will with a purpose that reached far beyond himself; and in Ephesians 5 the apostle Paul makes Christ's loving obedience the example for husbands to follow in relation to their wives.

Thus, we biblical feminists are not arguing that there is no room for Christian submission and service; instead, we are saying that there is no room for gender-based categories which define female persons exclusively in terms of subordination. After all, Christ taught the concept of service and mutual submission to *all* of his followers, male and female alike. Biblical feminists are returning to Christ's own emphasis by extending voluntary mutual submission to all believers. And we are saying that cooperation with the will of God is an internal and individual matter, not to be dictated to any individual by any other individual, and not to be blocked by human prejudice such as the prejudice which has barred women from the Christian ministry.

Finally, biblical feminism is grounded in the doctrine of the new creation in Christ Jesus. The context of Genesis 3:16 makes clear that dominance and submission in human society constitute a curse, a sinful condition resulting from the fall of humanity. But "if any man be in Christ, he is a new creature" (2 Corinthians 5:17); "as many of you as have been baptized into Christ have put on Christ" (Galatians 3:27); and "ye have been called unto liberty; only use not liberty for an occasion to the flesh, but by love serve one another" (Galatians 5:13). The Old Testament prophet Joel looked forward to a day when the Spirit of God would be poured out on all flesh so that men and women alike would prophesy (Joel 2:28-30); at Pentecost Peter said that on that very day Joel's prophecy had been fulfilled (Acts 2:16). Thus by implication Peter announced that with the advent of the Spirit had come the end of patriarchal limitations upon the ministry of women. Paul followed through with his vision of no male and female in Christ (Galatians 3:28). Yet most Christian churches have failed to implement the glorious insights of Peter and Paul, choosing to imitate certain first-century cultural conditions rather than to *revolutionize* them.

We Christian feminists face an important task of teaching the churches and the secular society to interpret the Bible with greater attention to its overall message and with an awareness of cultural background and the limitations of the human channels. In this task we may find guidance in Christ's own behavior as recorded in Matthew 10:3-9. When the Pharisees tried to trap Jesus by pitting his view of divorce against Mosaic law, Jesus pointed out that Mosaic law did not represent God's original glorious intention for man and woman, but rather that the law enunciated in Deuteronomy 24:1-3 was given to a patriarchal culture "because of the hardness of your hearts," although "from the beginning it was not so." Thus by his own practice Jesus showed us that sacred scripture concerning man's behavior toward woman does not always reflect God's highest intentions for the human race.

Jesus himself harks back to God's original intention, when "God made them male and female," as the basis for love and loyalty and equal partnership between male and female. By playing off Deuteronomy against Genesis, Jesus is not impugning the inspiration of the Old Testament but is showing that certain passages were inspired to meet specific needs in response to human hardness, while other passages (recognizable by context) convey God's ultimate intentions for the human race.

Women and Freedom

Letty M. Russell

"How can we speak of women and freedom?" Letty Russell chooses to speak of freedom in terms of liberation, and she uses Paul's description of the struggle toward freedom in Romans 8:14-27 to provide clues that women can use as they seek their liberation. One of the lessons is that "women have come to recognize sexism for what it is—a false ideology which declares that people are inferior because of their sex." It is Dr. Russell's conviction that "liberation is not a passing fad. It will not disappear even when the media ignore it, or when it is no longer a fashionable subject for speeches." Women, she urges, should "act now as if we were free . . . by living in anticipation of God's future." Letty Russell, Associate Professor of Theology at Yale Divinity School, is the author of *Human Liberation in a Feminist Perspective—A Theology* (Westminster Press, 1974). Her article, from vol. 22, no. 1 (1975) of *Lutheran World* (Geneva, Switzerland), originally was prepared for the World Council of Churches' consultation on "Sexism in the 1970s," held in West Berlin in June 1974.

Freedom is a journey with others and for others towards God's future. Freedom cannot be defined. It can only be experienced as it breaks into our lives as new awareness of hope in God's future and confidence in the growing ability to experience and share love with others.

Thus when we try to describe freedom in our lives as women in a world and a church in change, we usually turn to the word "liberation." Not because we have been any more specific about what it means, but because liberation helps us to think of a process, a struggle with ourselves and others towards a more open future for humanity. The exact description of that struggle varies for each woman, and for each human being in each situation.

This situation variability of liberation means that in every situation, every subculture, the things from which we would be free, and the things for which we long, are different. If some American middle-class women long to get out of the house and get a job, there are other women in the United States and in every continent who long to be free from grinding work at jobs, so that they can be at home with their children!

So how can we talk of women and freedom? Not by definitions or blueprints, because there are none. Rather by sharing clues and stories of liberation which can help each of us to search out our own road, our own journey, towards the future which God holds open for us. Or by sharing our common longing and speaking of the "hope that is in us" (I Pet. 3:15). In the words of Billy Taylor's haunting jazz melody:

I wish I knew how it would feel to be free
I wish I could break all these chains holding me
I wish I could say all the things I should say
Say 'em loud, say 'em clear, for the whole world to hear!

Perhaps one way to begin is to return to another haunting description of the journey towards freedom which we find in Romans 8:14-27, and to look together at how groaning for freedom, discovery of freedom, and horizons of freedom appear to be happening in the experience of women in today's world.

1. In Paul's description of the struggle towards liberation, the first thing that strikes us is his vivid picture of the whole universe groaning for freedom.

In Romans 8:22-23 Paul tells us: "As we all know, up to the present time, the creation in all its parts groans with pain like the pain of childbirth. But not just creation alone groans; we ourselves, although we have tasted already the aperitif of the Spirit, we groan inwardly because we are still anticipating our adoption as children and the full liberation of our human existence."

What a relief! We discover that there is a solidarity of groaning. We are not the only ones who feel trapped and frustrated. Our sisters and brothers, even our environment, share together in the oppressive structures of our society. All the universe longs for the fulfilment of God's new creation where all the parts will be born again in harmony, where the New Age promised by God and begun in Jesus Christ will be fulfilled.

We also discover as Christians that we are not saved out of this groaning world, but as part of it. We are saved in hope because we have already tasted the first fruits of the spirit of freedom (the aperitif).

Our heightened restlessness and longing can only direct us towards participating in God's solidarity with humankind. They thrust us to join with Christ who "emptied himself, taking the form of a servant," in order to be part of this journey with others and for others towards God's future (Phil. 2:7).

The women's liberation movement in the United States and other nations helps to underline this experience of solidarity in groaning. Through a steady flow of documents, papers, stories, and actions, women testify that they have discovered that male domination and the submission of women is a sign of personal and social groaning, brought about, not by God's design for creation, but by human disobedience and dislocation.

Certainly this experience in oppression is not quite the same as the classic forms of political and racial oppression, because women tend to share the social status of their husbands. Where men have had access to the goods of life, women have not been bred to inferiority, because they were destined to be the mothers of the next generation of sons. Yet the domination of women by men is an ancient and persistent form of the subjection of one human being to a permanent status of inferiority.

In this growing realization that they can participate more fully in shaping their own destiny and that of the world, women join in what Jürgen Moltmann describes as the "Revolution of Freedom."[1] Their rising expectations are leading them, along with the many oppressed peoples of the world, to participate together with others in the struggle for humanization of our global society.

And it is no surprise that it is often white, middle-class

women in the United States who are so vocal in the struggle for human liberation. They have, as it were, tasted initial kinds of freedom, and just because of this, they know that they are not free. In the very freedom from want which they experience has come a desire for more freedom, freedom to share with others in a better distribution of the goods of the earth, freedom to use their gifts to help serve the needs of others.

Christian women are no exception to this experience. They know that they are called to service: to diakonia. But what form should this diakonia take? How can they use their new experience of groaning and longing to be free to work out better ways of expressing their solidarity with others?

The service of Christ is a calling to be instruments of God's help, not a calling to be subservient. This in turn means that genuine service of others takes the form of solidarity in groaning and working with others to gain their freedom to shape their own future. Service which perpetuates dependence, we now know from our own experience, is not service at all. It is a form of domination.

This is not new, but it now takes on urgency because of the hope in our own hearts, and because of the demands of others that they find out their own journey to freedom. Diakonia (service or ministry) has traditionally taken three forms:[2]

Curative: the healing of the wounds of those who have become victims of life; providing help to the sick, the hungry, and homeless.

Preventive: attempting to forestall developments which might easily lead to curtailment of full freedom for life; working through social action to provide vocational training centers, drug prevention programs, etc.

Prospective: attempting to open the situation for a future of free realization in life; helping those who are outcasts from the dominant culture, the outsiders, to participate fully in culture and in shaping their own liberation.

Until recently, the church has specialized in curative or "band aid" tasks, and women have strongly supported these causes. Gradually we have realized that diakonia is genuine

solidarity in groaning only when it moves towards preventive
programs and finally into prospective advocacy of the rights of
people to decide for themselves how to work out their own
political and social liberation.

Prospective diakonia is what we would like for ourselves.
Many of us have discovered that having the basic necessities of
life, without a way to help in shaping life, does not necessarily
lead to liberation. The same discovery means that serving
young people, or aged, or ghetto residents, or Third World
people begins with their participation in setting the agenda and
picking the battles, so that we can be advocates in a solidarity of
groaning and a revolution of freedom.

2. If we return to Paul's story of the journey towards freedom,
   we notice a striking description of the discovery of freedom.

In Romans 8:18-19 he tells us: "I consider that whatever
we suffer now cannot be compared at all with the splendor as
yet not revealed, which is in store for us. The created universe
is waiting on tiptoe for the children of God to show what they
are. In fact, the fondest dream of the universe is to catch a
glimpse of real live children of God." In his poetic image, we
find that everyone who is working and longing for freedom is
eagerly longing (waiting on tiptoe) to catch a vision of what "it
means to be free." For to be set free is to become "real live
children of God!"

Because we are all in this journey together, we do not know
exactly what children of God look like! Certainly if the members
of the Christian church are presumed to represent them in any
finished character, there is little to be expected! Yet as Christians we have tasted the apertif of the Spirit. We trust that in
Jesus Christ God has made known the beginnings of the love
and obedience and true humanity which is the destiny of a restored creation.

As we begin to share the life style of Jesus of Nazareth in
giving our lives for others in diakonia and solidarity, we discover the cost of freedom and the struggle of obedience. We
also catch a glimpse of what it would mean to be a whole human
race in the words of Galatians 3:23-29, which speak of the bar-
riers Christ has already broken so that "there is neither Jew nor

Greek, there is neither slave nor free, there is neither male nor female." And because we are led by the Spirit of Christ, we have hope that we may be able "to distinguish between the spirits" which lead towards new freedom (I Cor. 12:10).

Again it may be the "ferment of freedom" in the women's liberation movement and in other liberation movements which puts this question before us with new urgency: What do real live children of God look like? What does it mean to be human?

Too long the image of what it means to be human has been patterned after the image of the white, Western male; all other people (non-white, non-Western, and women) appear as only partly human because they don't measure up to this mythical norm.

Women have come to recognize sexism for what it is—a false ideology which declares that people are inferior because of their sex—just as the non-white majority of the world has come to recognize racism as a cancerous ideology which declares that people are inferior because of the color of their skin. Eliminating sexism and racism means the restructuring of our whole world society, not just saying "it isn't so." It involves politics, economics, education, business, and family life styles. Such a struggle begins with us, in our own hearts where we have to learn first to be pro-woman, so that we can become pro-human. But it must stretch around the world to all humanists (men, women, and children) who are looking for the freedom to shape their own futures and participate in the search for what it means to be children of God.

As women in the church, we are called to share in this critical process of discerning what it means to be human and trying to live out our discoveries of freedom. Paul tells us in I Corinthians 12:10 that the ability to discern the signs of the time and to be thus able to work towards freedom is a gift of the Holy Spirit. The word he uses for discernment is *diakrisis*.[3]

This function of *diakrisis* can help women and the church to take a prophetic stance over against society, as they seek to discern God's actions and to criticize those parts of the world (including themselves) which deny God's plan and purpose of justice, freedom, and peace for humanity. In this way, we can join others in helping to shape society and discovering new freedom, rather than being shaped by society and old cultural assumptions which close off the future. This "diakritical" role is difficult especially for women. To begin with, it means having courage to be a *misfit* in society, acting and thinking according to a solidarity with those who are groaning and "disturbing the status quo." The cost of this may mean that we become "marginal women," those who don't fit with our peers or into accepted norms.

Secondly, Christian responsibility in the political and in all sectors of society calls for both theological discernment and technical know-how. This means that we will have to do our homework and be willing to take concrete actions for social change based on our own new consciousness of the social and theological issues at stake.

Raising our own consciousness is not enough. We must learn to act together with others to transform the societies in which we live by all the means necessary; constantly asking God through the power of the Spirit (in the words of Julius Lester) not only to raise our consciousness, but to raze our consciousness, so that our hearts are restless to work for the revealing of what real live children of God might look like.

3. Finally, if we return again to Paul's description of the journey towards freedom, we become aware that we live constantly in the horizon of freedom.

In Romans 8:20 he says: "The creation is in the grip of frustration and futility. Not by its own choice; God made it so, and therefore there is always hope that one day the universe will be set free from the shackles of mortality and decadence and share the glorious freedom of the children of God."

The horizon of freedom is hope: hope that God's promised future will become a reality. This "hope is not the opium of the people, but an impulse to change the world in the perspective of God's promise."[4] The nature of a horizon is that as we move towards it, it always disappears and a new one appears. The horizon of freedom constantly changes and looks different as we journey with others and for others towards God's future.

Because of the problems and difficulties and plain "mess" of the world we live in, there appears to be "no hope." The horizon closes in and there is no vision. Often our best planning and efforts bring little change in the immense problems of our world and the great problems of our own lives. Yet the future which we plan is not the last word. There is always the horizon of the future which comes towards us as God' future. When we act now as if that anticipated future of God is breaking into our lives, we discover new horizons of freedom.[5] God is hoping for us, and it is up to us to live as if God's freedom were already present in our lives (I Cor. 7:25-31).

The women's liberation movement can help us to move towards new horizons of freedom by teaching us some of the fundamental facts of liberation.

The first fact is that no one is free until all are free. This means that the horizon changes, but does not disappear, because a few privileged people gain new privileges. Sisterhood is a constant reminder of our responsibility for others. Whatever gains we have made, they are only partial unless society is structured so that other women have equal access to these changes, be they economic, political, social, or private. Those who have made it, however they have made it, have the responsibility to share the task of building new life styles with all women and men.

The second is that women's liberation is not the cause of disruption in our societies. It is a result of the changes in technology and family patterns which are freeing women from traditional biological roles of child raising and maintenance of the household. Many women are seeking new patterns of family life as partnership, and new life styles in society, because they have the courage to see that the old patterns are not working well for many men and women, and they are willing to risk working for a more humane way of life.

The last is that liberation is not a passing fad. It will not disappear even when the media ignore it, or it is no longer a fashionable subject for speeches. As long as people are oppressed, there will be a "groaning for freedom," whether in acts of rebellion, or in actions to build a new future of justice for all. And we are called to keep the "rumor going." The world can be different. God intends it to be so, and we can begin by acting out that intention here and now.

For women in the church, freedom began long ago, and it is time to act now as if we were free. We are called according to Paul to live now in the horizon of the new age. The words he uses for this in I Corinthians 7:25-31 are *hos me:* to live "as if not"; to live as if the facts of the situation are not the end of the matter, because a new world is breaking in on us.

We can begin now by living in *anticipation of God's future.* The Greek word for this is *prolepsis:* an anticipation of a hoped-for future in the present. Proleptic actions anticipate the situation for which they work; those who take them live as if the situation, at least in part, had already arrived.

The dictionary definition of prolepsis is a "chronological mistake," or the dating of an event before it actually happened. It is the opposite of anachronism, which is a chronological mistake which dates an event after it actually happened. For a long time the church has often appeared anachronistic. Today we and the church are called to be a chronological mistake, not a backward mistake, but a mistake which is proleptic because it establishes signs of hope, horizons of the future, in the midst of the present.

As members of the church, we are called to be a sign of the Kingdom of God, a "lived out" beatitude of the future of humanity. We can become signs in small or large ways by contradicting injustice, promoting peace, standing in solidarity with the poor. By living out new life styles of partnership with men in home, society, and church, we can become proleptic signs. By working in critical and concrete ways along with those who are oppressed in other nations as well as our own, we can begin to build world solidarity now. Women are free, and they can act freely and responsibly together for others now.

Conclusion

I have been trying to describe for you what it means to journey on the road towards freedom with others, for others, towards God's future. The clues I have given are few, because ultimately each woman must liberate herself. But I would suggest that these clues might help in the search: that the universal groaning for freedom calls us towards suffering and service (diakonia) with others; that the discovery of freedom means a continuing and "diakritical" search or discernment into how to be human beings, real live children of God; that the horizon of freedom leads us to hope against hope in God's promise, and to add our own limited efforts to the business of prolepsis or anticipation: bringing the future of God into the present.

I trust that women and freedom belong together. Perhaps simply, as Zechariah puts it, because I am "a prisoner of hope" (9:12) I cannot escape the facts of my situation, yet I trust in the reality of my freedom as a gift of God. God cares for us. God is a "humanist," and, therefore, we "can know how it feels to be free."

We are already on the road towards freedom, caught up in the process of liberation. But there are many roads, and I cannot give you or myself a map. All I can say is that there is a solidarity of groaning for freedom among all our sisters and brothers of the world who find themselves oppressed, and invite you who would be free to join in the very universal symphony of groaning, so that we can all play our part.

NOTES

1. *Religion, Revolution and the Future* (New York: Scribner's, 1969), p. 77.

2. Hans Hoekendijk, *Horizons of Hope* (Nashville: Tidings, 1970), pp. 32-33.

3. Letty M. Russell, "Rapidation in the Church," *Risk*, Vol. 5, No. 4, 1969, pp. 58-67.

4. Ferdinand Kerstiens, "Hope," *Sacramentum Mundi* (New York: Herder and Herder, 1969), III, p. 65.

5. Ernst Käsemann, *Jesus Means Freedom* (Philadelphia: Fortress Press, 1970), p. 73.

IV: Asian American Experience

Ethnic Liberation Theology: Neo-Orthodoxy Reshaped or Replaced?

Roy I. Sano

Roy I. Sano, Director of the Asian Center for Theology and Strategies in Berkeley, California, provides a study in practical hermeneutics. He explains why Asian Americans and other ethnic minorities try "to make better sense of our experiences" by identifying with the ethnic particularism in the story of Esther, rather than the cultural assimilation in the story of Ruth. Ethnic theologies of liberation also find in Scripture that the apocalyptic writers are more helpful to their cause than the prophets. Finally, Sano contends that "ethnic theologies of liberation place a priority on liberation rather than reconciliation. Theologically speaking, this means redemption comes before reconciliation." These emphases demonstrate "what has become outdated in neo-orthodoxy," and how ethnic theologies of liberation are moving beyond it. His essay is reprinted from the November 10, 1975 issue of *Christianity and Crisis* (New York City).

I write as an Asian American reshaping the contributions of the neo-orthodox phase of Protestant theology by means of the emerging ethnic theologies of liberation. Three distinguishable tasks inform this process: an analysis of Asian American experiences and our locus in American society, a comparison of these observations with other ethnic minorities at home and Third World peoples abroad, and reflections on the implications these analyses have for the neo-orthodoxy that was developed through my training and a decade of work in the church and various communities.

At this stage of the undertaking the theological method associated with neo-orthodoxy persists, but its contents have changed. I will discuss the method first.

The theological method common to ethnic theologies of liberation and neo-orthodoxy is the use of stories. Whereas in neo-orthodoxy the history of a people dominated and in the current vogue biographies of individuals have risen to prominence, ethnic theologies are likely to make equal use of both. Ethnic consciousness has made us sensitive to the story of our people, and participation in the struggles of a people makes personal identity possible. In this perspective the history of a community is mirrored in the biography of the individual, and vice versa.

The use of stories in theology should not surprise us. People throughout history have conveyed the religious dimensions of their cultures in this way. When we are able to reduce their diverse stories to skeletal outlines and classify them, we have isolated the cultural myths that enable them to organize their past, present and future into a coherent whole.

Myth writers and their audiences interact. Sometimes myth writers only *reflect* their people; at other times they *shape* the consciousness of their people. Both roles can serve humane ends. The first task is a descriptive one. Poets, dramatists, novelists, historians and even musicians and painters make visible to us the stories by which we live. The second task is prescriptive. The same myth writers can be myth makers, offering us as alternatives other stories that may be more appropriate to our setting.

In working on an ethnic theology of liberation I find myself practicing both these tasks. I have had to clarify the myths, stories, histories and biographies that have been paradigmatic for us. It has been equally important to experiment with other myths that may offer a more humanizing understanding of our past, a more honest reading of our present situation and a prospect for our future self-fulfillment.

These two tasks are not unique to ethnic theologies of liberation. I do claim, however, that the prescriptive task has produced some new contents. In order to survey the impact of ethnic theologies of liberation, I will illustrate the shift in two applications of the descriptive and prescriptive tasks. The first speaks to the role of ethnicity in the identity of individuals and groups; the second illuminates the place liberation has in reconstructing our stories.

If there is any biblical account that describes the story behind Asian Americans' dreams in America, it appears in the book of Ruth. Ruth came from Moab to Israel. The Moabites did not practice the law of hospitality when the Israelites made their trek through the wilderness, and this serious offense prompted animosity toward them. The Israelites refused at various stages of their history to permit the Moabites entry into their temple and prohibited intermarriage with them.

The story of Ruth, however, recalls her acculturation and assimilation. She made the Israelite God her God, the Israelite people her people. Despite reverses in her life she became the grandmother of King David, the towering symbol of Israel's national achievements and religious ideals. A rejected immigrant survived in an alien land, gained acceptance and made a notable contribution.

No other story describes so well the dreams by which immigrants from Europe, Africa and Latin America have lived in the United States of America. Asian Americans are no different. The greater part of our people came with a determination to live the same story in its secular or religious versions. However, an analysis of our actual situation suggests that another story would be more honest and humanizing. But first a review of our experiences, and then a look at the story that might be prescribed.

Testing the Story of Ruth

The experiences of Asian Americans are summarized in two colorful phrases: the yellow peril and the red scare. The first points to the low level of tolerance for Pacific Basin peoples in American society. Whenever we threaten white Americans, we are seen as a peril that must be driven back or at least put in its place. This dominates the first century of our experience from 1850 to 1950, as successive waves of Chinese, Japanese, Filipinos, Koreans and Pacific Islanders immigrated here. The yellow peril syndrome assigned us to the lower of two categories through restrictive immigration, residential segregation, underemployment, lower income, distorted education and restricted options for cultural expression.

More recently the red scare has affected our stay here. When the People's Republic of China threatened to invade Quemoy and Matsu in the 1950's, Chinese Americans prepared for a wartime concentration camp because they remembered the imprisonment of 110,000 Japanese Americans in the 1940's without due process of law. In those grim days Bishop Wilbur W. Y. Choy, then a minister in Sacramento, was asked by Chinese American leaders to speak to key whites to oppose another attempt to evacuate Asian Americans. Civil rights, though inalienable in theory, are in fact elusive for Asian Americans whenever a crisis arises in American society. Our rights can be jettisoned in order to keep this nation in orbit.

Other overseas observations lead to similar conclusions. In Viet Nam the U.S. abandoned restraint and turned Asian people into cannon fodder and Asian soil into a dumping yard for outdated military hardware. Even worse, the Government eventually used their lands as testing grounds for increasingly accurate systems for the delivery of ever more destructive weapons. Finally, we shall not forget that the atomic bomb was used first in East Asia.

Asian Americans can see how differently they are treated when comparisons are drawn with whites in Europe and America. These inequities lead them to speak of a "two category system." Harry H. L. Kitano and Roger Daniels first outlined this analytic model in *American Racism: The Nature of Prejudice* (Prentice-Hall, 1969). Dr. Kitano then elaborated the theory in *Race Relations* (Prentice-Hall, 1974). After a review of race relations and an analysis of contemporary American society, he concludes that a "two category system" persists. The upper category is colorless, privileged and powerful; the lower category is colorful, less privileged and only partially enfranchised. Furthermore, these boundaries have been maintained despite all efforts to obliterate or minimize them.

Christians are especially adept at self-delusion along these lines. The espousal of the universal Gospel and crusading social pronouncements blind them to the realities of these persisting categories. They think a few exceptional cases of superqualified minorities who penetrate the upper category refute the analytical model. They suppose the experiences of fellowship in the church discredit the analysis, failing to recognize that the church is at best a pocket in American society and is peripheral to the crucial centers that society at large protects more effectively.

Furthermore, even when minorities penetrate a sector of the upper category, whites have the power to redraw the boundaries and enforce the categories in new forms. Residential patterns, educational institutions and vocational turfs are cases in point.

Esther: Recovering our Ethnic Particularism

Given the two category system, ethnic minorities have been saying for at least half a decade that the story of Ruth is at best a dream, if not a delusion. Hence the search for another story. We are finding it in the book of Esther. It was Lloyd Wake of Glide Memorial United Methodist Church in San Francisco who first called the attention of Asian Americans to the potentialities of this story.

You may recall the book of Esther. Talk about making it in an alien society, she was making it there by denying her Jewishness during a "beauty contest." Her uncle Mordecai advised her to do so (Esther 2:10, 20). But after she was accepted into the inner circles, she discovered she had joined a society where people with power had promulgated a decree to exterminate her people. Mordecai reminded her of the realities of the situation. "Think not that in the king's palace you will escape any more than all other Jews . . .Who knows whether you have not come to the kingdom for such a time as this?" (Esther 4:13-14). As a person who had obtained an entrance into an alien society, it was time for her to recover her ethnic identity and reverse the decree against her people. At the risk of her own life she broke the law and resisted the king's decree.

This story enables us to make better sense of our experiences. As light-skinned minorities we have often denied our ethnic status while penetrating existing structures in American society. Even if a few appear to have succeeded, we are discovering decrees that would exterminate our peoplehood and cultures. Examples are numerous: Federal agencies, financial institutions and realtors destroy our neighborhoods through renewal projects. No provisions are made for self-determination in the reconstruction of our centers of economic, social and cultural activities. Welfare legislation frequently overlooks our problems, while public schools and universities turn our assets of bilingual skills and bicultural experiences into handicaps and problems. The reversal of these overt and covert decrees requires concerted effort—and sometimes illegal action, as in the case of Esther.

What enables us to make better sense of our past and present could benefit the predominantly white heirs of neo-orthodoxy as well. Their record is shallow and narrow when it comes to the struggles of Asian Americans. Though several explanations may be offered, the one worth pursuing here is the lack of biblical and theological foundations for ethnic particularism and social pluralism.

Like Protestant liberalism before it, neo-orthodoxy was a child of its culture. Both fell victim to the dream and the duplicities associated with the melting pot theory. The theory operated on two levels: the explicit one promised unity and acceptance of all peoples and their distinctive contributions; the hidden one promoted a monochrome, or colorless, culture and society dominated by whites.

The best indicator of this failure to offer religious resistance to the melting pot theory appears in the truncated canon that has operated in liberalism and neo-orthodoxy. In their reconstruction of the biblical drama of salvation, both highlighted universalism and rejected those high moments that assert particularism and imply pluralism. They used Ruth and overlooked the ethnicity that Esther espoused. They preached about Jonah's conversion to preach grace to the hated Ninevites, but they failed to preach about the glee Nahum felt when he saw the doom that threatened the oppressive Assyrians centered in

Nineveh. They gravitated toward the universalism of Isaiah and Amos and the historians who wrote from their viewpoint, but they found no use for Chronicles, Ezra and Nehemiah. The latter school sought fortifications around Jerusalem, restoration of the Temple within which the divine would manifest itself, and refinement of rituals that celebrated their ethnic histories.

If the genius of the Jewish canon were allowed to operate in the social theory of American Protestant theology and social ethics, liberalism and neo-orthodoxy would have the foundations for genuine pluralism. They would be prepared to handle the assertions of ethnicity among Asian Americans who are the nation's most rapidly growing ethnic minority, representing the majority of the world's populations. Asian Americans are dismissed as Johnny-come-latelies because they have not been heard, despite the years they have raised their voices. They have been treated as a nuisance to be assimilated.

From Prophecy to Apocalypticism

What is happening is that ethnic theologies of liberation have uncovered stories that are quite different from the ones operative in neo-orthodoxy, which still lives with the story of Ruth. The appropriation of the story of Esther and others like it would enable neo-orthodoxy to obtain the religious foundations for its best intentions, namely, the promotion of justice for neglected peoples and provision for the cultural pluralism it claims to offer.

In examining the second shift in the application of the descriptive and prescriptive tasks, we cannot be as generous with neo-orthodoxy. In this case it is not so much a shift in stories as it is a change in focus on a different stage in the history of Israel's religious development. White theologians of the neo-orthodox school gravitated toward the prophets; colorful people who recognize their oppression find the heirs of prophecy, the apocalyptic writers, more helpful. A comparison between the historical periods will explain the contrast.

The prophets became prominent after the Israelites had established their nation. By that time the priests had a well-established function to perform, the kings exercised their power, and economic and social leaders had secured their positions. The prophets came at that point as critics who challenged and corrected their society. They pleaded with their leaders to mend their ways so that God could again restore wholeness to their nation.

Whites would understandably use the prophets, for they were in control when this nation came into its full power. Neoorthodox whites were among the elites in a society where they had access to the mass media and a voice in the electoral process. They could be expected to amend the evils of their society. A rereading of Reinhold Niebuhr will reveal how much of his writings sought to convince fellow whites that they were in a position of power and could influence the course of history.

Ethnic minorities that style themselves as persons within earshot of leaders also appeal to the prophetic model. However, what happens when ethnic minorities find that appealing to leaders does not produce appropriate changes? A continued addiction to the heady wine of power implicit in the prophetic ministry turns ethnic minorities into imposters. An analysis of the place Asian Americans assume in America's power structures will lead them away from prophetism. The time has come to proceed through history with Israel, to move from prophecy to apocalypticism.

Apocalyptic literature is associated with the period when Israel lost its nationhood and became a vassal of a foreign country. Since other nations operated with interests far removed from the Israelites' needs, the literature of this period depicts a dualism between the enemy and the children of God. The writers portray these alien rulers as weird and deplorable creatures fit for imaginations mixed with pious hopes and smoldering hatred. Since no persuasion and appeals would correct the situation and since alterations in evil systems would be insufficient anyway, the writings prompted visions of wholesale changes, of an overthrow of existing social and political regimes.

Solutions of this sort relied on assistance from outside sources. Nothing within their environment offered them hope. Hence they looked to a "Son of Man" who reigned in the distant heavens to descend on clouds to accomplish their liberation, or redemption (Dan. 7:13; Rev. 14:14; Mt. 24:30; Acts

7:56). Since they hoped for conditions that departed greatly from their present experiences, they envisioned radical discontinuities in the course of history, which was schematized into radically distinguishable periods. Finally, people with visions of subverting tyrannical regimes would understandably employ pseudonyms and coded language.

Class consciousness largely determines the responses of readers to the apocalyptic tradition in the Old and New Testaments. In what follows here I note the contradictory reactions to the determinism of the future, the drastic changes seen in history, the dualistic world view and the use of pseudonyms associated with apocalyptic literature.

The deterministic element contradicts the neo-orthodox vision of the open texture of history and the free will it presupposed was the ground for action. Oppressed people, by contrast, read the deterministic element as an assurance of better things to come. Rather than inducing a debilitating fatalism, deterministic elements in the picture of the future promote courageous action designed to overthrow the powers of evil.

For neo-orthodox followers the drastic changes in history that apocalyptic literature portrays prompt unrealistic hopes. During its recent turn at the helm the middle class has not been able to alter significantly the course of events. Having grown weary of trying, and also perhaps recognizing that it has more to lose than to gain, the neo-orthodox middle class in this context counsels more acquiescence or mild alterations rather than the subversion of existing systems.

Oppressed people at home and abroad have caught the fever of the "revolution of rising expectations." How else could they depict the systemic changes in history but by means of radical discontinuities? We move from the kingdom of darkness to the kingdom of light. Asian Americans entertain their own version of the radical changes the course of history has brought. In 1945 Emperor Hirohito was forced to board the USS Missouri and sign an unconditional surrender. Less than a decade later East Asian military action forced the United States into a negotiated stalemate in Korea. And in 1975 the U.S. was forced to accept an unconditional surrender in Southeast Asia. It was in a position not to negotiate and deal but simply to leave.

Asian Americans have no illusions concerning the continuing presence and power of the U.S. in East Asia and the Pacific Basin. But the apocalyptic vision in Revelation 13 concerning the paradoxical figure of the beast, which is at once mortally wounded but yet allowed to live temporarily, suggests a realistic estimate of American power while lending courage to work for its eventual demise. The destruction of the American Empire is more likely to happen with a whimper than a bang, reminiscent of the decline of England from the British Empire to Commonwealth and now virtually to a colony in less than half a century.

History never followed exactly the scenarios of the apocalyptic readings. We recognize apocalyptic literature as poetry and religious rhetoric rather than as the empirical reports of a positivist historian that both its defenders and detractors mistake it to be. Despite these limitations this body of literature promises to generate a wholly different Asian American and East Asian consciousness.

Liberation and Reconciliation

The overthrow of the power of evil that we associate with the apocalyptic tradition provides ethnic theologies of liberation with a biblical foundation for one of their most important theological contributions. In what is surfacing as a historic breakthrough in the development of theology, ethnic theologies of liberation place a priority on liberation rather than reconciliation. Theologically speaking, this means redemption comes before reconciliation.

Such a proposal alters a practice associated with Western Christianity ever since the Middle Ages which even the Reformation did not change. Whereas the Medievalists claimed that correct conduct would assure us of God's acceptance, the Reformers claimed acceptance by God would facilitate the correct conduct the Medievalists sought. But the issue was the same: acceptance or reconciliation with the Maker. Both failed to narrate the event that would make possible an authentic reconciliation, namely, redemption or liberation. Karl Barth, following the Medieval and Reformation preoccupation with reconciliation, proceeded on dubious exegetical grounds from reconciliation in volume four of his *Church Dogmatics* to redemption in volume five. From the perspective of liberation theology Barth proceeded backwards. In current parlance there can be no genuine reconciliation, peace and understanding without liberation from political, economic, cultural and religious oppression.

The American Empire increasingly has become the focus for these forms of oppression and the need for liberation. Its practice of neocolonialism abroad and internal colonialism at home through racism, sexism and classism has reorganized our theological reflection and social action. Unfortunately, the heirs of Reinhold Niebuhr have not always been at the forefront of those who recognized the potential use of the category of empire for Christian thought and action. They talked about particular evils, and even if they spoke of institutional or systemic evils, they failed to employ the category of empire as an organizing principle, much less locate the seat of the empire in their own country.

The term empire suggests a monolithic structure that sounds simplistic, if not paranoid. Understandably. People in power who may have promoted efforts to relieve the suffering of people in the lower category may have found segments of the upper category unruly and uncooperative. By contrast people in the lower category have frequently observed collusion between labor and management, financial and educational institutions, and ecclesiastical and governmental bodies to keep them out of the upper category. Oppressed people know how the apparently competitive segments of the upper category work in concert against them. The apocalyptic books, written under the foreign domination of Babylonia, Persia, Greece or Rome, offer them an analytical model and a foundation for action when they face an empire.

If "the monolithic structures of evil" sounds simplistic and paranoid, the dualism, or distance, felt between sovereign and subject sounds unreal and neurotic. The neo-orthodox who come from the ruling class, or think they are in touch with those who govern, feel no distance between themselves and the centers of power. They fail to appreciate the boundaries between the two categories of people referred to earlier. When they conduct their own expeditions into the lower category on "rescue" operations, they encounter little difficulty crossing the boundary; when the pressure rises they push the panic button, and an emergency system returns them safely to the upper category.

No wonder they do not recognize that the boundary they cross so easily might represent a barrier to those of the lower category. This helps explain why they live with the compulsion to "deapocalypticize" articulated by Rudolf Bultmann and continued by his disciples: The task of theology is to eliminate the dualistic world view and the schematic outlines of history. When the middle-class neo-orthodox scholars discover the immunity of multinational corporations to nation-states and all others but the selected elites, they will find reason to appropriate the dualism of the apocalyptic perspective.

For oppressed people it would be unrealistic and neurotic not to operate with a consciousness of the boundaries between the two categories, with a "we-they" dichotomy. It should not surprise us that they find their experiences mirrored in the dualism of the apocalyptic orientation.

The final contrast appears in the use of pseudonyms. Scholars associated with people in power hold that the use of pseudonyms betrays the author's acknowledgement of the low quality of his/her work. Pseudonyms from this perspective lend to the literature the credibility of a recognized revealer of God's word. But none of us who have carried bits and pieces of paper out of Korea or who have smuggled papers into the Philippines would hold that view. We know that subverters of repressive regimes must employ false names to conceal their identity and engage in double talk with coded language so that their message will go undetected by the authorities. No Oxford don, Cambridge scholar or Tübingen professor could convince us that apocalyptic literature represents second-rate religious writings. For oppressed people it is the means of survival and hope, not suicide and despair as some suggest.

In conclusion, neo-orthodoxy's methodology has introduced into theology contents which are so alien to it that it may no longer be possible to speak of reshaping neo-orthodoxy. We are quite clearly moving beyond it under the impact of ethnic theologies of liberation. These theologies clarify not only what has become outdated in neo-orthodoxy but also something we may begin to use constructively: namely, new stories.

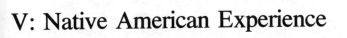

V: Native American Experience

A Native American Perspective on Liberation

Vine Deloria, Jr.

Arguing that "liberation theology is simply the latest gimmick to keep minority groups circling the wagons with the vain hope that they can eliminate the oppression that surrounds them," Sioux Indian Vine Deloria, Jr., charges that liberation theology "does not seek to destroy the roots of oppression, but merely to change the manner in which oppression manifests itself." The problem, according to Deloria, is "a general attitude toward the world that underlies the Western approach to human knowledge." What is needed, he proposes, is "the destruction of the whole complex of Western theories of knowledge and the construction of a new and more comprehensive synthesis of human knowledge and experience. . . . Then we are speaking truly of liberation. For it is the manner in which people conceive reality that motivates them to behave in certain ways." Deloria illustrates his thesis with an old Indian saying: "The white man . . . has ideas; Indians have visions. Ideas have a single dimension. . . . The vision, on the other hand, presents a whole picture of experience and has a central meaning that stands on its own feet as an independent revelation." Theologian, lawyer, and son of an Episcopal clergyman, Vine Deloria, Jr., is Chairman of the Institute for the Development of Indian Law in Washington, D.C. His best known books are *Custer Died for Your Sins* (1969), *We Talk, You Listen* (1970), *God Is Red* (1973) and *The Indian Affair* (1974). His article is taken from the July 1977 *Occasional Bulletin of Missionary Research,* published by the Overseas Ministries Study Center, Ventnor, New Jersey.

Liberation theology assumes that the common experience of oppression is sufficient to create the desire for a new coalition of dissident minorities. Adherents of this movement indiscriminately classify all minorities—racial, ethnic, and sexual—in a single category of people seeking liberation. Such classification is an easy way to eliminate specific complaints of specific groups and a clever way to turn aside efforts of dissenting groups to get their particular goals fulfilled. For instead of listening to their complaints, observers—and particularly liberal observers who pose as sympathetic fellow-travelers—can tie up the conversation endlessly by eliciting questions, framed within the liberation ideology, that require standard and nonsensical answers. Liberation theology, then, was an absolute necessity if the establishment was going to continue to control the minds of minorities. If a person of a minority group had not invented it, the liberal establishment most certainly would have created it.

The immediate response to such an accusation is one of horrified refusal to believe that there could be any racial or sexual minority that does not consider itself to be under oppression. This is followed by the perennial suggestion that if dissident minorities "got organized" instead of remaining separate they would be able to get things done. Those who reject that concept of oppression merely prove that they are so completely the victims of oppression that they do not even recognize it. The circular logic closes neatly in upon them, making them victims indeed. Liberation theology is simply the latest gimmick to keep minority groups circling the wagons with the vain hope that they can eliminate the oppression that surrounds them. It does not seek to destroy the roots of oppression, but merely to change the manner in which oppression manifests itself. No winner, no matter how sincere, willingly surrenders his power over others. He may devise clever ways to appear to share such power, but he always keeps a couple of aces up his sleeve in case things get out of control.

If there were any serious concern about liberation, we would see thousands of people simply walk away from the vast economic, political, and intellectual machine we call Western civilization and refuse to be enticed to participate in it any longer. Liberation is not a difficult task when one no longer finds value in a set of institutions or beliefs. We are liberated from the burden of Santa Claus and the moral demand to be "good" when, as maturing adolescents, we reject the concept of Santa Claus. Thereafter we have no sense of guilt in late November that we have not behaved properly during the year, and no fear that a lump of coal rather than a gift will await us Christmas morning. In the same manner, we are freed and liberated once we realize the insanity and fantasy of the present manner of interpreting our experiences in the world. Liberation, in its most fundamental sense, requires a rejection of everything we have been taught and its replacement by only those things we have experienced as having values.

But this replacement only begins the task of liberation. For the history of Western thinking in the past eight centuries has been one of replacement of ideas within a framework that has remained basically unchanged for nearly two millennia. Challenging this framework of interpretation means a rearrangement of our manner of perceiving the world, and it involves a reexamination of the body of human knowledge and its structural reconstruction into a new format. Such a task appears to be far from the struggles of the present. It seems abstract and meaningless in the face of contemporary suffering. And it suggests that people can be made to change their oppressive activity by intellectual reorientation alone.

All these questions arise, however, because of the fundamental orientation of Western peoples toward the world. We assume that we know the structure of reality and must only make certain minor adjustments in the machinery that operates it in order to bring our institutions into line. Immediate suffering is thus placed in juxtaposition with abstract metaphysical conceptions of the world and, because we can see immediate suffering, we feel impelled to change conditions quickly to relieve tensions, never coming to understand how the basic attitude toward life and its derivative attitudes toward minority groups continues to dominate the goals and activities that appear designed to create reforms.

Numerous examples can be cited to show that our efforts to bring justice into the world have been short-circuited by the passage of events, and that those efforts are unsuccessful because we have failed to consider the basic framework within

which we pose questions, analyze alternatives, and suggest solutions. Consider the examples from our immediate past. In the
early sixties college application forms included a blank line on
which all prospective students were required to indicate their
race. Such information was used to discriminate against those
of a minority background, and so reformers demanded that the
question be dropped. By the time all colleges had been forced to
eliminate questions concerning the race of applicants, the Civil
Rights Movement had so sensitized those involved in higher
education that scholarships were made available in great numbers to people of minority races. There was no way, however,
to allocate such scholarships because college officials could no
longer determine the racial background of students on the basis
of their applications for admission.

Much of the impetus for low-cost housing in the cities was
based upon the premise that in the twentieth century people
should not have to live in hovels but that adequate housing
should be constructed for them. Yet in the course of tearing
down slums and building new housing projects, low-income
housing areas were eliminated. The construction cost of the
new projects made it necessary to charge higher rentals. Former
residents of the low-income areas could not afford to live in the
new housing, so they moved to other parts of the city and
created exactly the same conditions that had originally provoked the demand for low-rent housing.

Government schools had a very difficult time teaching
American Indian children the English language. (One reason
was the assumption of teachers that all languages had Latin
roots, and their inability to adapt the programs when they discovered that Indian languages were not so derived.) Hence programs in bilingual teaching methods were authorized that would
use the native language to teach the children English, an under-
handed way of eliminating the native language. Between the
time that bilingual programs were conceived and the time that
they were finally funded, other programs that concentrated on
adequate housing had an unexpected effect on the educational
process. Hundreds of new houses were built in agency towns,
and Indians moved from remote areas of the different reservations into those towns where they could get good housing. Since

they were primarily younger couples with young children, the housing development meant that most Indian children were now growing up in the agency communities and were learning English as a first language. Thus the bilingual programs, which began as a means of teaching English as a second language, became the method designed to preserve the native vernacular by teaching it as a second language to students who had grown up speaking English.

Example after example could be cited, each testifying to the devastating effect of a general attitude toward the world that underlies the Western approach to human knowledge. The basis of this attitude is the assumption that the world operates in certain predetermined ways, that it operates continuously under certain natural laws, and that the nature of every species is homogeneous, with few real deviations. One can trace this attitude back into the Western past. Religious concepts, which have since been transformed into scientific and political beliefs, remain objects of belief as securely as if they had never been severed from their theological moorings.

Let us trace a few examples. Originally the continuity of the world was conceived as a demonstration of the divine plan and God, conceived as a lawgiver in the moral sense, became a lawgiver in the scientific sense also. Scientific data was classified in certain ways that in the eyes of Western peoples became a part of the structure of nature. Phenomena that did not fit into the structure that had been created were said to "violate" the laws of nature and hence to be untrue in the religious sense and unimportant in the scientific sense. When evolution replaced the concept of creation in the book of Genesis, it became an inviolable law in the eyes of Western people in much the same way that the literal interpretation of the biblical story had been accepted by Western people in former centuries.

The world was originally conceived in terms of the Near East as the center of reality. As awareness extended to other peoples, this world gradually expanded until by the Middle Ages it encompassed those regions that were in commercial contact with Western Europe. The discovery of the Western Hemisphere created a certain degree of trauma, for suddenly there was an awareness of lands and peoples of which Western

Europeans had no previous knowledge. The only way that these people could be accounted for was by reference to the Scriptures. So it was hypothesized that the aboriginal peoples in North and South America must have been the Ten Lost Tribes of Israel who had crossed into the New World over a land bridge somewhere in northern Asia. The basic assumption of this theory was the creation of the human species as a single act, performed by the Christian God, with its subsequent history one of populating the planet.

The rise of social science, and the downgrading of theological answers to what were considered scientific questions concerning the nature and history of human societies, meant that social science had to provide answers to questions formulated within the theological context. With virtually no reconsideration of the basic question of the creation (or origination in scientific terms) of our species as the product of a single act, anthropologists promptly adopted the old theological explanation of the peopling of the Western Hemisphere, developing the Bering Straits theory of migration to account for the phenomenon. Whether secular or sacred, the classification of American natives as a derivative, inferior group of Asian-European peoples, albeit far removed from those roots by the postulation of many millennia of wandering, became a status from which American Indians have been unable to escape.

The emphasis on objective knowledge by Western peoples has meant the development of an attitude that sees reality as basically physical, the knowledge thereof basically mental or verbal, and the elimination of any middle ground between extremes. Thus religion has become a matter of the proper exposition of doctrines, and non-Western religions have been judged on their development of a systematic moral and ethical code rather than the manner in which they conducted themselves. When a religion is conceived as a code of verbal importance rather than a way of life, loopholes in the code become more important than the code itself since, by eliminating or escaping the direct violation of the code by a redefinition of the code or a relaxation of its intended effect, one can maintain two types of behavior, easily discerned in a practical way, as if they were identical and consistent with a particular picture of reality.

In recent decades Western science has made an important discovery, important at least for Western peoples who had formerly confused themselves with their own belief system. Western science was premised upon the proposition that God had made the world according to certain laws. These laws were capable of discovery by human reason, and the task of science was to discover as many of these laws as possible. So human knowledge was misconceived as the only description of physical reality, a tendency Alfred North Whitehead called the principle of "misplaced concreteness." With the articulation of theories of indeterminancy in modern physics, this naïve attitude toward human knowledge radically shifted and became an acknowledgement that what we had formerly called nature was simply our knowledge of nature based upon the types of questions we had decided to use to organize the measurements we were making of the physical world.

The shift in emphasis meant that all knowledge became a relative knowledge, valid only for the types of questions we were capable of formulating. Depending upon the types of information sought, we could measure and observe certain patterns of phenomena, but these patterns existed in our heads rather than in nature itself. Knowledge thus became a matter of cultural preference rather than an indication of the ultimate structure of reality. Presumably if one culture asked a certain type of question while another asked another type of question, the two different answers could form two valid perspectives on the world. Whether these two perspectives could be reconciled in one theory of knowledge depended upon the broader pattern of interpretation that thinkers brought into play with respect to the data. When this new factor of interpretation is applied specifically to different cultures and traditions, we can see that what have been called primitive superstitions have the potential of being regarded as sophisticated insights into the nature of things, at least on an equal basis with Western knowledge. The traditional manner in which Western peoples think is now only one of the possible ways of describing a natural process. It may not, in fact, even be as accurate, insofar as it can relate specific facts without perverting them, as non-Western ways of correlating knowledge.

This uncertainty is liberating in a much more fundamental way than any other development in the history of Western civilization. It means that religious, political, economic, and historical analyses of human activities that have been derived from the Western tradition do not have an absolute claim upon us. We are free to seek a new synthesis that draws information from every culture, and every period of human history has as a boundary only the requirement that it make more sense of more data than any other synthesis. Even the initial premises of such a synthesis can be different from what we have previously used to begin our formulation of a picture of reality.

When we apply this new freedom to some of the examples cited above, we see that the proper question we should have asked with respect to housing did not concern housing at all, but covered the more general question of the nature of a community. We discover that the college applications and the bilingual programs should have been transcended by questions concerning the nature of knowledge, how it is transmitted, and how it can be expanded, rather than how specific predetermined courses of action can be implemented. Once we reject the absolute nature of Western conceptions of problems, we are able to see different types of questions inherent in our immediate problem areas. The immediacy we feel when observing conditions under which people live should enable us to raise new issues that contain within themselves new ways of conceiving solutions.

An old Indian saying captures the radical difference between Indians and Western peoples quite adequately. The white man, the Indians maintain, has ideas; Indians have visions. Ideas have a single dimension and require a chain of connected ideas to make sense. The connections that are made between ideas can lead to great insights on the nature of things, or they can lead to the inexorable logic of Catch-22 in which the logic inevitably leads to the polar opposite of the original proposition. The vision, on the other hand, presents a whole picture of experience and has a central meaning that stands on its own feet as an independent revelation. It is said that Albert Einstein could not conceive of his problems in physics in conceptual terms but instead had visions of a whole event. He then spent his time attempting to translate elements of that event that could be separated into mathematical and verbal descriptions that could be communicated to others. It is this difference, the change from inductive and deductive logic to transformation of perceived realities, that becomes the liberating factor, not additional information or continual replacement of data and concepts within the traditional framework of interpretation.

Let us return, then, to our discussion of the manner in which racial minorities have been perceived by the white community, particularly by the liberal establishment, in the past decade and a half. Minority groups, conceived to be different from the white majority, are perceived to be lacking some critical element of humanity that, once received, would bring them to some form of equality with the white majority. The trick has been in identifying that missing element, and each new articulation of goals is immediately attributed to every minority group and appears to answer the question that has been posed by the sincere but unreflective liberal community.

Liberation is simply the manner in which this missing element is presently conceived by people interested in reform. It will become another social movement fad and eventually fade away to be replaced with yet another instant analysis of the situation. Until fundamental questions regarding the assumptions that form the basis for Western civilization are raised and new articulations of reality are discovered, the impulse to grab quickly and apparently easy answers will continue. Social conditions will continue to be described in a cause-and-effect logic that has dominated Western thinking for its entire intellectual lifetime. Programs will be designed that fail to account for the change in conditions that occurs continually in human societies. Ideas will continue to dominate our concerns and visions will not come.

If we are then to talk seriously about the necessity of liberation, we are talking about the destruction of the whole complex of Western theories of knowledge and the construction of a new and more comprehensive synthesis of human knowledge and experience. This is no easy task and it cannot be accomplished by people who are encompassed within the traditional Western logic and the resulting analyses such logic provides. If we change the very way that Western peoples think, the way they collect data, which data they gather, and how they arrange that information, then we are speaking truly of liberation. For it is the manner in which people conceive reality that motivates them to behave in certain ways, that provides them with a system of values, and that enables them to justify their activities. A new picture of reality, a reality conceived as a vision and not as a series of related or connected ideas, can accomplish over a longer period of time many changes we have been unable to effect while conceiving solutions as short term remedies.

More important for our discussion is the recognition that all parts of human experience are related and the proposed solution to any particular problem overlooks the changes that will occur in related activities because of their relationship. Fundamental changes initiated by a new picture of reality will create a transformation, and will avoid the traditional replacement of words with new words. In summary we now challenge the basic assumptions of Western man. To wit:

1) that time is uniform and continuous;
2) that our species originated from a single source;
3) that our descriptions of nature are absolute knowledge;
4) that the world can be divided into subjective and objective;
5) that our understanding of our species is homogeneous;
6) that ultimate reality, including divinity, is homogeneous;
7) that by projection of present conditions we can understand human history, planetary history, or the universe;
8) that inductive and deductive reasoning are the primary tools for gaining knowledge.

As we create a new set of propositions that transcend these theses we will achieve liberation in a fundamental sense and the synthesis that emerges will be a theology. But it will transform present feelings of sympathy to shared experiences, it will transform tolerance to understanding, and it will transform appreciation of separate cultural traditions into a new universal cultural expression. And everyone will become liberated.

VI: Hispanic American Experience

Inhuman Treatment
of Farm Workers Must End

Cesar Chavez

Liberation theology, properly understood, originates in the struggle of the poor and the oppressed, not in the academy. Praxis (read: action/reflection) gives rise to social analysis or Christopraxis, and in the process liberation theology is born. It has been called "the verbalization of praxis." This article from the *Los Angeles Times* for February 11, 1974, illustrates the process at work in the crucible of suffering among migrant farm workers, a great many of whom are Mexican Americans. Roman Catholic Cesar Chavez, President of the United Farm Workers of America, with headquarters at La Paz in Keene, California, is noted for his commitment to non-violence.

In Florida, Gulf & Western Products Co., a major sugar-cane grower, hauls Jamaican cane workers in 8-by-35-foot aluminium vans with no windows, no seats and no inside lighting. The company says it has a policy of carrying only 80 men per vehicle but, in the pre-dawn darkness of Monday, Jan. 7, 1974, upward of 130 farm workers were jammed into a van headed for Gulf & Western's Oakeelanta mill near South Bay. The truck's steering failed, and the vehicle overturned in a ditch. One cane cutter died and eighty-six were injured.

Like most Florida cane growers, Gulf & Western imports Jamaican labor through an arrangement between the United States and Jamaican governments. If a cutter does not fulfill his quota—200 feet of cane per hour or eight tons per day—or if he complains about his working conditions or food, he is likely to be summarily deported to Jamaica—and charged for his passage. The *Miami News* quoted one Florida grower who summed up the process this way: "We used to own our slaves; now we rent them."

Florida is not alone in allowing such inhuman treatment of farm workers. Many California and Arizona growers have their own system for "renting" them.

They go to "The Pit" in Mexicali, a crude dump where hungry people from Mexico offer themselves to employers from the rich American croplands. From 2 a.m. on, hundreds of men, women and children show up to hear the prices that growers are willing to pay for that day. Then they climb aboard buses provided by labor contractors, who take them to work at distant points in the Imperial, Coachella, Yuma and Palo Verde valleys.

On Monday, Jan. 14, 1974, Pablo Arellanos, 54, started picking up farm workers at 2 a.m. for Jesus Ayala, a labor contractor. By 3:00 or 3:30 a.m. Pablo had a busload of people and began his 135-mile trip to High and Mighty Farms lettuce fields near Blythe. Then, after a full day working in the fields himself, Pablo drove the workers back to Mexico at night and cleaned the bus before trying to get some sleep for the next day.

Early Tuesday, he again picked up a crew of farm workers and headed north. On approacing Blythe shortly before sunrise, the bus missed a turn and careened off the road into a drainage ditch. On impact, seats and farm workers were thrown to the front of the bus, crushing Pablo to death and trapping many others who soon drowned in the ditch.

On the day of the accident, I was in Atlanta—along with other farm workers—taking part in services marking the death of Dr. Martin Luther King. When we heard of the tragedy in Blythe, we canceled the day's meetings with Coretta King and other black leaders, and took the first flight to Los Angeles. That night we drove to Calexico.

For the next three days we visited the families of the dead workers and sought more information about the causes of the accident.

Among the dead, we discovered, were men, women and children. In one family, a father and his three teen-age children were killed.

Amid the grief there was great bitterness. The workers were—and still are—bitter because they've been through this kind of tragedy too many times before. The workers learned long ago that growers and labor contractors have too little regard for the value of any individual worker's life.

The trucks and buses are old and unsafe. The fields are carelessly sprayed with poisons. The laws that do exist are not enforced. How long will it be before we take seriously the importance of the workers who harvest the food we eat?

On Saturday, Jan. 19, two-thousand farm workers crowded into the Calexico National Guard Armory for a funeral Mass celebrated in Spanish. Afterward, at the request of the farm workers' families, on behalf of their union, I made the following remarks in Spanish, printed here in English for the first time:

"Brothers and Sisters: We are united here in the name of God to pay final tribute to our brothers and sisters who lost their lives in a tragic bus accident. We are here also to show our love and solidarity for the families who have lost so much in the deaths of their loved ones.

"We are united in our sorrow but also in our anger. This tragedy happened because of the greed of the big growers who do not care about the safety of the workers and who expose them to grave dangers when they transport them in wheeled coffins to the fields. . . .

"There have been so many accidents—in the fields, on trucks, under machines, in buses—so many accidents involving farm workers.

"People ask if they are deliberate. They are deliberate in the sense that they are the direct result of a farm labor system that treats workers like agricultural implements and not as human beings. These accidents happen because employers and labor contractors treat us as if we were not important human beings.

"But brothers and sisters, the men and women we honor here today are important human beings. They are important because they are from us. We cherish them. We love them. We will miss them.

"They are important because of the love they gave to their husbands, their children, their wives, their parents—all those who were close to them and who needed them.

"They are important because of the work they do. They are not implements to be used and discarded. They are human beings who sweat and sacrifice to bring food to the tables of millions and millions of people throughout the world.

"They are important because God made them, gave them life, and cares for them in life and death.

"Now that they are gone, how can we keep showing how important they are to us? How can we give meaning to their lives and their sacrifice?

"These terrible accidents must be stopped! It is our obligation—out duty to the memory of those who have died—to see to it that workers are not continually transported in these wheeled coffins, these carriages of death and sorrow. The burden of protecting the lives of farm workers is squarely on our shoulders.

"The farm workers' union is . . . demanding a full investigation by the grand jury in Riverside County. We are also asking for hearings by the California Legislature as a first step toward stronger legislation.

"Let the whole world know that the pain that today fills our hearts with mourning also unifies our spirits and strengthens our determination to defend the rights of every worker.

"Let the labor contractors and the growers know that our union . . . will never stop working and struggling until there is an end to the inhuman treatment of all farm workers."

One dead in a Florida cane workers' truck accident . . . nineteen in a California drainage ditch . . . when will it all end?

Toward a Chicano Theology of Liberation

Leo D. Nieto

"The outstanding reality for Chicanos and other ethnic minority groups in the United States," according to Leo D. Nieto, "is that we are basically an oppressed people and that we, therefore, form a part of the Third World living within the bowels of the First World." Nieto, who serves on the staff of the National Farm Workers Ministry in New York, proposes that "a theological statement peculiar to the Chicano experience . . . will of necessity be similar in its main lines to other theologies of liberation." After establishing four criteria or guidelines for this task, he offers "a first attempt at such a statement of a Chicano theology of liberation." Nieto's statement, part of a longer article, first appeared in the Fall 1975 issue of the Perkins *Journal,* published by Perkins School of Theology, Southern Methodist University, Dallas, Texas.

A theological statement peculiar to the Chicano experience is much needed. Such a statement will of necessity be similar in its main lines to other theologies of liberation, such as those coming out of Black, Latin American, and other Third World currents of thought. I do not pretend to be making such a statement in this paper; however, I would like to make some suggestions which I hope will stimulate such a process among Chicano Christians wherever they may be.

First, I would suggest that such statements must be made by Chicanos themselves, who have lived the Chicano experience in the barrios and who have demonstrated a commitment to Chicano and Christian values and assumptions. Secondly, such a statement should be grounded in biblical theology, as this is a part of the Chicano Christian experience at its best. I believe that Tillich's assertion that religion forms the basis for cultural development is applicable to this situation. Thirdly, I would hope that such a statement would not be merely reflective but that it be related to action or *praxis* both in its analysis and in its proposals. Finally, I would hope that all such efforts at theological statements of the Chicano experience will resist attempts at cooperation by those who are not Chicanos. (Mexican Americans who find the term "Chicano" offensive are not a part of the Chicano Movement, and therefore do not qualify for making such statements.) Such statements should be authentic and should resist being used to further other ends. As a conclusion I will make a first attempt at such a statement of a Chicano theology of liberation.

It is necessary to recognize, first, that ours is a dual heritage stemming from our Spanish and Indian ancestors—one of them basically an oppressive cultural group, the other an oppressed one. There is a tendency on the part of many Chicanos to account for their Indian heritage with much pride, to the exclusion of any recognition of their Spanish heritage. On the other hand, there have been many Mexican Americans who, perhaps because of a relatively fair complexion, have chosen to emphasize their Spanish heritage to the exclusion of the Indian. Often this may have been an effort to identify with white or European stock in order to avoid receiving discriminatory treatment because of racial origin.

The truth, if we are willing to face it, is that we are meztizos, the product of both Indian and European stock and cultural tradition. This dual heritage often results in cultural ambivalence which is expressed on the one hand by vehement support of Indian-ness while at the same time adhering to racist attitudes regarding skin color and a subtle preference for European-ness. The meztizo reality must be faced and affirmed as "la nueva Raza cósmica" of Vasconcelos with all of the anti-racist implications involved. The concept of "el nuevo hombre" being proclaimed throughout Latin America must be studied along with its relationship to St. Paul's concept of the new man which was similar. Another aspect of the ambivalence from which we often suffer is that we adopt the thought patterns and values of the conquerors from Spain, while at other times our sentiments and visceral reactions are those of the Indian in us.

Since we find ourselves now living in a land controlled by the gringos, we find this same tendency to adopt the ways of the oppressor as our own; thus, we become coopted by the educational and other sytems into believing in the prevalent economic, social and political values even though they may be detrimental to us as a group. We find ourselves believing that we form an integral part of a privileged class, when in reality we are often used as "token Mexicans" for the sole purpose of keeping the masses of the Mexican people in a subservient status. We are coopted, bought off and used as pawns for the maintenance of the *status quo*. This is especially true of Mexican American Protestants as a group, since Protestantism has functioned so effectively as an acculturating device, alienating us from our own culture and people.

In spite of these pitfalls, we must realize that the outstanding reality for Chicanos and other ethnic minority groups in the United States is that we are basically an oppressed people and that we, therefore, form a part of the Third World living within the bowels of the First World. When we become aware of this fact, then we realize that we have this status in common with the majority of the earth's population and we can stand in solidarity with them, and in particular with our brothers and sisters in Latin America.

As we move toward this awareness there seem to be several steps we must take. The first is to become aware of our cultural and historical particularity with all that this implies: accept and affirm ourselves as we are, children of God and his creation. But we must be careful not to stop at this step and become merely cultural nationalists.

Another step we must take, which has to do with intra-cultural structures, has to do with the role of women in the struggle for liberation. As Chicanos, we have inherited certain patterns and values we refer to as "machismo." As a group we constitute a classic case of male supremacy, a concept and an

ideology which is not unique to us, but which is a disease prevalent throughout the world and for ages past. It is also one of the
most subtle and most difficult aspects of the struggle for liberation with which to deal, especially for "machos," but also for
many women who prefer to remain subordinate "happy
slaves." If the matter of equality between the sexes is not dealt
with and resolved, their true liberation cannot be achieved by
Chicanos. If all of us are not free, then none of us is free.

One last problem I shall enumerate is still something of a
mystery to me, but it is an important problem. It has been
recently pointed out to some Chicanos that we tend to be anar-
chistic, being suspicious and often opposed to structures and
organizations which are supposed to help us, even those of our
own creation. This phenomenon has been observed recently as
various Latino groups have made efforts to form a coalition on
a national level.

One explanation given to explain this phenomenon is that
Chicanos suffer from a lack of observable, significant victories
in the recent past, beginning with the bitter defeat of the Mexican War of 1848, which created the Chicano Southwest. Since
that time there have been few, if any, significant victories by the
Chicanos, says this explanation, the most recent failure being
the government's "War on Poverty." Therefore, it is stated, the
Chicanos now seem suspicious of any and all efforts at organi-
zation or structuring. The result is a curious tendency toward
anarchism. This is a recent problem for pondering.

If we are to be clear, then, on the task ahead, we can no
longer afford the luxury of ambivalence. We must choose what
we shall be and do. It is at this point that our biblical heritage
shows us the way. Christ was not ambivalent on what he was to
be or do, nor was he so in his charge to his followers:

> No servant can serve two masters; for either he will hate
> the one and love the other, or he will be devoted to the one
> and despise the other.

Christ demanded of his followers a certain commitment, to
"preach good news to the poor, to proclaim the acceptable year
of the Lord, to set at liberty the oppressed." His demands were

constantly, consistently, that Christians take the side of the suffering, the poor, the oppressed with the strength and the assurance of the "arm of God."

What are some of the implications of this "good news" for our situation today as Christian Chicanos? Keeping in mind that we must be "innocent as doves, and wise as serpents," it may mean that in order to achieve some semblance of justice, liberation and human fulfillment as a people, we must seek coalitions with other oppressed groups in the United States, expressing in so doing our solidarity with each other as well as with similar groups throughout the world. This would include people of other races, nationalities and colors, including white people. The common factor bringing about this solidarity is a commitment to the same objective of liberation for all people. Such an ideology has to be clarified and refined, together with its theological implications before meaningful coalitions can be formed.

We must continually engage in mutual and self-criticism as we seek to clarify such an ideological position, thus seeking to avoid self-complacency.

There must be a conscious decision for commitment to the ideals of justice and liberation in the context of love. This commitment must be at a life and death level so that one is willing to risk much for its achievement, even to the giving of one's life.

We cannot be afraid of freedom, for herein lies the ultimate meaning of life. To be afraid and to "play it safe" is to lack freedom and to choose slavery instead. For *La Raza* to live means for *La Raza* to risk being free. So it is that slogans which came out of Emiliano Zapata's struggle for the freedom and dignity of *campesinos* in Mexico a half century ago take on religious meaning for us today: "Prefiero morir de pie, que vivir de rodillas." ("I would rather die on my feet than live on my knees.")

Other words of Zapata ought to take on a meaningful challenge to us today: "Que has hecho tu para que nuestra muerte no haya sido en vano?" ("What have you done so that our death might not have been in vain?")

As Chicano Christians in the United States we must identify ourselves unequivocally with the poor from whom we have come and from whom we are seeking to escape. This means that we must abandon and redirect in a radical way our efforts to identify with the values and standards of the middle and upper classes. We must put away our striving for the accumulation of material possessions, prestige and high position. Instead we must find ways not only of providing services for the poor, but we must become ourselves the servants of the poor. This can only be done through definite decision and follow-through with action. It has implications for life style, and for a struggle to change dehumanizing structures.

It can probably be assumed that not all Chicano Christians will take this direction, nor that even a large number will do so. However, if even a small but significant number do so, it will mean a change in the historical pattern of the churches' allying themselves with the powerful, the oppressors, at least for this small segment of the church.

Selected Bibliography of Books in English

Mission and Liberation

Adler, Elisabeth. *A Small Beginning. An Assessment of the First Five Years of the Programme to Combat Racism* (Geneva: World Council of Churches, 1974).

Anderson, Gerald H. and Thomas F. Stransky, eds. *Mission Trends No. 3*—"Third World Theologies." (New York: Paulist Press; and Grand Rapids, Mich.: Wm. B. Eerdmans Publishing Co., 1976).

Armerding, Carl E., ed. *Evangelicals and Liberation* (Nutley, N.J.: Presbyterian and Reformed Publishing Co., 1977).

Brown, Robert McAfee. *Theology in a New Key: Responding to Liberation Themes* (Philadelphia: Westminster Press, 1978).

Bucher, Glenn A., ed. *Straight/White/Male* (Philadelphia: Fortress Press, 1976).

Dickinson, Richard D. N. *To Set at Liberty the Oppressed. Towards an Understanding of Christian Responsibilities for Development/Liberation* (Geneva: World Council of Churches, 1975).

Goulet, Denis. *A New Moral Order. Studies in Development Ethics and Liberation Theology* (Maryknoll, N.Y.: Orbis Books, 1974).

Gremillion, Joseph. *The Gospel of Peace and Justice. Catholic-Social Teaching since Pope John* (Maryknoll, N.Y.: Orbis Books, 1976).

Guinan, Edward, ed. *Redemption Denied. An Appalachian Reader.* (Washington, D.C.: Appalachian Documentation [ADOC], 1976).

Herzog, Frederick. *Liberation Theology* (New York: Seabury Press, 1972).

IDOC. *Church Within Socialism. Church and State in East European Socialist Republics*. Edited by Erich Weingärtner, based on the work of Giovanni Barberini. IDOC Europe Dossiers Two and Three (Rome: IDOC, 1976).

IDOC. *Mission in America in World Context*. "The Future of the Missionary Enterprise," Dossier No. 16 (Rome and New York: IDOC, 1976).

Kee, Alistair. *A Reader in Political Theology* (Philadelphia: Westminster Press, 1974).

McFadden, Thomas M., ed. *Liberation, Revolution, and Freedom* (New York: Seabury Press, 1975).

Mencarelli, James and Steve Severin. *Protest 3: Red, Black, Brown Experience in America* (Grand Rapids, Mich.: Wm. B. Eerdmans Publishing Co., 1975).

Ogden, Schubert M. *Faith and Freedom: Toward a Theology of Liberation* (Nashville: Abingdon Press, 1979).

Reist, Benjamin A. *Theology in Red, White, and Black* (Philadelphia: Westminster Press, 1975).

Ruether, Rosemary R. *Liberation Theology* (New York: Paulist Press, 1973).

————. *The Radical Kingdom: The Western Experience of Messianic Hope* (New York: Paulist Press, 1970).

Soelle, Dorothee. *Political Theology* (Philadelphia: Fortress Press, 1974).

Torres, Sergio and John Eagleson, eds. *Theology in the Americas* (Maryknoll, N.Y.: Orbis Books, 1976).

Wallis, Jim. *Agenda for Biblical People* (New York: Harper & Row, 1976).

Yoder, John Howard. *The Politics of Jesus* (Grand Rapids, Mich.: Wm. B. Eerdmans Publishing Co., 1972).

Black Experience

Bruce, Calvin E. and William R. Jones, eds. *Black Theology II. Essays on the Formation and Outreach of Contemporary Black Theology* (Lewisburg, Pa.: Bucknell University Press, 1978).

Cleage, Albert B. *Black Christian Nationalism* (New York: Morrow, 1972).

Cone, Cecil W. *The Identity Crisis in Black Theology* (Nashville: African Methodist Episcopal Church, 1975).

Cone, James. H. *Black Theology and Black Power* (New York: Seabury Press, 1969).

_____. *A Black Theology of Liberation* (Philadelphia: Lippincott, 1970).

_____. *God of the Oppressed* (New York: Seabury Press, 1975).

Jones, Major J. *Black Awareness: A Theology of Hope* (Nashville: Abingdon Press, 1971).

_____. *Christian Ethics for Black Theology* (Nashville: Abingdon Press, 1974).

Jones, William R. *Is God a White Racist? A Preamble to Black Theology* (Garden City, N.Y.: Anchor Press/Doubleday, 1973).

Lincoln, C. Eric, ed. *The Black Experience in Religion* (Garden City, N.Y.: Anchor Press/Doubleday, 1974).

Massie, Priscilla, ed. *Black Faith and Black Solidarity* (New York: Friendship Press, 1973).

Mitchell, Henry. *Black Beliefs* (New York: Harper & Row, 1975).

_____. *Black Preaching* (Philadelphia: J. B. Lippincott, 1970).

Nelson, Hart M., Raytha L. Yokley, and Anne K. Nelson, eds. *The Black Church in America* (New York: Basic Books, 1971).

Pannell, William E. *My Friend, The Enemy* (Waco, Texas: Word Books, 1968).

Roberts, J. Deotis, Sr. *A Black Political Theology* (Philadelphia: Westminster Press, 1974).

_____. *Liberation and Reconciliation: A Black Theology* (Philadelphia: Westminster Press, 1971).

_____ and James J. Gardiner, eds. *Quest for a Black Theology* (Philadelphia: Pilgrim Press, 1971).

Skinner, Tom. *How Black Is the Gospel?* (Philadelphia: Lippincott, 1970).

Thibodeaux, Sister Mary Roger. *A Black Nun Looks at Black Power* (New York: Sheed & Ward, 1972).

Thomas, Latta R. *Biblical Faith and the Black American* (Valley Forge, Pa.: Judson Press, 1976).

Traynham, Warner R. *Christian Faith in Black and White. A Primer in Theology from the Black Perspective* (Wakefield, Mass: Parameter Press, 1973).

Wilmore, Gayraud S. *Black Religion and Black Radicalism* (Garden City, N.Y.: Anchor Press/Doubleday, 1972).

The Word in the World. Divine Word Missionaries, '76 Black Apostolate. Edited by John Boberg, S.V.D. (Techny, Illinois: Society of the Divine Word, 1976).

Feminist Experience

Bianchi, Eugene C. and Rosemary Ruether. *From Machismo to Mutuality: Essays on Sexism and Woman-Man Liberation* (New York: Paulist Press, 1976).

Bruns, J. Edgar. *God as Woman, Woman as God* (New York: Paulist Press, 1973).

Burkhardt, Walter, ed. *Woman: New Dimensions* (New York: Paulist Press, 1977).

Clark, Elizabeth and Herbert Richardson, eds. *Women and Religion: A Feminist Sourcebook of Christian Thought* (New York: Harper Forum Book, 1976).

Coriden, James, ed. *Sexism and Church Law: Equal Rights and Affirmative Action* (New York: Paulist Press, 1977).

Collins, Sheila D. *A Different Heaven and Earth: A Feminist Perspective on Religion* (Valley Forge, Pa.: Judson Press, 1974).

Daly, Mary. *Beyond God the Father. Toward a Philosophy of Women's Liberation* (Boston: Beacon Press, 1973).

Doely, Sarah Bentley, ed. *Women's Liberation and the Church* (New York: Association Press, 1970).

Emswiler, Sharon and Thomas N. *Women and Worship: A Guide to Non-Sexist Hymns, Prayers, and Liturgies* (New York: Harper & Row, 1974).

Ermath, Margaret S. *Adam's Fractured Rib. Observations on Women in the Church* (Philadelphia: Fortress Press, 1970).

Fischer, Clare Benedicks, Betsy Brenneman, and Anne McGrew Bennett, eds. *Women in a Strange Land: Search for a New Image* (Philadelphia: Fortress Press, 1975).

Grana, Janice, ed. *Images: Women in Transition* (Nashville: The Upper Room, 1976).

Hageman, Alice L., ed. *Sexist Religion and Women in the Church: No More Silence* (New York: Association Press, 1974).

Heyer, Robert J., ed. *Women and Orders* (New York: Paulist Press, 1974).

IDOC. *The Mission of Women.* Edited by Marilyn Weingärtner. Dossier No. 15/16 in "The Future of the Missionary Enterprise" Series (Rome and New York: IDOC, 1976).

Jewett, Paul K. *Man as Male and Female* (Grand Rapids, Mich.: Wm. B. Eerdmans Publishing Co., 1975).

Mollenkott, Virginia R. *Women, Men, and the Bible* (Nashville: Abingdon Press, 1977).

Pro Mundi Vita. *Women, the Women's Movement, and the Future of the Church.* Bulletin No. 56 (Brussels: Pro Mundi Vita, 1975).

Ruether, Rosemary R. *New Woman/New Earth* (New York: Seabury Press, 1975).

_____, ed. *Religion and Sexism: Images of Women in the Jewish and Christian Traditions* (New York: Simon and Schuster, 1974).

Russell, Letty M. *Human Liberation in a Feminist Perspective—A Theology* (Philadelphia: Westminster Press, 1974).

_____. *The Liberating Word: A Guide to Nonsexist Interpretation of the Bible* (Philadelphia: Westminster, 1976).

Scanzoni, Letha and Nancy Hardesty. *All We're Meant to Be: A Biblical Approach to Women's Liberation* (Waco, Texas: Word Books, 1974).

Stendahl, Krister. *The Bible and the Role of Women* (Philadelphia: Fortress Press, Facet Books, 1966).

Swidler, Arlene. *Sistercelebrations: Nine Worship Experiences* (Philadelphia: Fortress Press, 1974).

_____. *Woman in a Man's Church: From Role to Person* (New York: Paulist Press, 1972).

———— and Leonard Swidler, eds. *Women Priests: A Catholic Commentary on the Vatican Declaration* (New York: Paulist Press, 1977).

Tavard, George H. *Woman in Christian Tradition* (Notre Dame, Indiana: University of Notre Dame Press, 1973).

Wahlberg, Rachel C. *Jesus and the Freed Woman* (New York: Paulist Press, 1978).

Native American Experience

Deloria, Vine, Jr. *Custer Died for Your Sins, An Indian Manifesto* (New York: Macmillan, 1969).

————. *God Is Red* (New York: Grosset & Dunlap, 1973).

————. *The Indian Affair* (New York: Friendship Press, 1974).

Starkloff, Carl F. *The People of the Center: American Indian Religion and Christianity* (New York: Seabury Press, 1974).

Asian American Experience

Sano, Roy I., ed. *Amerasian Theology of Liberation: A Reader* (Oakland, Calif.: Asian Center for Theology and Strategies, Pacific School of Religion, 1973).

————, ed. *The Theologies of Asian Americans and Pacific Peoples. A Reader* (Oakland, Calif.: Asian Center for Theology and Strategies, Pacific School of Religion, 1976).

Hispanic American Experience

Acuna, Rodolfo. *Occupied America: The Chicano's Struggle Toward Liberation* (San Francisco: Canfield Press, a Division of Harper and Row, 1972).

Day, Mark. *Forty Acres: Cesar Chavez and the Farm Workers.* Introduction by Cesar Chavez (New York: Praeger, 1971).

Matthiessen, Peter. *Sal Si Puedes: Cesar Chavez and the New American Revolution* (New York: Random House, 1970).

Rendon, Armando B. *Chicano Manifesto: The History and Aspirations of the Second Largest Minority in America* (New York: Macmillan, 1971).

MISSION TRENDS NO. 1

Contents

ISBN: 0-8091-1843-2

MISSION TRENDS NO. 2

Contents

I: MANDATE AND MEANING OF EVANGELIZATION

II: PRIORITIES AND STRATEGIES

III. COMMON FAITH AND DIVIDED WITNESS

IV. NEW PERSPECTIVES ON OTHER FAITHS AND IDEOLOGIES

APPENDIX

MISSION TRENDS NO. 3

Contents

I. THEOLOGY IN CONTEXT

II: LATIN AMERICAN PERSPECTIVES

III. AFRICAN PERSPECTIVES

IV. ASIAN PERSPECTIVES

SELECTED BIBLIOGRAPHY OF BOOKS IN ENGLISH

(Paulist ISBN: 0-8091-1984-6) (Eerdmans ISBN: 0-8028-1654-1)